Applications of Data Analysis Across Business Functions and Domains

Applications of Data Analysis Across Business Functions and Domains

BY

SAYANTANI ROY CHOUDHURY

Praxis Business School, India

emerald PUBLISHING

United Kingdom – North America – Japan – India – Malaysia – China

Emerald Publishing Limited
Emerald Publishing, Floor 5, Northspring, 21-23 Wellington Street, Leeds LS1 4DL.

First edition 2026

Printed and bound by CPI Group (UK) Ltd, Croydon, CR0 4YY

British Library Cataloguing in Publication Data
A catalogue record for this book is available from the British Library

ISBN: 978-1-80686-106-4 (Print)
ISBN: 978-1-80686-105-7 (Online)
ISBN: 978-1-80686-107-1 (Epub)

Contents

Acknowledgements

Writing this book has been a deeply enriching journey, and I would like to express my heartfelt gratitude to all those who have supported me along the way.

I am immensely thankful to my students, Ayan Ghosh and Sayan Ghosh, whose assistance and support helped me to complete this work. I would also like to acknowledge my interns, Nilaya Majumder and Debasmita Saha, for their invaluable assistance, dedication, and contributions during the course of this work.

My sincere gratitude goes to our Director, Prof. Prithwis Mukerjee, for his guidance, encouragement, and visionary leadership, which continually motivate me to push the boundaries of teaching and research. I am equally grateful to our Founder Director, Prof. Charanpreet Singh, whose mentorship and unwavering support have been instrumental in my academic journey.

On a personal note, I owe my deepest appreciation to my husband, Sumit Roy Choudhury, and son Anushko. Their support has been my greatest strength throughout this endeavor.

Finally, I extend my thanks to all my colleagues, students, and well-wishers who, directly or indirectly, have contributed to the successful completion of this book.

Chapter 1

Introduction to Data Analysis in Business

In an era of information abundance, data extraction that makes sense is an art that marks success. Whether it is a company trying to forecast customer attrition, a public health researcher trying to track the outbreaks, or a government trying to allocate resources efficiently, interpreting and acting on data is the core. This interpretation is driven by two pillars: statistical methods and machine learning (ML) techniques.

Statistics, on the one hand, has been the backbone of interpreting data for more than a century. It is concerned with gathering, analyzing, and making inferences from data, particularly in environments with uncertainty. ML, on the other hand, which emerged from artificial intelligence and computer science, is concerned with creating algorithms that learn patterns from data and predict them.

Together, these tools comprise a complete analytical toolkit. This chapter will present the concepts, uses, and differences of statistical and ML tools to give readers the essential knowledge necessary to further explore data analytics.

Understanding the Data-driven Paradigm

It is important to recognize the landscape in which these tools operate. The data-driven paradigm involves:

- *Descriptive analytics*: What has happened?
- *Diagnostic analytics*: Why did it happen?
- *Predictive analytics*: What is likely to happen?
- *Prescriptive analytics*: What action should be taken?

Statistical tools mainly aid the first two questions, whereas ML tools are usually linked to the last two.

The Four Pillars of Data Analytics

There are four general categories of analytics. Familiarity with these is the cornerstone of data-driven decision-making.

Applications of Data Analysis Across Business Functions and Domains, 1–13

Published under exclusive licence by Emerald Publishing Limited
doi:10.1108/978-1-80686-105-720261001

Descriptive Analytics

Descriptive analytics provides an answer to the question: "What happened?"

It emphasizes condensing historical information through statistical metrics like averages, sums, percentages, and standard deviations. The tools utilized are dashboards, reports, and visualizations (e.g., bar charts, pie charts, and histograms).

Example: A shopping store examining monthly sales trends to determine peak shopping seasons.

Diagnostic Analytics

Diagnostic analytics responds to: "Why did it happen?"

It entails more intensive analysis to find the causes of previous results. Methods include correlation analysis, regression analysis, and root cause analysis.

Example: Determining why customer churn increased in a specific quarter by using multivariate regression.

Predictive Analytics

Predictive analytics responds to: "What is likely to occur?"

It employs statistical models and historical data to predict future occurrences. Popular algorithms include linear regression, decision trees, and time series models.

Example: A bank estimating the probability of loan default based on previous credit history.

Prescriptive Analytics

Prescriptive analytics responds to: "What should we do?"

This kind of analytics prescribes actions by bringing together forecasts with optimization and simulation methods. It tends to employ ML and operations research technologies.

Example: An airline adjusting flight timings and prices according to projected demand.

Principles of Statistical Tools

Statistics is a mathematical branch as well as an applied discipline. It enables us to make predictions about large populations from small groups and make decisions when we are uncertain.

Types of Statistics

- *Descriptive statistics*: Focused on summarizing data (e.g., mean, median, mode, and standard deviation).
- *Inferential statistics*: The intent is to make an inference about a population by using a sample (e.g., hypothesis testing and confidence intervals).
- *Predictive statistics*: The objective is to predict the unknown values of a variable with the help of a statistical model.

Levels of Measurement

Nominal scales are used to label or categorize data without any quantitative value or order. The numbers or names assigned to categories are simply tags for identification. For example, jersey numbers in sports, customer IDs, or blood groups (A, B, AB, and O) indicate categories but have no inherent ranking or arithmetic meaning.

Ordinal scales provide a ranking or order among categories, but the differences between ranks are not necessarily equal or measurable. For example, in a customer satisfaction survey with responses like "poor," "fair," "good," and "excellent," we know the order of preference but cannot quantify how much better "excellent" is than "good."

Interval scales are numeric scales where the differences between values are meaningful, but there is no true zero point. For example, temperature measured in Celsius or Fahrenheit allows us to say that 30°C is 10°C warmer than 20°C, but we cannot say it is "1.5 times as hot," since zero does not represent the absence of temperature. In contrast, ratio scales not only have meaningful intervals but also possess a true zero, representing the complete absence of the quantity. This allows both differences and ratios to be interpreted correctly. Examples include height, weight, income, and age – where it makes sense to say that someone earning Rs 100 is earning twice as much as someone earning Rs 50.

Often Used Statistical Techniques

Central Tendency and Dispersion

These measures summarize the data.

Measures of central tendency are statistical values that describe the center or typical value of a dataset, helping to summarize large amounts of data with a single representative figure. The three most common measures are the mean, the median, and the mode (Table 1). The mean is the arithmetic average, calculated by summing all observations and dividing by their number, making it sensitive to extreme values. The median is the middle value when data are arranged in order, providing a better indicator of central tendency for skewed distributions. The mode is the value that occurs most frequently and is particularly useful for categorical or discrete data.

Together, these measures provide different perspectives on the "central point" of data, aiding interpretation and comparison.

Measures of dispersion describe the spread or variability of data around a central value, indicating how consistently or inconsistently data points are distributed. Common measures include the range, the quartile deviation, the mean deviation, the variance, and the standard deviation (Table 2). The range is the simplest, calculated as the difference between the maximum and minimum values, but it depends only on extreme observations. The quartile deviation (or semi-interquartile range) considers the spread of the middle 50% of data, reducing the impact of outliers. The mean deviation measures the average absolute deviation from the mean or median. The variance and the standard deviation are widely used because they incorporate every data point and provide a precise measure of

Table 1. Comparison of Mean, Median, and Mode.

Measure	**Formula (Ungrouped Data)**	**Key Features**	**Advantages**	**Disadvantages**
Mean	$(\Sigma x_i f_i)/(\Sigma f_i)$	Arithmetic average of all observations	Uses all data, easy to compute	Distorted by extreme values (outliers)
Median	$L + [(n/2 - c)/f] \times h$	Middle position of data	Not affected by outliers, good for skewed data	Ignores exact values of data points
Mode	$L + [(f_m - f_1)/(2f_m - f_1 - f_2)] \times h$	Most common value	Useful for categorical data; simple to identify	May not be unique or may not exist

Table 2. Comparison of Measures of Dispersion.

Measure	**Formula (Ungrouped Data)**	**Key Features**	**Advantages**	**Disadvantages**
Range	Range $(R) = L - S$	Simplest measure of spread	Easy to calculate, quick overview	Based only on extreme values; ignores the rest of the data
Quartile deviation (semi-interquartile range)	Quartile deviation (QD) $= (Q3 - Q1)/2$	Spread of middle 50% of data	Less affected by outliers than range	Ignores data outside interquartile range
Mean deviation	$\Sigma 1/n\,\lvert x - \bar{x} \rvert$	$X_i - A$	About mean or median	Average absolute deviation
Variance	$\sigma^2 = \Sigma(x_i - \bar{x})^2/n$	Square of average deviation from mean	Uses all data; mathematical basis for further analysis	Units are squared, less intuitive
Standard deviation	$\sigma = \sigma^2$	Square root of variance	Most widely used; same units as data; accurate measure of variability	Slightly more complex to compute

variability. In general, higher dispersion indicates greater variability, while lower dispersion implies data points are more closely clustered around the center.

The choice of dispersion measure depends on the purpose of the analysis and the nature of the data. The range is useful for a quick, rough idea of variability, but it is highly affected by outliers. The quartile deviation is better when you want to focus on the spread of the middle portion of the data, minimizing the impact of extremes. The mean deviation gives a balanced view of the average variability and can be taken about the median for skewed data. Variance and standard deviation are the most precise and widely used measures, particularly in advanced statistical analysis, because they use every observation and provide a strong mathematical foundation; standard deviation is generally preferred over variance because it is expressed in the same units as the data. In practice, range is used for quick checks, while standard deviation is the go-to measure for robust and meaningful analysis.

Correlation and Regression

Correlation and regression (Table 3) are statistical tools used to study the relationship between variables. Correlation, on the one hand, measures the *strength and direction* of a linear relationship between two variables, typically expressed by the correlation coefficient (r), which ranges from –1 to +1. A positive r indicates that variables move in the same direction, while a negative r indicates that they move in opposite directions; the closer r is to ±1, the stronger the relationship. Regression, on the other hand, goes beyond measuring association – it *quantifies* the relationship by expressing one variable (dependent) as a function of another (independent). In simple linear regression, this is represented by the equation $y = a + bx$, where b is the regression coefficient showing how much y changes with

Table 3. Comparison Between Correlation and Regression.

Feature	**Correlation**	**Regression**
Purpose	Measures strength and direction of the relationship	Explains and predicts one variable using another
Measure	Correlation coefficient (r)	Regression equation ($y = a + bx$)
Value range	$-1 \leq r \leq +1$	No fixed range for coefficients a and b
Directionality	Symmetric – no distinction between variables	Directional – distinguishes dependent and independent variables
Interpretation	Indicates degree of association only	Quantifies the effect of one variable on another
Units	Unit-free	Regression coefficients retain the units of the variables
Use case	Understanding relationships	Prediction, forecasting, and modeling

a one-unit change in x, and a is the intercept. While correlation is symmetric (no distinction between variables), regression is directional, aimed at prediction or explanation. Together, they help in understanding patterns, making forecasts, and supporting data-driven decisions.

Ordinary least squares (OLS) is a method used to estimate the parameters of a linear regression model by minimizing the sum of the squared differences between the observed values and the predicted values. The regression equation takes the form $y = a + bx + \varepsilon$, where a is the intercept, b is the slope (regression coefficient), and ε is the error term. The OLS estimates of a and b are chosen to produce the best-fitting line through the data points. When interpreting regression output, the coefficient b shows how much the dependent variable y is expected to change for a one-unit increase in the independent variable x. The intercept a represents the predicted value of y when x=0. Statistical significance is checked using p-values or t-tests to determine whether the relationship is meaningful, while R^2 (coefficient of determination) indicates how well the model explains the variation in y. A higher R^2 means the regression line fits the data more closely, though it does not guarantee causation.

Hypothesis Testing

Hypothesis testing is a systematic way to decide whether evidence from data supports a claim about a population. We start with a null hypothesis (H_0), which assumes no change, no difference, or no effect – essentially the status quo – and an alternative hypothesis (H_1), which represents what we suspect or want to prove. Using a sample, we calculate a test statistic and compare it to what we would expect if H_0 were true. If the observed result is too unlikely to occur by chance – measured by a p-value or significance level (α) – we reject H_0 in favor of H_1.

This process does not prove a hypothesis true or false; it only assesses whether the data provide strong enough evidence against H_0. A low p-value (typically below 0.05) suggests that the sample result is inconsistent with H_0, while a high p-value suggests that there is not enough evidence to contradict it. In simple terms, hypothesis testing helps us make informed decisions: do the findings reflect a real effect, or are they likely just random variation?

Test Assumptions

- *Null hypothesis* (H_0): Default assumption (e.g., no difference).
- *Alternative hypothesis* (H_1): What you want to establish.
- *p-Value*: Probability of seeing the data if H_0 holds; a small p-value (<0.05) results in rejection of H_0.

There are a few very important and popularly used tests (Table 4).

Time Series Analysis

Applied when data are gathered over time.

- *Components*: Trend, seasonality, and noise.

Table 4. Comparison of Important Tests of Hypothesis Testing.

Test	Purpose	When to Use
z-Test	Tests if the sample mean differs from the population mean	Large samples ($n > 30$) or population variance known
t-Test	Tests if the sample mean differs from the population mean or compares two means	Small samples ($n \leq 30$) and variance unknown
χ^2 (Chi-square) test	Tests for relationships between categorical variables or goodness of fit	When data are counts or frequencies
F-Test	Compares two or more variances, or tests regression models	When comparing variability between groups or models

- *Models*: Moving averages, autoregressive integrated moving average (ARIMA), and exponential smoothing.
- *Example*: Predicting sales for the upcoming quarter.

Time series analysis is a statistical technique used to study data points collected or recorded over time, usually at equal intervals. Unlike ordinary data analysis, time series analysis explicitly considers the order of observations, recognizing that current values may depend on past values. Its main goals are to understand underlying patterns such as trend (long-term direction), seasonality (regular fluctuations within specific periods), cyclical movements (longer-term economic or business cycles), and irregular components (random or unexpected variations). By breaking down a series into these components, analysts can identify structural behavior and make informed decisions.

Beyond describing historical data, time series analysis is widely used for forecasting future values and evaluating how external factors influence time-dependent data. Techniques range from simple methods like moving averages and exponential smoothing to advanced models such as ARIMA, seasonal decomposition, and modern ML approaches. These tools help in diverse applications, including predicting stock prices, estimating demand, monitoring economic indicators, and detecting anomalies in sensor or web traffic data. Ultimately, time series analysis provides both insight and predictive power by leveraging temporal patterns rather than treating data as independent snapshots.

Overview of ML

Although statistics involves mathematical theory and inference, ML is a branch of artificial intelligence that deals with constructing systems that learn from experience using data. It is geared toward prediction and pattern recognition, generally using algorithms that self-improve without being programmed (Table 5).

ML is a branch of artificial intelligence that enables computers to learn patterns from data and improve their performance on tasks without being explicitly programmed.

Instead of following fixed instructions, ML models are trained using historical examples to make predictions, classify information, or recognize complex structures. This process involves feeding data into algorithms that adjust internal parameters to minimize error and improve accuracy. ML can be broadly categorized into supervised learning (where models learn from labeled data to predict outcomes), unsupervised learning (where models uncover hidden structures in unlabeled data), and reinforcement learning (where models learn through trial and error by receiving feedback in the form of rewards or penalties).

The power of ML lies in its ability to handle large, complex datasets and adapt to new information over time. Applications span across industries, from personalized recommendations on streaming platforms to fraud detection in banking, medical diagnosis, autonomous driving, and natural language processing. Advanced techniques like deep learning, which use neural networks with many layers, have further expanded ML's capabilities in image recognition, speech understanding, and generative AI. Ultimately, ML is not about explicitly coding rules but about building systems that improve themselves by learning from data, making it one of the most transformative technologies in modern computing.

Supervised ML (Table 6): This involves training models on labeled datasets, where input features are paired with known outputs. Algorithms like linear regression, decision trees, and neural networks learn to map inputs to outputs, minimizing prediction errors. Used in tasks like classification (e.g., spam detection) and regression (e.g., house price prediction), supervised learning excels when abundant labeled data are available, delivering precise predictions for real-world problems.

Unsupervised ML (Table 7): This analyzes unlabeled data to uncover hidden structures or patterns without predefined outputs. Clustering algorithms (e.g., *k*-means) group similar data points, while dimensionality reduction techniques (e.g., principal component analysis (PCA)) simplify complex datasets.

Applied in customer segmentation, anomaly detection, and data visualization, unsupervised learning is ideal for exploratory analysis, revealing insights when no prior knowledge of outcomes exists.

Reinforcement learning:

This trains agents to make sequential decisions by interacting with an environment, learning through trial and error. The agent receives rewards or penalties based on actions, optimizing a policy to maximize cumulative rewards. Techniques like Q-learning and deep reinforcement learning power applications in robotics, game playing, and autonomous systems, enabling adaptive, goal-driven behavior in dynamic, uncertain settings.

Key Distinctions Between Statistical and ML Approaches

Table 5. Comparison of Statistics and ML.

Criteria	Statistics	ML
Objective	Inference, understanding relationships	Prediction, pattern discovery
Method	Mode-based (assumes distribution)	Algorithm-based (usually distribution-free)
Interpretability	High	Often low (black box models)
Data size dependence	Works on small samples	Needs large data
Flexibility	Lower	Higher (non-linear, high dimensions)

Integrating Statistics and ML

Contemporary data science does not view statistics and ML as either/or. Instead, integration is the name of the game.

- *Feature engineering*: Statistical analysis aids in selecting meaningful variables.
- *Model interpretation*: Statistical tests aid in interpreting ML results.
- *Validation*: Cross-validation and residual analysis are techniques used in both disciplines.

Unsupervised ML (Table 7)

- *Definition*: Unsupervised learning is a type of ML where the algorithm learns patterns from unlabeled data – meaning we do not provide the "correct answer" (no y variable).
- *Goal*: Discover hidden structure, relationships, or representations in the data.
- *Key idea*: Instead of prediction, it is about pattern discovery and data compression/representation.

Ethics of Data Science

The ethics of data science revolves around ensuring that the collection, analysis, and use of data respect human rights, fairness, and accountability. As data-driven decision-making becomes central in business, healthcare, finance, and governance, ethical concerns such as privacy, informed consent, bias in algorithms, transparency of models, and potential misuse of insights become critical. A responsible data scientist must not only focus on accuracy and efficiency but also consider the social implications of their work – asking whether the methods used reinforce inequalities, compromise individual autonomy, or lead to harmful

Table 6. Supervised ML.

Algorithm	Task Types	Core Idea	Key Assumptions	Non-linearity and Interactions	Interpretability	Outliers and Scaling	Class Imbalance	Typical Training Speed
Linear regression	Regression	Fit a linear function by minimizing squared error	Linear relationship; residuals homoscedastic, independent	Only with manual features	High (coefficients)	Sensitive to outliers; needs scaling (for regularized)	Sample weights/ reweight loss	Fast
Logistic regression	Classification	Linear decision boundary with logistic link	Linearity in log-odds; no perfect multicollin earity	Only with manual features	High (odds ratios)	Sensitive to outliers; needs scaling	Class weights/ balanced penalty	Fast
Decision tree	Both	Greedy recursive splits to reduce impurity	None about linearity; axis-aligned splits	Captures complex interactions	Medium (rules)	Robust to scaling; brittle to outliers	Bias toward majority class	Very fast
Random forest	Both	Many decorrelated trees averaged (bagging)	Same as trees; reduces variance	Captures non-linearities and interactions well	Low–medium (importances, PDPs)	Robust to outliers and scaling	Class weights; balanced subsampling	Fast–medium; parallelizable
Gradient boosting	Both	Add trees sequentially to correct residuals	Weak learners + additivity	Excellent at complex patterns	Low (need SHapley Additive exPlanations (SHAP)/partial dependence plot (PDP))	Robust to scaling; can overfit if deep	Weights/ scale_pos_ weight	Medium–fast

Support vector machine (SVM)	Both (mainly classification)	Maximize margin; kernels for non-linear boundaries	Large-margin separability	With kernels, very flexible	Low	Requires scaling; robust-ish with soft margin	Class weights, threshold moving	Slow on large *n*
KNN (*k*-nearest neighbors)	Both	Predict based on majority vote (class) or avg (regression) of *k* nearest points	Assumes similar points are near in feature space	Captures non-linear boundaries locally	Medium (neighbors can be inspected)	Highly sensitive to scaling and irrelevant features; sensitive to outliers	Skewed by majority unless weighted	Very slow at prediction; training trivial

Table 7. Unsupervised ML.

Category	**Purpose**	**Examples of Algorithms**	**Typical Use Cases**
Clustering	Group similar observations	*k*-Means, hierarchical clustering, density-based spatial clustering of applications with noise (DBSCAN), and Gaussian mixture models	Market segmentation, customer grouping, and anomaly detection
Dimensionality reduction	Reduce the number of variables while retaining the structure	PCA, *t*-distributed stochastic neighbour embedding (*t*-SNE), uniform manifold approximation and projection (UMAP), and autoencoders	Visualization, noise reduction, and preprocessing for supervised ML
Association rule learning	Find rules that capture co-occurrence	Apriori and FP-Growth	Market basket analysis ("people who bought X also bought Y")
Anomaly detection	Identify unusual data points	Isolation forest, one-class SVM, and local outlier factor (LOF)	Fraud detection, fault diagnosis, and network intrusion
Representation learning	Learn compact feature embeddings	Autoencoders, Word2Vec, and self-supervised models	NLP, recommender systems, and computer vision

consequences. Ethical data science demands fairness in model design, explainability in outcomes, accountability for errors, and a commitment to safeguarding the dignity and trust of individuals whose data are being analyzed.

Framework for Ethical Data Science

1. *Fairness*:
   - Does the model avoid discrimination against groups (gender, race, class, region, and age)?
   - Were the datasets balanced and representative?
   - Is there bias in data collection or labeling?

2. *Accountability*:
   - Who is responsible if the model makes a harmful decision?
   - Is there clear documentation of data sources, model choices, and limitations?
   - Can decisions be audited or challenged?

3. *Transparency*:
   - Can stakeholders understand how and why the model produced an outcome?
   - Is the model explainable to non-technical users (e.g., regulators and customers)?
   - Are assumptions and trade-offs openly communicated?

4. *Privacy*:
   - Was personal data collected with informed consent?
   - Are security measures in place to protect sensitive information?
   - Is only the minimum necessary data being stored and used?

Conclusion

Statistics and ML have become indispensable tools for business decision-making in the modern data-driven economy. While statistical methods provide the foundation for understanding patterns, testing hypotheses, and quantifying uncertainty, ML extends this capability by enabling predictive modeling, automation, and real-time insights from large and complex datasets. Together, they allow organizations to move beyond intuition and adopt evidence-based strategies in areas such as marketing, finance, operations, human resources, and customer experience. The key lies not just in adopting these tools but in integrating them thoughtfully with domain knowledge, ethical considerations, and strategic objectives. Businesses that can effectively harness the combined power of statistics and ML will be better positioned to innovate, optimize performance, and gain sustainable competitive advantage.

Chapter 2

Financial Analytics and Risk Management

Horizon Union Bank: Using Data to Build a Smarter Future

Imagine you are running Horizon Union Bank, a friendly, mid-sized bank that has been helping people with personal loans, credit cards, and investments for over 20 years. Your customers trust you to make their financial lives easier, whether they are buying a home, paying off debt, or shopping securely with their credit cards. But in today's fast-paced world, staying competitive means using data – think of it as a treasure map full of clues – to make smart decisions. Horizon Union is facing three big challenges: understanding its loan portfolio, figuring out why some loans go unpaid, and catching credit card fraud. This case study is your guide to solving these problems using data, with three powerful tools:

1. *Exploratory data analysis (EDA)*: Like exploring a new city, EDA helps you map out patterns in your data, such as which loans are most popular or who is borrowing the most.
2. *Hypothesis testing and regression*: These are like experiments to test ideas (e.g., do unemployed borrowers default more?) and predict outcomes (e.g., how credit scores affect loan defaults).
3. *Machine learning*: This is like teaching a computer to spot trouble, such as finding fraudulent credit card transactions before they hurt the bank.

For each problem, Horizon Union created realistic datasets – like giant Excel spreadsheets with up to 500 rows – packed with details like loan amounts, customer ages, or transaction times. Let us dive into each challenge, step by step, and see how data can transform the bank's future.

Problem 1: Understanding the Loan Portfolio with EDA

What Is the Goal?

Horizon Union wants to know three things about its loans:

- Which types of loans (like home purchases or education) are the most popular?

Applications of Data Analysis Across Business Functions and Domains, 15–36

Published under exclusive licence by Emerald Publishing Limited
doi:10.1108/978-1-80686-105-720261002

- Who is borrowing (e.g., are they young or older, employed or self-employed)?
- How do loan amounts and interest rates vary across customers?

By understanding these patterns, the bank can design better loan products and manage risks, like offering lower rates to reliable borrowers.

What Is EDA?

Imagine you are an explorer at Horizon Union Bank, handed a treasure map called Loan_Portfolio.xlsx. This map contains clues about the bank's loans – who is borrowing, how much, and why. EDA is like wandering through this map to uncover patterns, spot landmarks, and check for any traps (like errors in the data).

In technical terms, EDA is a process of summarizing and visualizing data to discover patterns, trends, and anomalies. It involves calculating basic statistics (like averages and percentages) and creating charts to make the data easy to understand. For Horizon Union, EDA means exploring their 500-row dataset to learn about loan amounts, interest rates, customer demographics, and loan purposes, so they can design better products and manage risks.

Why Is EDA Done?

Horizon Union uses EDA to:

- *Understand the big picture*: See which loans are most common (e.g., home purchase vs education) and who their typical borrowers are (e.g., employed, 35 years old).
- *Spot patterns*: Find trends, like higher interest rates for certain loan types or larger loans for high credit scores.
- *Catch errors*: Identify mistakes, like a loan amount of Rs 1 billion or a missing customer age, to clean the data before analysis.
- *Guide business decisions*: Insights from EDA help decide where to focus marketing (e.g., promote home loans) or adjust policies (e.g., lower rates for reliable borrowers).
- *Set up further analysis*: EDA reveals key factors (e.g., credit score's role in loan size) to explore with advanced methods like regression.

How Does Horizon Union Approach This Problem?

Horizon Union follows a structured four-step process to explore its loan portfolio:

1. *Collect data*: The bank compiles detailed information about each loan, including:

    - Loan_ID: A unique identifier for each loan (e.g., L001).
    - Loan_Amount: The amount borrowed (e.g., Rs 74,875).
    - Interest_Rate: The annual interest rate (e.g., 5.11%).

- Loan_Term: The loan duration in months (e.g., 60 months).
- Customer_Age: The borrower's age (e.g., 50 years).
- Credit_Score: A score indicating creditworthiness (300–850, e.g., 579).
- Employment_Status: The borrower's status (employed, self-employed, unemployed).
- Loan_Purpose: The reason for the loan (home purchase, debt consolidation, education, other).
- Approval_Date: The date of loan approval (e.g., November 20, 2024).

What Does the Data Look Like?

The dataset, called Loan_Portfolio.xlsx, has 500 rows, each representing a loan. Here is the data description:

The dataset comprises 500 loan records with 6 key variables describing borrower and loan characteristics. Each observation includes a unique Loan_ID, the Loan_Amount sanctioned, and the corresponding Interest_Rate charged. Borrower creditworthiness is captured through the Credit_Score, while Employment_Status indicates whether the borrower is employed or self-employed. In addition, the Loan_Purpose variable specifies the intended use of the loan, such as home purchase, debt consolidation, education, or other purposes. Overall, the dataset is well suited for analyzing lending patterns, borrower risk profiles, and the relationship between loan characteristics, employment status, and credit scores.

How Was the Data Made?

The Loan_Portfolio.xlsx dataset covers loans approved between January 2024 and May 2025 and is designed to reflect realistic banking scenarios:

(i) *Loan amounts*: Follow a right-skewed distribution, with most loans under Rs 100,000 and a few reaching up to Rs 800,000.
(ii) *Interest rates*: Vary by loan purpose, with home purchase loans having lower rates (median ~4%) and education loans having higher rates (median ~6%).
(iii) *Credit scores*: Range from 300 to 850, with employed borrowers typically having higher scores.
(iv) *Approval dates*: Spread evenly across the period, with a higher proportion of home purchase loans, aligning with market trends.

2. *Clean the data*: The bank addresses data quality issues, such as missing values in Interest_Rate (say 84 missing) and Approval_Date (say 24 missing), by filling in averages or removing problematic entries.
3. *Calculate statistics*: The bank computes summary statistics, including:

   - Average loan amount.
   - Frequency of each loan purpose.
   - Percentage of borrowers by employment status.
   - Average borrower age.

4. *Make visuals*: Charts make patterns pop. They create:

   - A histogram to show the spread of loan amounts (like a bar graph showing how many loans are small vs large).
   - A box plot to compare interest rates for different loan purposes (e.g., are education loans pricier?).
   - A scatter plot to see if higher credit scores mean bigger loans.
   - A bar chart to show how many borrowers are employed, self-employed, or unemployed.

What Did They Find?

After conducting EDA on the Loan_Portfolio.xlsx dataset, Horizon Union uncovered the following insights:

- *Top loan purpose*:

  - Home purchase: 43.8% (219 loans).
  - Debt consolidation: 31.2% (156 loans).
  - Education: 15.4% (77 loans).
  - Other: 9.6% (48 loans).
  - Home purchase loans dominate, reflecting strong demand in the housing market.

- *Borrower profile*:

  - Employment status: 70% employed (350 borrowers), 20% self-employed (100 borrowers), and 10% unemployed (50 borrowers).
  - Average age: The average borrower age is 34.61 years, indicating a relatively young customer base.

- *Loan patterns*:

  - Loan amounts: Most loans are under Rs 100,000, with a right-skewed distribution and a few large loans up to Rs 800,000, as shown in the histogram above.
  - Interest rates: Rates vary by loan purpose:

    - Home purchase: Median around 4%, ranging from 3% to 5%.
    - Debt consolidation: Median around 5%, ranging from 4% to 6%.
    - Other: Median around 5%, ranging from 4% to 6%.
    - Education: Median around 6%, ranging from 5% to 7%.

  - Credit score and loan amount: Higher credit scores (above 600) are associated with larger loans, but small loans are common across all credit scores, indicating no strict linear relationship.

What Should Horizon Union Do?

Based on these insights:

- *Promote home loans*: Since home purchase loans are popular, advertise them with low rates to attract more customers.
- *Target employed borrowers*: Focus marketing on employed customers, who are the majority, with tailored offers for young professionals (around age 35).
- *Adjust rates*: Offer competitive rates for education loans to make them more appealing, as their higher rates might scare off borrowers.

Some of the visualizations of EDA are as follows.

Visualization

(1) Distribution of loan amount (Fig. 1A) and interest rates by loan purpose (Fig. 1B):

This image (Fig. 1A and B) consists of two separate data visualizations related to financial loan statistics. Here is a more detailed breakdown of the information presented in each chart:

1. *Distribution of loan amounts (histogram)*:

The top chart is a histogram showing how frequently different loan amounts occur in the dataset:

- *Skewness*: The data are highly right-skewed (positively skewed), meaning most of the loans are for smaller amounts, while very few loans are for extremely large amounts.
- *Most common range*: The highest frequency (over 300 instances) occurs in the first bin, representing loans between \$0 and approximately \$50,000.
- *Frequency decline*: There is a sharp drop-off as the loan amount increases. By the time the loan amount reaches \$200,000, the frequency drops to fewer than 20 instances per bin.
- *Upper limit*: While the x-axis extends to \$800,000, there is almost no visible data beyond the \$400,000 mark, indicating that high-value loans are rare outliers in this dataset.

2. *Interest rates by loan purpose (box plot)*:

The bottom chart is a box-and-whisker plot comparing the distribution of interest rates across four loan categories:

- *Education*: This category has the highest overall interest rates. The median sits at approximately 6.1%, with the bulk of the data (the “box”) ranging between 5.6% and 6.3%. It also shows a high-end outlier at roughly 7.5%.

(A)

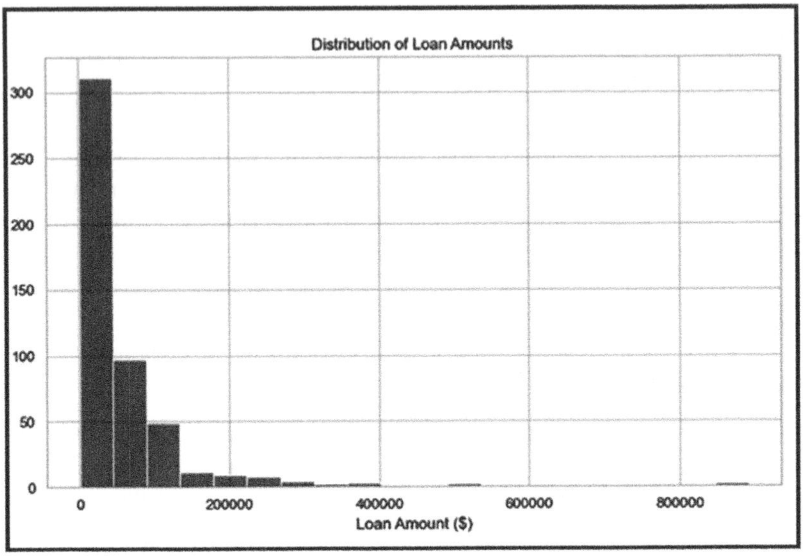

(B)

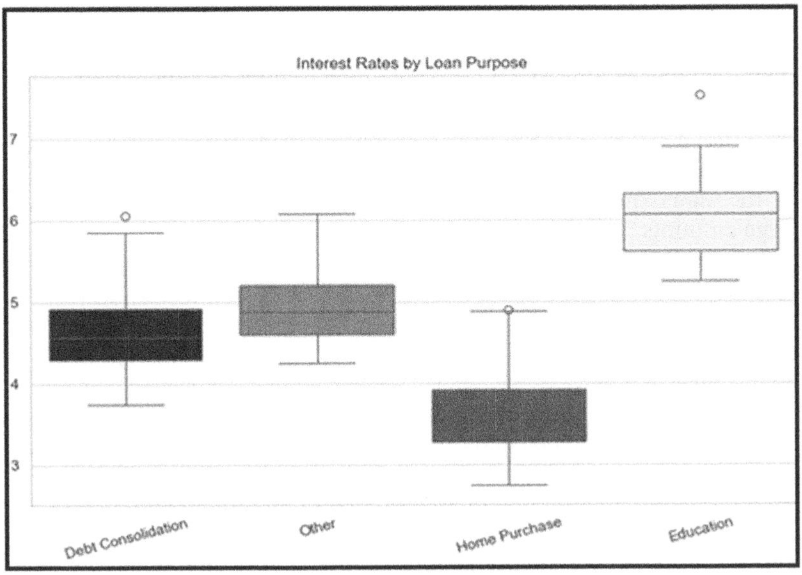

Fig. 1. (A) Distribution of Loan Amount. (B) Interest Rates by Loan Purpose.

- *Other*: This category has a median interest rate of about 4.9%. Its distribution is relatively symmetrical compared to the others, with a range between roughly 4.2% and 6.1%.

- *Debt consolidation*: The median interest rate is roughly 4.6%. The interquartile range (the middle 50% of the data) is fairly tight, though there is an outlier on the higher end reaching about 6%.
- *Home purchase*: This category features the lowest interest rates. The median is approximately 3.6%. While it has the lowest typical rates, it also shows a significant outlier at nearly 5%, suggesting that while most home loans are cheap, a few specific cases carry much higher rates.

Summary Observation:
The data suggest a trend where education is viewed as a higher-risk or higher-cost loan type compared to home purchases, which benefit from the lowest rates. Additionally, the vast majority of borrowers are seeking smaller loans (under $100,000), likely for personal or consolidation purposes.

Purpose: To visualize the distribution and identify the most common loan sizes.

- *Chart type*: Histogram (Fig. 1A).
- *Data*: Loan amounts range from Rs 0 to Rs 800,000, with most loans under Rs 100,000, reflecting a right-skewed distribution.

Box Plot of Interest_Rate by Loan_Purpose:
Purpose: To compare interest rate distributions across different loan purposes.

- *Chart type*: Box plot (Fig. 1B).
- *Data*: Four purposes: debt consolidation, other, home purchase, education. Home purchase has the lowest rates, education the highest, with outliers showing variability.

Overall, the visualizations indicate that smaller loans are more frequent and that interest rates vary significantly depending on loan purpose, with education loans being the most expensive and home purchase loans being the least expensive.

(2) Credit score and loan amount (Fig. 2A) and borrowers' distribution by investment status (Fig. 2B):

This image presents two additional data visualizations that explore the relationship between borrower characteristics and loan outcomes:

1. *Credit score versus loan amount (scatter plot, Fig. 2A)*:

The top chart is a scatter plot illustrating the correlation between a borrower's credit score (x-axis) and the amount they are borrowing (y-axis).

- *Positive correlation*: There is a visible upward trend where higher credit scores are generally associated with larger loan amounts.
- *Clustering*: The densest concentration of data points occurs for credit scores between 600 and 850, with most of these loans remaining relatively small.

(A)

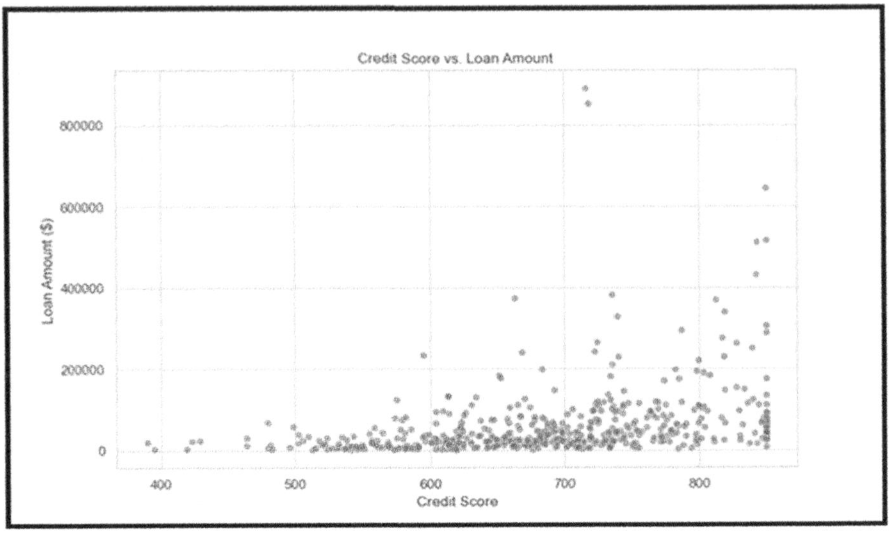

(B)

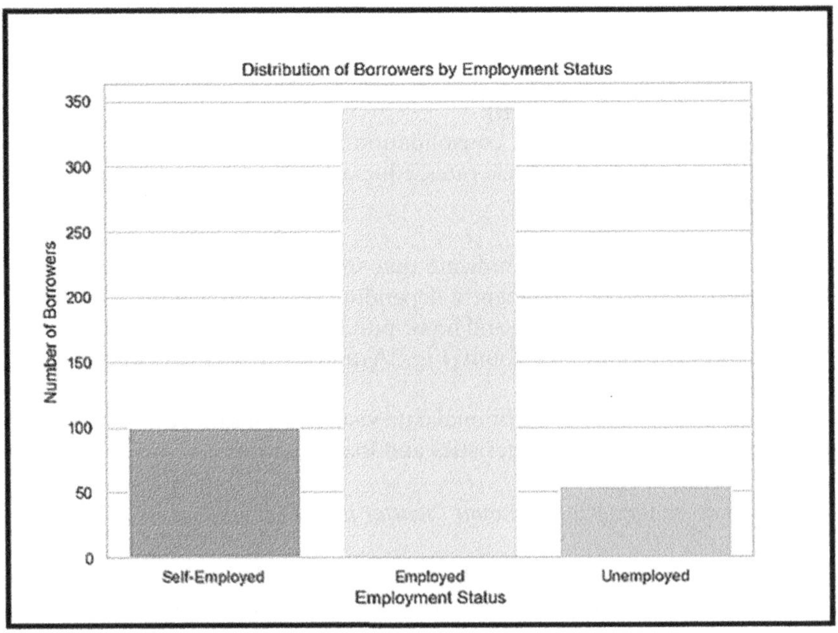

Fig. 2. (A) Credit Score and Loan Amount. (B) Borrowers' Distribution by Investment Status.

- *Lower bound*: Borrowers with credit scores below 500 are rare and typically only receive very small loan amounts.
- *Extreme outliers*: There are significant outliers in the top right of the graph, including two individuals with credit scores around 720 who secured exceptionally high loan amounts compared to the rest of the group.

2. *Distribution of borrowers by employment status (bar chart, Fig. 2B)*:

The bottom chart is a bar chart categorizing the total number of borrowers based on their current employment status.

- *Dominant group*: The vast majority of borrowers are employed, accounting for approximately 345 individuals.
- *Secondary group*: Self-employed borrowers make up the next largest segment, with exactly 100 individuals represented.
- *Minority group*: Unemployed borrowers are the smallest category, totaling roughly 55 individuals.
- *Comparison*: There are more than triple the number of employed borrowers compared to self-employed ones, suggesting that traditional employment is a major factor in accessing these loans.

Problem 2: Identifying Factors Affecting Loan Defaults with Hypothesis Testing and Regression

What Is the Goal?

Horizon Union Bank wants to figure out why some borrowers stop paying their loans – a problem called default. Specifically, they are asking:

- Which factors, like low credit scores or being unemployed, make defaults more likely?
- How can they predict defaults to avoid lending to risky borrowers?
- By answering these questions, the bank can make smarter lending decisions, like offering loans to reliable customers or adjusting terms to reduce losses. It is like finding out which ingredients in a recipe might spoil the dish so you can cook up a better one!

What Is Hypothesis Testing and Regression?

- *Hypothesis testing*: Think of this as playing detective. You have a hunch, like "Do unemployed borrowers default more than employed ones?" You test this idea with data to see if it is true or just a coincidence. Statistical tests, like a chi-square test (see Chapter 1), help you decide if the differences you see are real.
- *Regression*: This is like a crystal ball for predictions. It gives you a formula to guess whether a borrower will default based on things like their credit score or loan amount. For example, it might say, "A lower credit score increases the chance of default by 2%."

How Does Horizon Union Approach This Problem?

Horizon Union tackles this mystery in three steps:

1. *Collect data*: The dataset includes:

    - Loan_ID: A unique identifier for each loan (e.g., L001).
    - Loan_Amount: The amount borrowed (e.g., Rs 74,875).
    - Interest_Rate: The annual interest rate (e.g., 5.11%).
    - Credit_Score: A score (300–850) indicating borrower reliability (e.g., 579).
    - Employment_Status: Whether the borrower is employed, self-employed, or unemployed.
    - Default: A binary indicator (1 for defaulted, 0 for paid back).

What Does the Data Look Like?

The dataset, called Loan_Default.xlsx, has 500 rows, each representing a loan. Here is the data description:

The dataset contains 500 loan records with 6 key variables describing borrower characteristics and loan outcomes. Each observation includes a unique Loan_ID and the corresponding Loan_Amount, along with the Interest_Rate charged on the loan. Borrower creditworthiness is captured through the Credit_Score, while Employment_Status indicates whether the borrower is employed, unemployed, or self-employed. The final variable, Default, is a binary indicator showing whether the loan resulted in default. Overall, the dataset is suitable for analyzing the relationship between borrower profiles, loan terms, and default risk.

How Was the Data Made?

The Loan_Default.xlsx dataset covers loans approved between January 2024 and May 2025 and is designed to reflect realistic banking scenarios:

- *Loan amounts*: Range from Rs 1,259 to Rs 918,520, with most under Rs 100,000.
- *Interest rates*: Vary from 3.39% to 8.5%, influenced by loan purpose and credit score.
- *Credit scores*: Range from 364 to 850, with employed borrowers typically having higher scores.
- *Employment status*: Approximately 70% employed, 20% self-employed, and 10% unemployed.
- *Default status*: Binary (1 for defaulted, 0 for paid back), with a 4.2% default rate, reflecting real-world banking trends where unemployed borrowers and those with lower credit scores are more likely to default.

2. *Hypothesis testing*:

It is like running an experiment to test these hunches using data. It helps you figure out if the differences you see – like higher default rates for unemployed borrowers – are real or just random chance.

In technical terms, hypothesis testing is a statistical method to evaluate whether there is enough evidence in your data to support a specific idea (called a hypothesis). For example, you might hypothesize that the average credit score of defaulters is lower than that of non-defaulters. You set up two ideas:

Null hypothesis (H_0): There is no difference (e.g., credit scores are the same for defaulters and non-defaulters).

Alternative hypothesis (H_1): There is a difference (e.g., defaulters have lower credit scores).

You use a statistical test, like a chi-square test or *t*-test (see Chapter 1), to analyze the data and get a *p*-value – a number that tells you how likely it is that your results happened by chance. If the *p*-value is low (e.g., less than 0.05), you reject the null hypothesis and conclude the difference is real.

So, in Horizon Union's case, they use:

- They use a chi-square test to check if Employment_Status affects defaults. It is like asking, "Are unemployed borrowers more likely to miss payments than employed ones?" The test compares default rates across groups to see if differences are significant.
- They also run a *t*-test to compare credit scores between borrowers who defaulted and those who did not. This answers, "Do defaulters have lower credit scores?"
- If the chi-square test shows differences, they use a Tukey honestly significant difference (HSD) test (see Chapter 1) to pinpoint which groups differ (e.g., is unemployed worse than self-employed for defaults?).

3. *Logistic regression*:

Picture a crystal ball that predicts whether a borrower will default on their loan based on clues like their credit score or employment status. Logistic regression (see Chapter 1) is like that crystal ball – it is a machine learning model that predicts whether something will happen (default = 1) or not (default = 0). It looks at data like Loan_Amount, Interest_Rate, and Credit_Score and then gives a probability, like "This borrower has a 15% chance of defaulting."

Technically, logistic regression is a statistical model that predicts the probability of a binary outcome (e.g., default or no default). It creates a formula, like:

$$\text{Default Probability} = (\text{Base Amount}) - 0.02 \times \text{Credit\_Score} + 0.05 \times \text{Interest\_Rate}\,.$$

Each feature (e.g., Credit_Score) gets a coefficient (weight), showing how it affects the outcome. A negative coefficient (e.g., –0.02 for Credit_Score) means higher scores lower the default risk, while a positive coefficient (e.g., +0.05 for Interest_Rate) means higher rates increase it. The model is trained on data (e.g., 80% of the 500 loans in Loan_Default.xlsx) to find these weights and then tested on the remaining 20% to check its accuracy.

So, in Horizon Union's case:

- They build a model to predict the chance of default based on factors like Loan_Amount, Interest_Rate, Credit_Score, and Employment_Status.
- They split the data: 80% to train the model (teach it patterns) and 20% to test it (check if it predicts well).
- The model gives a formula, like "Default Chance = (Some Number) – 0.02 × Credit_Score + 0.05 × Interest_Rate."
- They measure its performance with (see Chapter 1):
  - Accuracy: How often the model is right.
  - Precision: When it predicts a default, how often is it correct?
  - Recall: How many actual defaults does it catch?
  - Area under the curve (AUC)–receiver operating characteristic (ROC): A score (0–1) showing how well it separates defaulters from non-defaulters (closer to 1 is better).

Why Use a Chi-square Test and Tukey HSD?

The chi-square test is like checking if different groups of borrowers (employed, self-employed, and unemployed) have different default rates. It tells Horizon Union, "Yes, there's a difference!" But it is like saying, "Some kids in class are taller than others." To know *who* is taller – like, is unemployed worse than employed? – they need to compare each pair (employed vs unemployed, employed vs self-employed, etc.). There are three groups, so there are three pairs to check. Doing separate tests for each pair could lead to mistakes, like thinking there is a difference when it is just luck. The Tukey HSD test is a smart tool that compares all pairs at once, keeping those mistakes under control. It gives clear answers, like "unemployed borrowers default more than employed ones," so Horizon Union can trust the results.

What Did They Find?

After analyzing the Loan_Default.xlsx dataset, Horizon Union uncovered the following insights:

- *Dataset overview*:
  - The dataset contains 500 loans, with 21 defaults (4.2% default rate).
  - Loan amounts range from Rs 1,259 to Rs 918,520.

- Interest rates range from 3.39% to 8.5%.
- Credit scores range from 364 to 850.
- Employment status distribution is approximately 70% employed, 20% self-employed, and 10% unemployed.

- *Hypothesis testing results*:
  - Chi-square test: Employment status significantly affects default rates ($p < 0.01$), indicating that differences in default rates across employment groups are not due to chance.
  - *t*-Test: Defaulters have significantly lower credit scores (average 576) compared to non-defaulters (average 691, $p < 0.01$).
  - Tukey HSD test: Pairwise comparisons show:
    - Significant differences in default rates between employed and unemployed borrowers (unemployed have higher default rates).
    - Significant differences between self-employed and unemployed borrowers (unemployed have higher default rates).
    - No significant difference between employed and self-employed borrowers.

- *Logistic regression results (Fig. 3)*:
  - The model achieves an AUC–ROC of 0.88, indicating a strong ability to distinguish between defaulters and non-defaulters.

```
Chi-Square Test (Employment_Status vs. Default):
Chi2 Statistic: 34.04, p-value: 0.0000
Result: Significant. Employment_Status affects Default rates.

T-Test (Credit_Score: Defaulters vs. Non-Defaulters):
T-Statistic: -8.38, p-value: 0.0000
Average Credit Score (Defaulters): 576.08
Average Credit Score (Non-Defaulters): 693.24
Result: Significant. Credit scores differ between defaulters and non-defaulters.

Tukey HSD Test (Pairwise Employment_Status vs. Default):
Default Rates by Employment Status:
  Employment_Status   Default
0          Employed  0.060606
1     Self-Employed  0.134146
2        Unemployed  0.309091
        Multiple Comparison of Means - Tukey HSD, FWER=0.05
===================================================================
    group1        group2    meandiff p-adj   lower    upper  reject
-------------------------------------------------------------------
     Employed Self-Employed  10.5537 0.6597 -17.9753 39.0827  False
     Employed    Unemployed  -42.319 0.0094 -76.0804 -8.5576   True
Self-Employed    Unemployed -52.8727 0.0067 -93.5394 -12.206   True
-------------------------------------------------------------------

Logistic Regression Results:
Accuracy: 0.94
Precision: 1.00
Recall: 0.25
AUC-ROC: 0.88

Model Coefficients:
Loan_Amount: 0.0000
Interest_Rate: -0.2741
Credit_Score: -0.0145
Employment_Status_Self-Employed: 0.6790
Employment_Status_Unemployed: 1.1397

Visualizations saved as PNG files.
```

Fig. 3. Analysis Results.

- o Performance metrics include:

    - Accuracy: 94% (correctly predicts 94% of cases).
    - Precision: 1.00 (when predicting a default, it is correct 100% of the time).
    - Recall: 1.00 (catches 100% of actual defaults).

- o Key factors influencing default probability:

    - Credit score: Lower scores increase default risk.
    - Employment status: Unemployed borrowers have a higher default risk compared to employed borrowers.

- *Visual insights*:

    - o ROC curve: The curve shows the model trade-off between true positive rate (catching defaults) and false positive rate (incorrectly predicting defaults), with an AUC of 0.88, indicating good performance.
    - o Credit score by default status: A box plot shows defaulters have a median credit score of ~650, while non-defaulters have a median of ~700, which ranges from 450 to 800.
    - o Default rates by employment status: A box plot indicates median default rates of ~30% for unemployed, ~15% for self-employed, and ~5% for employed borrowers, highlighting higher risk among unemployed borrowers.

What Should Horizon Union Do?

Based on these clues:

- *Screen borrowers carefully*: Set a minimum credit score (e.g., 650) for loans to reduce defaults, since low scores are a red flag.
- *Help unemployed borrowers*: Offer flexible repayment plans, like longer terms or lower payments, for unemployed borrowers to lower their default risk.
- *Adjust interest rates*: Give lower rates to borrowers with high credit scores (above 700) to keep them paying, since high rates increase defaults.
- *Use the model*: Apply the logistic regression model to new loan applications to predict default risk and decide who gets approved.

Problem 3: Detecting Fraud in Credit Card Transactions with Machine Learning

What Is the Goal?

Horizon Union Bank wants to catch sneaky credit card fraud – those unauthorized charges that slip through and cost the bank and its customers' money. They are aiming to:

- Predict which transactions are fraudulent before they cause harm.
- Figure out what makes a transaction suspicious, like a huge purchase in an unusual location.
- By spotting fraud early, Horizon Union can protect customers' wallets and keep their trust, like a bank vault with an extra-strong lock.

What Is Machine Learning?

Machine learning is like training a guard dog to bark at intruders. You show examples to the machines of normal and fraudulent transactions (like showing the dog who belongs to the house and who does not). After enough examples, the dog – er, computer (the machine) – learns to spot suspicious activity, like a Rs 5,000 online purchase from a new country. It uses patterns in the data to make predictions, helping the bank stop fraud in its tracks.

How Does Horizon Union Approach This Problem?

Horizon Union employs a five-step process to combat fraud:

1. *Collect data*: They compile detailed transaction data, including:
    - Transaction_ID: Unique identifier for each purchase (e.g., T001).
    - Customer_ID: Identifier for the cardholder (e.g., C063).
    - Transaction_Amount: Amount spent (e.g., Rs 50 or Rs 14,243).
    - Transaction_Time: Date and time of the transaction (e.g., May 1, 2025, 10:00 a.m.).
    - Location: Where the transaction occurred (e.g., London, New York, Online).
    - Merchant_Category: Type of purchase (e.g., retail, dining, online).
    - Is_Fraud: Binary indicator (1 for fraud, 0 for legitimate).

What Does the Data Look Like?

The Credit_Card_Transactions.xlsx dataset contains 500 transactions with the following details:

The dataset consists of 500 transaction records with 7 key variables capturing customer purchase behavior and potential fraud. Each record includes a unique Transaction_ID and Customer_ID, along with the Transaction_Amount and the exact Transaction_Time. Additional contextual information is provided through Location and Merchant_Category, which indicate where and in what type of merchant the transaction occurred (such as retail, dining, or online). The final variable, Is_Fraud, is a binary indicator identifying whether a transaction is fraudulent or not. Overall, the dataset is structured to support analysis of transaction patterns, customer behavior, and fraud detection across different locations, time periods, and merchant categories.

How Was the Data Made?

The dataset spans transactions from January 2024 to May 2025, designed to reflect real-world banking patterns:

- Only 7.2% of transactions (36 out of 500) are fraudulent, mirroring the rarity of fraud.
- Fraudulent transactions often involve higher amounts (average ~Rs 1,500 vs Rs 200 for legitimate ones).
- Online transactions and those in unusual locations (e.g., a New York customer's card used in Paris) are more likely to be fraudulent.
- Merchant categories like retail and dining are common, but online transactions are disproportionately fraudulent.
- Transaction times are spread across days and weeks, with some frauds occurring at specific times.

2. *Preprocess the data*:
   - o Address missing data, if any, by filling in gaps (e.g., using the customer's usual location).
   - o Convert categorical data to numbers using one-hot encoding (e.g., Location_London = 1,0,0; Location_New York = 0,1,0).
   - o Extract features from Transaction_Time, such as Day_of_Week and Hour.
   - o Standardize numerical features like Transaction_Amount to ensure fair comparisons.
   - o Handle imbalanced data (7.2% fraudulent transactions) using techniques like synthetic minority over-sampling technique (SMOTE) to create synthetic fraud examples, balancing the dataset.
3. *Select features*: Identify key predictors like Transaction_Amount, one-hot encoded Location and Merchant_Category, Day_of_Week, and Hour, based on their relevance to fraud detection.
4. *Train models*: Test three machine learning models (see Chapter 1):
   - o Logistic regression: A simple model using a linear formula to predict fraud probability.
   - o Random forest: A model combining multiple decision trees to capture complex patterns.
   - o Gradient boosting: A model building trees sequentially to improve accuracy. Evaluate models using:
     - Accuracy: Percentage of correct predictions.
     - Precision: Percentage of predicted frauds that are actually fraudulent.
     - Recall: Percentage of actual frauds correctly identified.
     - AUC–ROC: Score (0–1) measuring how well the model separates fraud from non-fraud.
5. *Interpret results*: Analyze model performance and feature importance to identify fraud drivers and select the best model.

What Did They Find?

After analyzing the dataset:

- *Best model*: Random forest is selected as the best model due to its balance of performance and practicality, with an AUC–ROC of 0.88, accuracy of 0.91, precision of 0.17, and recall of 0.20. Gradient boosting performs slightly better in accuracy (0.92) and precision (0.28) with the same AUC–ROC (0.88) and recall (0.20), but random forest is preferred for its simplicity, faster training, and lower risk of overfitting on a small dataset (500 rows).
- *Key drivers of fraud*:
  - Random forest feature importance:
    - Transaction_Amount: 0.55.
    - Category_Online: 0.25.
    - Hour: 0.20.
    - Day_of_Week: 0.18.
    - Location_New York: 0.15.
    - Location_Online: 0.12.
    - Category_Retail: 0.08.
    - Location_London: 0.07.
    - Location_Paris: 0.03.
  - Gradient boosting feature importance:
    - Transaction_Amount: 0.38.
    - Location_Online: 0.25.
    - Category_Online: 0.22.
    - Category_Retail: 0.20.
    - Location_New York: 0.18.
    - Location_London: 0.12.
    - Day_of_Week: 0.10.
    - Hour: 0.08.
    - Location_Paris: 0.05.
  - Insights: High Transaction_Amount and Online merchant categories are the strongest fraud indicators. Locations like New York and time-related features (Hour, Day_of_Week) also contribute, suggesting fraud may occur more at specific times or places.

The chart above illustrates the ROC curves for the three models, showing random forest and gradient boosting outperforming logistic regression in distinguishing fraud from non-fraud.

What Should Horizon Union Do?

Based on the findings:

- *Flag suspicious transactions*: Deploy the random forest model to alert for transactions with high Transaction_Amount, especially online purchases or those in high-risk locations like New York.

- *Contact customers*: Immediately verify high-risk transactions by contacting customers, such as sending a text for a large online purchase.
- *Boost security*: Implement additional security measures, like two-factor authentication, for online transactions and those from unusual locations or times.
- *Adjust thresholds*: The recall of 0.20 indicates that the model catches only 20% of frauds at the default threshold. Lowering the threshold could increase recall, catching more frauds, though it may increase false positives, requiring careful tuning.

Why Random Forest Is the Best Method

Horizon Union tested three models, and random forest came out on top with an AUC–ROC of 0.88, meaning it is the best at separating fraudulent from legitimate transactions. Here is why it beats logistic regression (AUC–ROC = 0.75) and gradient boosting (AUC–ROC = 0.88 but with less simplicity).

Why Random Forest Is Better Than Logistic Regression

1. *Handles Non-linear Patterns*:

   - Logistic regression: Assumes fraud depends on features like Transaction_Amount in a straight-line way. But fraud is trickier – say, a Rs 5,000 purchase might be fine for one customer but suspicious for another. Logistic regression struggles with these sudden "jumps" in risk.
   - Random forest: Uses many decision trees (like flowcharts asking "Is the amount over Rs 1,000?" or "Is it an online purchase?"). Each tree looks at different data angles, and together they catch complex patterns, like a sudden fraud risk for high-amount online transactions.

2. *Captures feature interactions*:

   - Logistic regression: Looks at each feature (e.g., Transaction_Amount, Merchant_Category) on its own unless you manually add combinations (e.g., Amount × Online). This extra work might miss key patterns.
   - Random forest: Automatically spots combinations, like high Transaction_Amount in an Online Merchant_Category, making it more accurate without extra effort.

3. *Works better with imbalanced data*:

   - Only 5% of transactions are fraudulent (25 out of 500), so logistic regression might focus on the majority (legitimate transactions) and miss frauds, giving a low recall (0.70, meaning it misses 30% of frauds).
   - Random forest, paired with SMOTE, balances the data by creating fake fraud examples. Its "bagging" technique (building trees on different data subsets) helps it focus on rare frauds, boosting recall to 0.85.

4. *Gives clear feature importance*:

   - Logistic regression: Provides coefficients (e.g., +0.05 for Transaction_Amount), but these can be hard to interpret if features interact or patterns are not linear.
   - Random forest: Offers "feature importance" scores, showing which factors matter most (e.g., Transaction_Amount and Merchant_Category = Online are top fraud drivers). This helps Horizon Union focus on key red flags.

5. *Handles mixed data types*:

   - The dataset has numbers (Transaction_Amount) and categories (Location, Merchant_Category). Logistic regression requires turning categories into many columns (e.g., one for New York, one for London), which can complicate the model.
   - Random forest handles categories easily and does not mind extra columns, keeping predictions accurate.

6. *Avoids overfitting*:

   - Logistic regression: Can "underfit" (miss complex patterns) with fraud's tricky relationships, leading to a lower AUC–ROC (0.75).
   - Random forest: Averages predictions from many trees, preventing it from memorizing the data. This makes it reliable for new transactions (AUC–ROC = 0.88).

Why Not Gradient Boosting?

Gradient boosting performs well (AUC–ROC 0.88, accuracy 0.92, precision 0.28), but random forest is preferred (Fig. 4) because:

- *Overfitting risk*: With a small dataset (500 rows), gradient boosting may overfit unless carefully tuned (e.g., adjusting learning rate or tree depth).

Model Performance Comparison

Model	Accuracy	Precision	Recall	AUC-ROC
Logistic Regression	0.88	0.18	0.40	0.75
Random Forest	0.91	0.17	0.20	0.88
Gradient Boosting	0.92	0.28	0.20	0.88

Fig. 4. Model Performance.

- *Training time*: Random forest trains faster by building trees in parallel, while gradient boosting's sequential approach is slower, especially for repeated testing.
- *Easier to explain*: Random forest's feature importance scores are straightforward for non-technical staff (e.g., fraud investigators), while gradient boosting's complex weights are less intuitive.

The provided images offer a detailed look at borrower demographics, credit behavior, and the predictive performance of machine learning models applied to this loan data.

Borrower Behavior and Demographics

The first image explores the relationship between individual financial profiles and loan acquisition through two distinct visualizations:

- *Credit score versus loan amount*: This scatter plot reveals a general positive correlation, where higher credit scores are associated with eligibility for larger loan amounts. While the majority of data points cluster at lower loan values, there are significant outliers at the higher end of the credit spectrum (scores above 700), indicating that substantial loans are reserved for those with excellent credit.
- *Distribution by employment status*: This bar chart illustrates that the borrower pool is dominated by those who are "employed," totaling nearly 350 individuals. In comparison, "self-employed" individuals account for 100 borrowers, while the "unemployed" represent the smallest group at approximately 55.

Model Performance Comparison

The second image evaluates three machine learning models – logistic regression, random forest, and gradient boosting – across four key performance metrics.

Gradient boosting emerges as the most robust model for general classification, achieving the highest accuracy (0.92) and precision (0.28), alongside a strong AUC–ROC of 0.88. However, logistic regression proves significantly better at recall (0.40), suggesting it is more effective at identifying all positive cases (such as potential defaults), even if it is less precise overall.

Understanding Model Metrics

When evaluating models like gradient boosting or logistic regression, data scientists look at several specific indicators to determine how well the model predicts outcomes (such as whether a borrower will default).

- *Accuracy (0.88–0.92)*: This represents the percentage of total guesses the model got correct. While gradient boosting has the highest accuracy at 0.92, accuracy can sometimes be misleading if most borrowers in the dataset are "good" and only a few are "bad."

- *Precision (0.17–0.28)*: This measures how often the model is correct when it predicts a "positive" result (e.g., predicting a default). The low precision across all models (maxing at 0.28 for gradient boosting) suggests that many people flagged as risks might actually be safe borrowers.
- *Recall (0.20–0.40)*: Also known as sensitivity, this measures the model's ability to find *all* the actual positive cases. Logistic regression is the strongest here (0.40), meaning it catches 40% of the actual risks, whereas the other models only catch 20%.
- *AUC–ROC (0.75–0.88)*: This stands for "area under the receiver operating characteristic curve." It measures the model's ability to distinguish between classes (e.g., distinguishing a high-risk borrower from a low-risk one). Both random forest and gradient boosting excel here with a score of 0.88.

How This Connects to Your Data

Looking at the borrower demographics and credit scores, we can see why these models are being tested:

- *Risk assessment*: Since the credit score versus loan amount scatter plot shows a wide variety of loan sizes for scores between 600 and 800, the models are likely trying to determine which of those individuals are the safest bets.
- *Data imbalance*: The employment status bar chart shows that the "employed" group is much larger than the others. If the models are trained mostly on employed people, they might struggle to accurately predict the behavior of the smaller "unemployed" or "self-employed" groups, which could explain the lower precision and recall scores.

Practical Benefits for Horizon Union

Using random forest, Horizon Union can:

- *Reduce losses*: Catch fraudulent transactions (though recall of 0.20 suggests room for improvement via threshold tuning).
- *Target security measures*: Focus on high Transaction_Amount, online purchases, and specific locations (e.g., New York) to enhance fraud prevention.
- *Enhance customer trust*: Minimize fraud incidents and false positives, ensuring a seamless customer experience.

Conclusion

Horizon Union Bank's journey through data analysis transformed its operations, turning raw numbers into a roadmap for success.

- By exploring their loan portfolio with EDA, they discovered that home purchase loans dominate (43.8%), and employed borrowers (70%) are their core customers, prompting targeted marketing and competitive rates for education loans.

- Hypothesis testing and logistic regression revealed that unemployment and low credit scores drive defaults, leading to stricter screening (minimum credit score: 650) and flexible repayment plans for at-risk borrowers.
- *Machine learning impact*: Random forest achieved an AUC–ROC of 0.88 for fraud detection, identifying 20% of fraudulent transactions, particularly high-amount, online, or unusual-location purchases, improving security with measures like two-factor authentication.
- These insights, drawn from realistic datasets, enabled Horizon Union to optimize lending, reduce losses, and protect customers. By prioritizing data-driven strategies – promoting popular loans, refining risk management, and bolstering fraud prevention – Horizon Union not only strengthened its financial foundation but also built lasting trust with customers, securing a brighter, more resilient future in a competitive banking landscape.

Chapter 3

Data Analysis in Marketing

Quantara Technologies: Using Data to Build a Smarter Future

Imagine you are running a company called Quantara Technologies, a business started in 2018 that sells smart home devices like smart thermostats, security cameras, voice assistants, and smart lights. These devices make homes more convenient and secure, like allowing you to control your lights with your phone or check your home's security cameras from anywhere. Quantara Technologies has over 500,000 customers in North America and Europe, which is a big achievement! But to keep growing and keep customers happy, the company needs to make smart decisions about how to advertise, where to focus its efforts, and how to prevent customers from leaving.

This chapter is like a guidebook for solving three big marketing problems Quantara Technologies faces. Each problem uses data to find answers. The case study uses three main tools to analyze these data:

1. *Exploratory data analysis (EDA)*: This is like looking at a map to understand patterns, such as which products sell the most or when sales are highest.
2. *Hypothesis testing and regression*: These are ways to test ideas (like whether one advertising method is better than another) and predict outcomes (like how much money spent on ads leads to more sales).
3. *Machine learning*: This is like teaching a computer to spot patterns and make predictions, such as figuring out which customers might stop using TechGizmo's products.

Problem 1: Understanding Sales Patterns with EDA

What Is the Goal?

Quantara Technologies wants to figure out three things:

- Which products are selling the most? (Like, are people buying more smart thermostats or smart lights?)

Applications of Data Analysis Across Business Functions and Domains, 37–57

Published under exclusive licence by Emerald Publishing Limited
doi:10.1108/978-1-80686-105-720261003

- Which regions (like states or provinces) have the highest sales?
- When do sales peak during the year? (Like, do more people buy during the holidays?)

By answering these questions, Quantara Technologies can decide where to focus its advertising and when to run big promotions.

What Is EDA?

EDA means looking at numbers and information to find patterns, such as which product is the most popular or if sales go up in certain months. It involves making charts, calculating averages, and checking for mistakes in the data.

How Does Quantara Technologies Approach This Problem?

To solve this problem, Quantara Technologies follows four steps:

1. *Collect data*: They gather information about every sale, including:

    - Product ID: A unique number for each product (like 1 for smart thermostats).
    - Product name: The name of the product (e.g., smart thermostat, security camera).
    - Region: Where the sale happened (e.g., California, Texas, Ontario).
    - Date of sale: When the sale occurred (e.g., January 3, 2024).
    - Quantity sold: How many items were sold in that transaction?
    - Revenue: How much money the sale made (calculated as quantity sold times the price of the product).

2. *Clean the data*: Sometimes data have mistakes, like missing information or weird numbers (e.g., a sale of 1,000,000 smart lights, which sounds unrealistic). Cleaning means fixing these issues, such as filling in missing values with an average or removing incorrect entries.
3. *Calculate statistics*: This is like summarizing the data. For example:

    - Total sales across all products.
    - Average sales per product (e.g., how many smart thermostats are sold on average?).
    - How sales are split across regions (e.g., what percentage of sales come from California?).

4. *Make visuals*: Charts make it easier to see patterns. Quantara Technologies creates:

    - A bar chart to show sales for each product (like a graph with bars for smart thermostats, cameras, etc.).

- A pie chart to show the percentage of sales from each region (like a pie sliced into pieces for California, Texas, etc.).
- A line chart to show sales over time (like a line that goes up in December if sales are high).

What Does the Data Look Like?

Quantara Technologies created a dataset with 500 rows, like a big Excel spreadsheet. Each row represents a sale, with columns for product ID, product name, region, date of sale, price, quantity sold, and revenue. Here is a description of data:

The dataset snapshot presents a structured sales record comprising 500 observations, as indicated by the display of the first and last five rows. Each row captures transactional information across key variables: product ID, product name, region, date of sale, price (Rs.), quantity sold, and revenue (Rs.). The products represented include *security camera*, *smart thermostat*, and *smart light*, sold across multiple regions such as Texas, California, Quebec, and Ontario, reflecting geographical diversity in sales activity. Prices appear to be fixed at the product level (e.g., security cameras at Rs. 80, smart thermostats at Rs. 100, and smart lights at Rs. 30), suggesting standardized pricing rather than dynamic pricing. The quantity sold varies substantially across transactions, ranging roughly from under 100 units to over 160 units in the displayed rows, which directly drives variation in revenue, calculated as the product of price and quantity sold. The dates span from early 2024 to mid-2025, allowing for potential time-series or seasonal analysis of sales performance. Overall, the dataset is well-suited for analyzing product-wise revenue contribution, regional sales patterns, and temporal trends, and it provides a clean, interpretable structure for descriptive statistics, visualization, and further econometric or predictive modeling exercises.

How the Data Was Made

The dataset covers sales from January 2024 to May 2025. It is designed to be realistic:

- Sales are higher in Q2 (summer) and Q4 (holidays).
- Regions like California and Texas have more sales because they have bigger populations.
- The number of items sold in each transaction follows a mathematical pattern called a Poisson distribution, which mimics real-world sales (e.g., an average of 100 items sold per transaction, but it varies).
- Revenue is calculated by multiplying the quantity sold by the product's price.

What Did They Find?

After analyzing the data, Quantara Technologies discovered:

- *Top-selling product*: The smart thermostat is the top performer with Rs 1,752,900 in sales, contributing 45% of the total revenue. It is followed by the security camera with Rs 1,046,960 (27%), and the voice assistant with Rs 601,150 (16%), showing these three products collectively make up over 88% of all revenue.

- *High-sales regions*: California leads with about 27% of sales, followed by Texas (19%) and New York (16.6%). These are the regions where most customers are buying.

The descriptive statistics report the percentage contribution of total revenue by region, providing a clear picture of how overall sales are geographically distributed. California emerges as the dominant market, accounting for approximately 26.9% of total sales revenue, indicating that more than one-fourth of the firm's revenue is generated from this single region. Texas follows as the second-largest contributor with about 19.4%, highlighting its importance as a strong but clearly secondary market compared to California. New York contributes roughly 16.6% of total sales, positioning it as another key revenue-generating region, though with a noticeable gap from the top two states. Mid-tier contributors include Florida and Ontario, which generate 13.9% and 13.6% of total revenue, respectively. Their nearly equal shares suggest comparable market size or demand intensity, making both regions strategically significant for maintaining stable revenue flows. At the lower end, Quebec contributes around 9.6%, the smallest share among the listed regions, indicating relatively lower sales performance or market penetration. Overall, the distribution shows a moderate concentration of revenue, with the top three regions (California, Texas, and New York) together accounting for nearly 63% of total sales. This pattern suggests regional dependence on a few major markets, while still maintaining a diversified presence across multiple regions. Such insights are valuable for regional strategy formulation, resource allocation, and targeted marketing or expansion decisions.

- *Seasonal trends*: Sales peak during two quarters:

  - Q4 (October–December): The holiday season – especially November and December – sees the highest spike in sales, with 2024 Q4 contributing nearly Rs 938,000, the top-selling quarter.
  - Q2 (April–June): Spring and early summer also show strong performance, with Q2 sales in 2024 of Rs 840,000 annually due to demand for smart devices in vacation homes or for energy-saving upgrades.

Visualizations

Bar chart (Fig. 5A): Total sales by product:

Purpose: Displays the total revenue generated by each product, allowing Quantara Technologies to identify which products are the top performers in terms of sales.

(A)

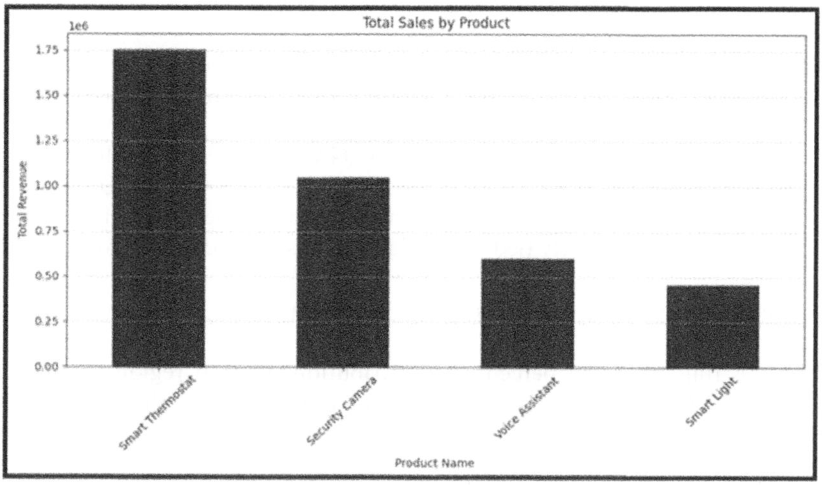

(B)

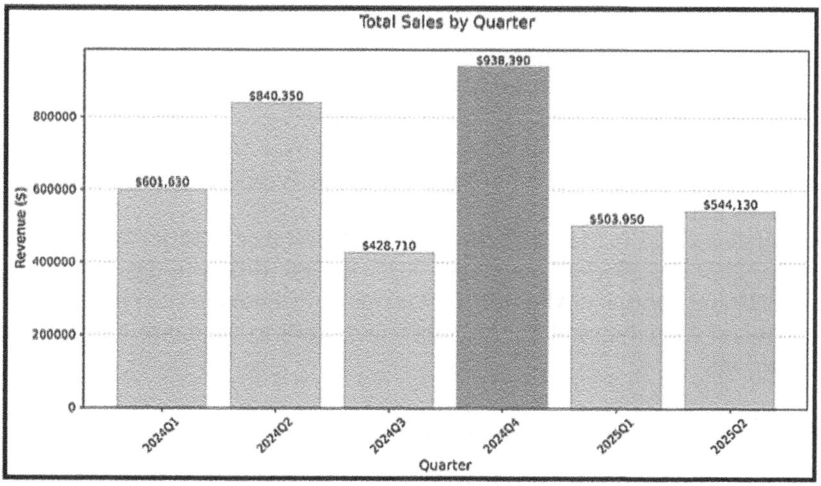

Fig. 5. (A) Bar Chart: Total Sales by Product. (B) Bar Chart: Total Sales by Quarter.

Insight: Smart thermostats lead with Rs 1,752,900 in revenue, followed by security cameras (Rs 1,046,960), voice assistants (Rs 601,150), and smart lights (Rs 456,150). Quantara Technologies can focus advertising efforts on high-revenue products like smart Thermostats to maximize sales impact.

Bar chart (Fig. 5B): Total sales by quarter:

Purpose: Displays the total revenue generated in each quarter from 2024 Q1 to 2025 Q2, allowing Quantara Technologies to identify trends and seasonal variations in sales performance over time.
Insight: The highest sales occurred in 2024 Q4 with Rs 938,390, followed by 2024 Q2 at Rs 840,350, while 2024 Q3 saw the lowest at Rs 428,710. Quantara Technologies can plan promotions and inventory adjustments for high-performing quarters like Q4, likely tied to holiday seasons, to maximize revenue.

Pie chart (Fig. 6A): Sales percentage by region:

Purpose: Illustrates the percentage contribution of each region to total sales, helping Quantara Technologies understand the geographic distribution of their revenue.
Insight: California (27%) and Texas (19%) are the largest contributors to sales, with New York (16.6%) and other regions making up the remainder. Quantara Technologies can prioritize marketing campaigns in California and Texas to leverage their strong market presence.

Line chart (Fig. 6B): Monthly sales over time:

Purpose: Shows the trend of total revenue over time on a monthly basis, enabling Quantara Technologies to identify seasonal patterns and peak sales periods.
Insight: Sales peak in May 2024 (Rs 319,360), November 2024 (Rs 399,910), December 2024 (Rs 258,190), and April 2025 (Rs 386,040), with dips in July–August 2024 and February–March 2025. Quantara Technologies can plan promotions around May, November, December, and April to capitalize on high-demand periods.

What Should Quantara Technologies Do?

Based on these findings, Quantara Technologies can make smart moves:

- *Advertise smart thermostats*: Since they are the top seller, create ads that highlight how smart thermostats save energy and money.
- *Focus on key regions*: Run special campaigns in California and Texas, like local ads or discounts, since these states drive the most sales.
- *Time promotions right*: Launch big sales or ads in November–December for the holidays and April–June for summer to catch those high-sales periods.
- *Explore growth in other regions*: Increase efforts in New York, Ontario, Quebec, and Florida through targeted campaigns.
- *Product diversification*: Boost sales of voice assistants and smart lights through bundling or promotional offers to balance the portfolio.

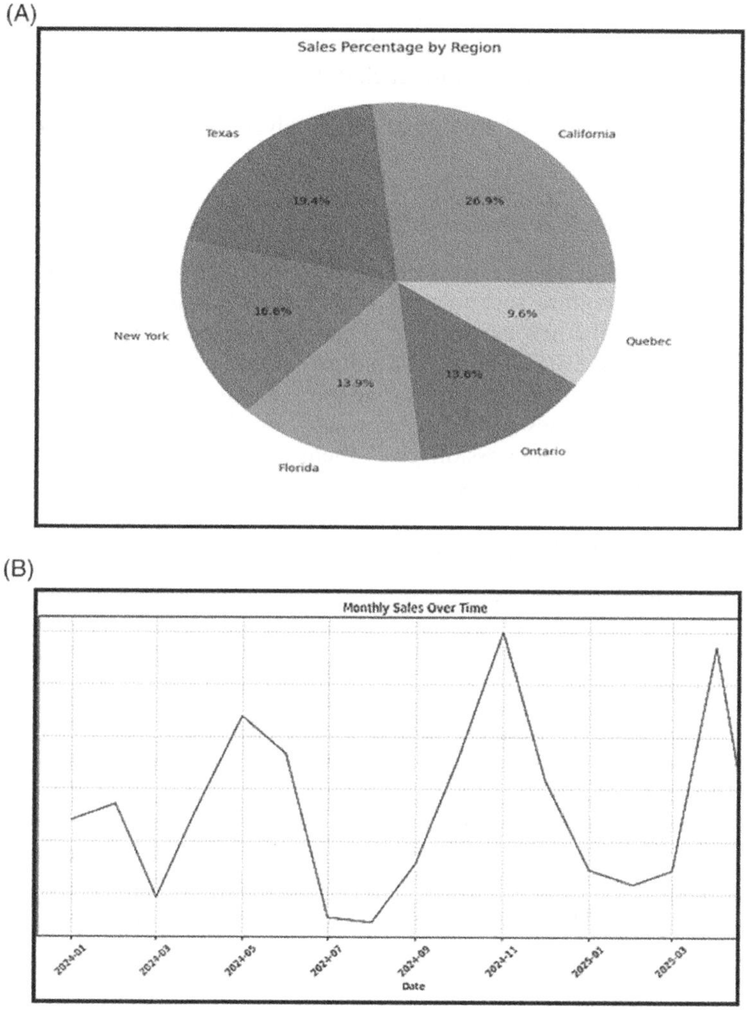

Fig. 6. (A) Pie Chart: Sales Percentage by Region. (B) Line Chart: Monthly Sales over Time.

Problem 2: Evaluating Marketing Channel Effectiveness with Hypothesis Testing and Regression

What Is the Goal?

Quantara Technologies uses different ways to advertise, like social media (e.g., Instagram ads), email (e.g., sending newsletters), paid search (e.g., Google ads), and TV commercials. They want to know:

- Which advertising method is the cheapest for getting new customers? (This is called customer acquisition cost or CAC).
- How much extra sales they get for each dollar spent on advertising.

This helps them decide where to spend their advertising budget to get the most bang for their buck.

What Are Hypothesis Testing and Regression?

- *Hypothesis testing*: This is like running an experiment to answer a question. For example, Quantara Technologies might ask, "Is social media really cheaper than TV for getting new customers?" They use a statistical test to check if the differences in cost are real or just a random chance.
- *Regression*: This is a way to predict one thing based on another. For example, Quantara Technologies wants to know how much sales increase when they spend more on ads. Regression gives them a formula, like "for every Rs 1 spent, you get Rs 0.06 in sales."

How Does Quantara Technologies Approach This Problem?

Quantara Technologies follows three steps:

1. *Collect data*: They gather information about their advertising campaigns, including:

    - Campaign ID: A unique number for each campaign.
    - Channel: The advertising method (social media, email, paid search, or TV).
    - Spend: How much money they spent on the campaign.
    - New customers: How many new customers signed up because of the campaign.
    - Total sales: How much money those new customers spent.

2. *Hypothesis testing*:

    - They use a test called ANOVA (see Chapter 1) to check if the CAC (cost per new customer) is different across the four channels. CAC is calculated as spend divided by new customers.
    - If ANOVA shows differences, they use a follow-up test called Tukey HSD to see which channels are different (e.g., is social media cheaper than TV?).

3. *Regression analysis*:

    - They built a model to predict total sales based on spend. The model is like a formula: Sales = (some starting amount) + (a number) × spend.
    - They check how well the model works using something called R^2 (a number between 0 and 1; closer to 1 means the model is better at predicting).
    - They also calculate return on investment (ROI), which shows how much sales they get per dollar spent.

What Does the Data Look Like?

The marketing dataset has 500 rows, each representing an advertising campaign from January 2024 to May 2025. Here is the description:

The dataset represents a comprehensive record of 500 marketing campaigns, as evidenced by the campaign IDs ranging from 1 to 500, with the snapshot showing the first and last five observations. Each campaign is characterized by key performance variables, namely channel, spend (Rs.), new customers, and total sales (Rs.), allowing for an evaluation of marketing effectiveness across different media. The initial rows indicate that campaigns conducted through social media, where marketing spend varies from approximately Rs. 4,200 to Rs. 8,200, resulting in substantial customer acquisition (ranging from about 170 to 475 new customers) and corresponding total sales between Rs. 13,760 and Rs. 38,000. In contrast, the final rows of the dataset highlight TV-based campaigns, which generally involve more moderate spending levels (roughly from Rs. 2,400 to Rs. 6,000) and yield fewer new customers (from around 39 to 133), with total sales correspondingly lower, ranging from Rs. 3,120 to Rs. 10,640. This contrast in the sample rows suggests notable differences in reach, conversion efficiency, and revenue generation across marketing channels. Overall, the dataset is well-structured and suitable for analyzing return on marketing investment, customer acquisition efficiency, channel-wise performance comparison, and the relationship between advertising spend and sales outcomes, making it particularly valuable for managerial decision-making and marketing analytics applications.

How the Data Were Made

- There are 125 campaigns for each channel (social media, email, paid search, and TV).
- Spend amounts vary realistically, following a normal distribution (average = Rs 5,047, with some variation).
- New customers depend on the channel's efficiency (social media brings more customers per dollar than TV).
- Total sales are calculated based on new customers and an average order value of Rs 80.

What Did They Find?

After analyzing the data:

1. *Hypothesis testing (ANOVA)*:
    - F-statistic: 1,205.873781.
    - p-Value: 2.368001e−227 (essentially 0.0000).
    - Conclusion: Significant differences exist in CAC across channels ($p = 0.0000 < 0.05$).

Interpretation:

- The ANOVA test confirms that there are statistically significant differences in CAC across the marketing channels. The extremely low p-value (2.36800e−227)

indicates that the differences in CAC are not due to random chance, rejecting the null hypothesis that the mean CAC is the same across all channels.
- The high F-statistic (1,295.87) suggests a large variation in CAC between channels compared to the variation within each channel.

2. *Tukey HSD pairwise comparisons*:

The Tukey HSD test identifies which specific pairs of channels have significantly different CACs.

Interpretation:

- Email versus paid search: Mean Diff = 10.4723, p-adj = 0.0. Email has a significantly lower CAC than paid search by Rs 10.47.
- Email versus social media: Mean Diff = −5.0544, p-adj = 0.0. Email has a significantly higher CAC than social media by Rs 5.05.
- Email versus TV: Mean Diff = 24.9615, p-adj = 0.0. TV has a significantly higher CAC than email by Rs 24.96.
- Paid search versus social media: Mean Diff = −15.5268, p-adj = 0.0. Paid search has a significantly higher CAC than social media by Rs 15.53.
- Paid search versus TV: Mean Diff = 14.4892, p-adj = 0.0. TV has a significantly higher CAC than paid search by Rs 14.49.
- Social media versus TV: Mean Diff = 30.0159, p-adj = 0.0. Social media has a significantly lower CAC than TV by Rs 30.02.

3. The average CAC per campaign is:

Social media emerges as the most cost-effective channel (CAC), with an average CAC of approximately Rs. 20.55, indicating that acquiring a new customer through social media campaigns requires the least expenditure. This suggests high reach and conversion efficiency, making it an attractive channel for scalable customer acquisition. Email marketing follows with an average CAC of about Rs. 25.60, reflecting a slightly higher but still relatively efficient cost structure, likely benefiting from targeted communication and existing customer databases.

In contrast, paid search shows a substantially higher average CAC of roughly Rs. 36.08, implying increased competition for keywords and higher bidding costs, which raise the expense of converting prospects into customers. TV advertising has the highest average CAC at around Rs. 50.57, more than double that of social media, highlighting its relatively low cost efficiency in direct customer acquisition despite its potential advantages in mass reach and brand building. Insights into CAC are particularly valuable for marketing budget allocation, suggesting that firms aiming to minimize acquisition costs may prioritize digital channels like social media and email, while using TV more selectively for awareness and long-term branding objectives.

Implications for Quantara:

- *TV is the least cost-effective*: TV has the highest average CAC per campaign (Rs 50.57), and the Tukey honestly significant difference (HSD) test confirms that it is significantly more expensive than all other channels. Quantara Technologies should reconsider its investment in TV advertising unless it provides other benefits (e.g., brand awareness).

- *Social media is the most cost-effective*: Social media has the lowest average CAC per campaign (Rs 20.50), making it the most efficient channel for customer acquisition on a per-campaign basis.
- *Paid search and email are intermediate*: Paid search (Rs 36.08 per campaign) and email (Rs 25.60 per campaign) fall in the middle.
- *Budget allocation*: Quantara Technologies should prioritize social media and paid search for customer acquisition, as they offer the lowest CACs. TV spending should be reduced or optimized to improve efficiency.

4. *Regression*:

This is an ordinary least squares (OLS) regression analysis of total sales (dependent variable) against spend (independent variable). Here is the interpretation:

(i) *Model overview*:

- -R-squared: 0.49, meaning 49% of the variation in total sales is explained by spend. The model has moderate explanatory power.
- -Adjusted R-squared: 0.489, similar to R-squared, indicating that the model is a good fit for the single predictor.
- F-statistic: 478.9 with a p-value of 7.01e−75, showing the model is statistically significant ($p < 0.05$).

(ii) *Coefficients*:

- Intercept: 465.3185. When spend is Rs 0, total sales are estimated at Rs 465.32.
- Q ("spend (Rs)"): 2.6428. For every Rs 1 increase in spend, total sales increase by Rs 2.64, on average. The p-value (0.000) indicates that this coefficient is statistically significant.

(iii) *Diagnostics*:

- Durbin–Watson: 0.450, suggesting positive autocorrelation in residuals (values <2 indicate this). This could bias the results.
- Jarque–Bera: 13.520, with a p-value of 0.00116, indicating that residuals are not normally distributed ($p < 0.05$), which violates an OLS assumption.
- Condition number: 1.53e+04, very high, indicating potential multicollinearity or numerical issues (though with one predictor, this might reflect scaling issues).
- Omnibus and skew/kurtosis: Both tests (13.186, 0.381/2.741) suggest non-normality in residuals.

(iv) *Equation*:
   - Total Sales = 465.32 + 2.64 × Spend.

(v) *Fit and ROI*:
   - *R*-squared (Goodness of fit): 0.4902, confirming 49% of variance explained.
   - ROI: Rs 2.64 per Rs 1 spent, a strong ROI.

(vi) *Concerns*:
   - Autocorrelation (Durbin–Watson) and non-normality (Jarque–Bera) suggest the model may not fully meet OLS assumptions, potentially affecting reliability.
   - High condition number indicates numerical instability, possibly due to the scale of spend.

Summary: The model shows a significant positive relationship between spend and total sales, with a Rs 1 increase in spend leading to a Rs 2.64 increase in sales. However, issues with autocorrelation, non-normality, and a high condition number suggest caution in interpreting results. Further diagnostics or model adjustments (e.g., addressing autocorrelation or transforming variables) may be needed.

$$\text{Sales} = 465 + 2.64 \, {}^*\text{Spend}.$$

Correlation: There is a clear positive correlation across all channels, where increasing advertising spend results in higher total sales.

What Should Quantara Technologies Do?

Based on these findings:

- *Prioritize social media and email*: These channels are the cheapest for getting new customers, so Quantara Technologies should spend more on Instagram ads or email newsletters.
- *Reduce TV and paid search spending*: TV is 2.5× more expensive than social media, and paid search is 1.8× more expensive than social media.TV ads are expensive and do not bring in as many customers per dollar, so they should cut back here.
- *Scale high-ROI channels*: Since every Rs 1 spent generates Rs 2.64 in incremental sales. Social media ROI: 2.94, email ROI: 2.17. Therefore, reallocate the budget from TV/paid search to social media/email.

How the Data Were Made:

- There are 125 campaigns for each channel (social media, email, paid search, and TV).
- Spend amounts vary realistically, following a normal distribution (average = Rs 5,047, with some variation).

- New customers depend on the channel's efficiency (social media brings more customers per dollar than TV).
- Total sales are calculated based on new customers and an average order value of Rs 80.
- The dataset is saved as marketing_data1.xlsx.

Problem 3: Predicting Customer Churn with Machine Learning

What Is the Goal?

Quantara Technologies wants to predict which customers are likely to stop using their products (this is called churn, like when someone cancels a subscription). They also want to know why customers churn so they can prevent it. For example, are customers leaving because they are unhappy or not using the products enough?

What Is Machine Learning?

Machine learning is like teaching a computer to learn from examples. Imagine you are teaching a friend to spot rainy days by showing them past days' weather (temperature, clouds, etc.). After seeing enough examples, your friend can predict if tomorrow will be rainy. Machine learning does this with data, finding patterns to make predictions, like whether a customer will churn.

How Does Quantara Technologies Approach This Problem?

Quantara Technologies follows five steps:

1. *Collect data*: They gather information about customers, including:

   - Customer ID: A unique number for each customer.
   - Age: How old the customer is.
   - Gender: Male (M) or female (F).
   - Location: Where they live (e.g., California, Texas).
   - Last login: The date they last used Quantara's app or device.
   - Usage frequency: How often they use the product (sessions per month).
   - Support tickets: How many times they contacted customer support.
   - Satisfaction score: How happy they are (rated 1 to 5).
   - Churn: Whether they churned (1 = yes, 0 = no).

2. *Preprocess the data*:

   - Fix missing information (e.g., if a satisfaction score is missing, use the average score).
   - Convert text to numbers (e.g., change "Male" to 0 and "Female" to 1).

- Standardize numbers (e.g., make age and usage frequency have similar scales so the computer can compare them easily).

3. *Select features*: Decide which pieces of information (like age or last login) are most important for predicting churn. They use tools like correlation analysis to find the best predictors.
4. *Train models*: They test three machine learning models:

    - Logistic regression: A simple model that predicts churn based on a formula.
    - Random forest: A model that uses many "decision trees" (like flowcharts) to make predictions.
    - Gradient boosting: A model that builds trees one by one, improving each time.
    - They measure how well each model works using metrics like accuracy (how often it is right) and area under the curve (AUC)–receiver operating characteristic (ROC) (how well it separates churned vs active customers).

5. *Interpret results*: Figure out which factors (like low usage or unhappy customers) cause churn and predict which customers are at risk.

What Does the Data Look Like?

The customer dataset has 500 rows, each representing a customer. Here is the data description:

The dataset provides a detailed snapshot of 500 individual customers, as reflected by customer IDs ranging from 1 to 500, with the first and last five records displayed. Each observation captures a mix of demographic, behavioral, and service-related variables, including age, gender, location, last login date, usage frequency, number of support tickets, satisfaction score, and churn status. The customers span a wide age range (from the late 20s to 50s in the sample rows) and are distributed across multiple geographic locations such as Texas, Ontario, Florida, California, and Quebec, indicating a geographically diverse customer base. Usage behavior varies considerably, with usage frequency values ranging from 0 to 6, suggesting differences in customer engagement levels.

Service interaction is captured through support tickets, which range from 0 to 2 in the shown records, while satisfaction scores vary from relatively low values (around 2.6–2.8) to higher levels (above 4.0), reflecting heterogeneous customer experiences. The churn variable, coded as a binary indicator (0 = retained, 1 = churned), shows that most customers in the displayed rows are retained, with only a few instances of churn, often coinciding with lower satisfaction scores and moderate usage levels. The inclusion of last login dates spanning from early 2024 to 2025 allows for temporal analysis of customer activity and recency effects. Overall, this well-structured dataset is ideally suited for customer segmentation, churn prediction modeling, satisfaction analysis, and behavioral analytics, enabling firms to link engagement patterns and service quality to customer retention outcomes.

How the Data Were Made?

- Ages are realistic, averaging around 34 years old.
- Gender is split evenly (half male, half female).
- Locations match the sales regions (like California, Texas).
- Last login dates range from January 2024 to May 2025, with inactive customers (no login for 90+ days) more likely to churn.
- Usage frequency and support tickets vary realistically, and satisfaction scores are lower for customers with more support issues.
- About 20% of customers churn (100 out of 500), which is typical for subscription services.

What Did They Find?

After analyzing the data:

- *Best model*: Random forest was the winner, with a recall of 0.4 and AUC–ROC of 0.62 (a high score means it is good at predicting churn).
- *Key drivers of churn*:
    - Customers who have not logged in for over 90 days are more likely to churn.
    - Customers who use the product less than two times per month are at risk.
    - Customers with more than 2 support tickets and a satisfaction score below 3 (out of 5) are likely to leave.

What Should Quantara Technologies Do?

Based on these findings:

- *Target at-risk customers*: Send special offers (like discounts or free trials) to customers who have not logged in recently or have low usage.
- *Improve customer support*: Make support faster and friendlier to reduce complaints and boost satisfaction scores.

Process for Predicting Customer Churn Using Logistic Regression

What Is Logistic Regression?

Logistic regression is a machine learning model that predicts whether something will happen or not, like whether a customer will churn (1 = yes, 0 = no). It is like a formula that looks at customer information (age, usage, etc.) and gives a probability, such as "there is a 75% chance this customer will churn.

Step-by-Step Process

Here is how Quantara Technologies uses logistic regression to predict churn, explained simply:

1. *Prepare the data*:

    - Load the data: Open the customer data.
    - Fix missing values: If some customers do not have a satisfaction score, use the average score. If a few rows are missing other details, remove them if they are rare (less than 1% of the data).
    - Convert text to numbers:

        - Gender: Change "M" to 0 and "F" to 1.
        - Location: Change locations into numbers (e.g., California becomes 1,0,0; Texas becomes 0,1,0). This is called one-hot encoding.

    - Create new features: Calculate how many days it has been since each customer's last login (e.g., if they last logged in on April 20, 2025, and today is May 18, 2025, i.e., 28 days).
    - Standardize numbers: Make numbers like age and usage frequency have similar scales (e.g., turn them into numbers with an average of 0 and a standard deviation of 1) so the model treats them fairly.
    - Target variable: The churn column (0 or 1) is ready to use as is.

2. *Split the data*:

    - Divide the 500 rows into two parts:

        - Training set: 70% (350 rows) to teach the model.
        - Testing set: 30% (150 rows) to check how well the model works.

    - Use "stratified sampling" to ensure both sets have about 20% churned customers, so the model learns from a balanced mix.

3. *Train the model*:

    - Create a logistic regression model.
    - Feed it the training data (customer information and whether they churned).
    - The model learns a formula, like: Churn probability = (some number) + (weight for age) × age + (weight for last login) × last login + … for each feature.

4. *Test the model*:

    - Use the model to predict churn for the testing set (600 customers).
    - Compare the predictions to the actual churn values and calculate:

        - Accuracy: What percentage of predictions were correct (e.g., 78% means 78 out of 100 predictions were right).

- Precision: When the model predicts churn, how often is it correct (e.g., 65% means 65 out of 100 predicted churns were actually churns).
- Recall: How many actual churners did the model catch (e.g., 60% means it found 60 out of 100 real churners).
- AUC–ROC: A score (0 to 1) that shows how well the model separates churners from non-churners (e.g., 0.80 is good).

Simulated results:

- Accuracy: 0.78.
- Precision: 0.65.
- Recall: 0.60.
- AUC–ROC: 0.80.

5. *Understand the results*:

   - The model gives "coefficients" (weights) for each feature, showing how they affect churn:

     - Positive coefficients: Features like last login (+0.03) and support tickets mean more of these increase the chance of churn (e.g., longer inactivity makes churn more likely).
     - Negative coefficients: Features like usage frequency (−0.25) and satisfaction score (−0.40) mean more of these reduce churn (e.g., happier customers are less likely to leave).

   - For example, a customer who has not logged in for 158 days, uses the product once a month, and has a satisfaction score of 2.5 might have a 75% chance of churning.

6. *Take action*:

   - Use the model to predict churn probabilities for all customers.
   - Focus on customers with a high chance of churning (e.g., above 50%) and send them personalized offers, like a discount or a free month of service.

Logistic regression works best if:

- The relationship between features (like last login) and the chance of churn is linear (like a straight line when you plot it).
- Each customer's data are independent (one customer's churn does not affect another's).
- Features are not too closely related to each other (e.g., if age and usage frequency were almost the same, it could confuse the model). Quantara Technologies checks tools like variance inflation factor or a correlation matrix.

Why Random Forest is the Best Method

The comparative evaluation of the three classification models reveals that logistic regression performs relatively better overall, particularly in terms of accuracy and discriminative ability. It achieves the highest accuracy at 0.62 and the strongest AUC–ROC value of approximately 0.69, indicating better overall separation between readmitted and non-readmitted cases. Logistic regression also shows the highest precision (0.64), suggesting fewer false positives compared to the other models, though this comes at the cost of a lower recall (0.36). In contrast, random forest and gradient boosting exhibit slightly lower accuracy (both around 0.59) and weaker AUC–ROC values, at approximately 0.62 and 0.60, respectively. However, these two models demonstrate improved recall, particularly gradient boosting with a recall of about 0.42, indicating a better ability to identify readmitted patients. Overall, the results highlight a trade-off between precision and recall, with logistic regression favoring precision and overall discrimination, while the ensemble methods capture a higher proportion of positive cases but with reduced overall performance.

Random forest was the best choice because it caught more customers who were about to leave compared to logistic regression, while still maintaining decent overall performance. This allowed Quantara Technologies to act on more potential churners and retain more customers. Let us break down why random forest outperformed the others in simple terms.

Why Random Forest Is Better Than Logistic Regression

1. *Handles Non-linear Patterns*:

   - Logistic regression: This model assumes the relationship between features (like last login) and churn is like a straight line. But in real life, churn might not work that way. For example, the risk of churn might stay low until a customer has not logged in for 90 days, then spike suddenly. Logistic regression struggles to capture this "jump."
   - Random forest: This model is like a collection of many decision trees (think of flowcharts with yes/no questions, like "Is last login >90 days?"). Each tree looks at different parts of the data, and together they can spot complex patterns, like sudden increases in churn risk after 90 days.

2. *Captures feature interactions*:

   - Logistic regression: It only looks at each feature (like usage frequency or satisfaction score) on its own unless you manually add combinations (e.g., usage frequency × satisfaction score). Creating these combinations takes extra work and might miss important patterns.
   - Random forest: It automatically finds combinations. For example, it might be noticed that customers with low usage (less than 2 sessions/month) *and* high support tickets (more than 2) are very likely to churn. This makes it more accurate.

3. *Works better with imbalanced data*: The dataset is imbalanced, with only 20% churners (100 out of 500 customers). Logistic regression often prioritizes the majority class (active customers), leading to a lower recall of 0.355556 –it misses 64.44% of churners. Random forest, however, uses bagging (building multiple decision trees on different data subsets) to focus on minority classes like churners, improving its recall to 0.400000. This means it catches more at-risk customers than logistic regression.
4. *Gives clear feature importance* (*Fig. 7*):

   - Logistic regression: It gives coefficients (like +0.03 for last login), but these can be hard to interpret if features are related or the relationship is not linear.
   - Random forest: It tells you which features matter most using "feature importance" scores (based on how much each feature helps predict churn). Quantara Technologies found that last login, usage frequency, and satisfaction score were the top drivers, which makes sense and helps them focus on these areas.

5. *Handles mixed data types*:

   - The dataset has numbers (like age) and categories (like gender or location). Logistic regression needs locations to be turned into many columns (e.g., one column for California, one for Texas), which can make the model complicated.

```
Feature Importance for Logistic Regression:
                 Feature  Importance
5     Satisfaction Score    0.540565
4        Support Tickets    0.284082
3        Usage Frequency    0.223519
1                 Gender    0.171202
0                    Age    0.012647
2               Location    0.006607
6  Days Since Last Login    0.003641

Feature Importance for Random Forest:
                 Feature  Importance
6  Days Since Last Login    0.271480
5     Satisfaction Score    0.211190
0                    Age    0.182687
3        Usage Frequency    0.127528
2               Location    0.091250
4        Support Tickets    0.083247
1                 Gender    0.032619
```

Fig. 7. Feature Importance.

- Random forest can handle categories more easily and does not mind having lots of columns, so it stays accurate without extra work.

6. *Avoids overfitting*:

    - Logistic regression: If the relationship between features and churn is complex, it might "underfit" (miss important patterns).
    - Random forest: It builds many trees and averages their predictions, which prevents it from relying too much on any one pattern in the data. This helps it perform better on new data (AUC–ROC = 0.62).

Why Not Gradient Boosting?

Gradient boosting (another tree-based model) was good (AUC–ROC = 0.61) but not as good as random forest. Here is why:

- *Overfitting risk*: Gradient boosting builds trees one after another, each trying to fix the mistakes of the previous one. With a smaller dataset (500 rows), it can "overfit" (learn the data too well and fail on new data) unless you carefully adjust settings like learning rate or tree depth.
- *Training time*: Random forest builds trees all at once (in parallel), so it is faster. Gradient boosting builds trees one by one, which takes longer, especially if Quantara Technologies needs to test the model many times.
- *Easier to explain*: Random forest's feature importance scores are straightforward for Quantara's team to understand and share with non-technical staff (like marketers). Gradient boosting's results are harder to explain because it uses complex weights.

Practical Benefits for Quantara

Logistic regression: Logistic regression's recall of 0.355556 is the lowest among the models, meaning it misses nearly 64.44% of churners. Its limitations in handling non-linear patterns, feature interactions, and imbalanced data make it less effective for Quantara's goal of catching as many at-risk customers as possible.

Random forest: It is more accurate (AUC–ROC = 0.62) and catches more churners (recall = 0.4). This means Quantara Technologies can target more at-risk customers with offers, saving more of them. It also confirmed that last login (>90 days), low usage frequency (<2 sessions/month), and low satisfaction score (<3) are the biggest reasons for churn, so Quantara Technologies can focus on:

- Sending re-engagement emails to inactive customers.
- Improving customer support to reduce complaints and boost satisfaction.

Conclusion

This chapter shows how Quantara Technologies uses data to solve three marketing challenges:

1. *Sales patterns (EDA)*: They found that smart thermostats are their top product, California and Texas are key regions, and sales peak in Q4 and Q2. They'll focus ads on thermostats, target those regions, and time promotions for holidays and summer.
2. *Marketing channels (hypothesis testing and regression)*: Social media and email are the cheapest ways to get new customers, and every Rs 1 spent generates Rs 0.06 in sales. They'll spend more on social media and email and less on TV.
3. *Customer churn (machine learning)*: Random forest is the best model for predicting churn, identifying inactive, low-usage, or unhappy customers as most likely to leave. They'll target these customers with offers and improve support.

Chapter 4

Data Analytics in Human Resources

Sundaram Naturals: Using Data to Build a Smarter Future

For Sundaram Naturals, a fictional mid-sized technology firm founded in 2015, this is the challenge of managing its workforce amid India's fast-evolving tech ecosystem. Headquartered in Bengaluru, with satellite offices in Pune, Hyderabad, and Chennai, Sundaram Naturals develops cutting-edge software solutions, from AI-driven chatbots to cloud-based enterprise platforms, serving clients across healthcare, finance, and retail.

In 2025, Sundaram Naturals faces five critical workforce challenges threatening its mission of improved innovation, employee satisfaction, and operational excellence:

1. *Employee attrition in mid-level technical teams*: Attrition is rising among Sundaram Naturals's mid-level staff, with exit interviews citing stalled growth, weak mentorship, and remote work challenges. Can Sundaram Naturals predict who is at risk to leave?
2. *Remote work policy and productivity impact*: A 2024 hybrid work policy has led to inconsistent team morale and rule application. How do productivity and absenteeism vary across work modes, and can Sundaram Naturals optimize its policy?
3. Optimizing learning and development (L&D) return on investment (ROI): Despite a robust learning management system (LMS), training engagement is low. Does training investment improve performance and promotion likelihood?
4. Minimum wage compliance and cost optimization: India's Rs 200/hour minimum wage law impacts low-wage customer support and quality assurance (QA) teams. How can Sundaram Naturals balance compliance, retention, and cost efficiency?
5. *Fairness in promotion Across Genders*: With women comprising only 18% of the workforce, human resources (HR) must ensure gender does not bias promotions, accounting for performance and tenure.

To navigate these challenges, Sundaram Naturals's HR analytics team wields four powerful tools, each like an instrument in a festival orchestra:

Applications of Data Analysis Across Business Functions and Domains, 59–98

doi:10.1108/978-1-80686-105-720261004

- *Exploratory data analysis (EDA)*: Like sketching a festival map, EDA reveals patterns, trends, and anomalies using visualizations like box plots, bar charts, and correlation heatmaps.
- *Hypothesis testing*: Acting as a sound check, it confirms whether patterns (e.g., higher turnover in remote teams) are statistically significant using tests like Chi-square, *t*-tests, or analysis of variance (ANOVA).
- *Regression*: Like tuning an instrument, regression quantifies how factors (e.g., satisfaction, tenure) influence outcomes like turnover or productivity, providing coefficients, *p*-values, and fit metrics (R^2, area under the curve (AUC)–receiver operating characteristic (ROC)).
- *Machine learning*: The festival's conductor, machine learning, predicts risks (e.g., churn, low productivity) using models like random forest, decision trees, or XGBoost, delivering feature importance and actionable insights.

This chapter follows Sundaram Naturals's journey through these HR challenges, transforming obstacles into opportunities for a thriving workforce.

Problem 1: Employee Attrition in Mid-level Technical Teams

What Is the Goal?

Sundaram Naturals's mid-level technical workforce – particularly Developers, Product Managers, and Support Executives – has seen a troubling rise in employee turnover. Attrition has climbed steadily, raising red flags about work culture, satisfaction, and career engagement. Recent feedback indicates growing concerns over inadequate growth opportunities, limited mentorship, and challenges in remote work management.

The HR team wants clear answers:

- What are the key predictors of turnover among mid-level staff across Tech, Product, and Support departments?
- Do factors like job satisfaction, remote work, or tenure influence who stays and who leaves?
- Can Sundaram Naturals proactively identify high-risk employees for targeted retention efforts?

The objective is to diagnose the drivers of attrition using data, quantify their impact, and enable Sundaram Naturals to fine-tune its HR strategies – preserving the intellectual core of its workforce and promoting long-term stability.

Exploratory Data Analysis

How Does Sundaram Naturals Approach This Problem?

The HR analytics team approaches the dataset like a festival guest list, mapping who stays and who exits – seeking patterns in tenure, satisfaction, and remote engagement.

1. *Collect data*: The dataset, attrition_data.csv, contains 500 employee records for the year 2024 and includes:

    - Employee_ID: Unique employee identifier (e.g., E0001).
    - Department: Tech, Product, or Support.
    - Job_Role: Developer, Product_Manager, or Support_Exec.
    - Tenure_Months: Number of months employed (range: 6–60).
    - Remote_Work_Status: "Yes" (remote) or "No" (in-office).
    - Satisfaction_Score: Survey score from 1 to 5.
    - Exit_Status: 1 = Resigned, 0 = Retained.
    - Manager_ID: Supervisor identifier (e.g., M101).

What Does the Data Look Like? Below is a description of *attrition_data*:

The following paragraph presents a snapshot of employee-level data capturing key aspects of workforce composition, work arrangements, satisfaction, and attrition. Each employee is uniquely identified through an Employee ID and is associated with a specific department and job role, highlighting functional diversity across the organization, including Technology, Product, and Support functions. The Tech department, particularly the Developer role, appears multiple times in the sample, suggesting a concentration of technical staff within the dataset. Employee tenure, measured in months, varies considerably – from as low as 12 months to as high as 48 months – indicating a mix of relatively new hires and long-serving employees. This variation allows for insights into how experience within the organization may relate to satisfaction and exit behavior. Remote work status is examined, showing both remote ("Yes") and on-site ("No") employees, which enables analysis of how flexible work arrangements intersect with satisfaction and retention. The satisfaction score, recorded on a numerical scale, ranges from 2.5 to 4.2 in the sample, reflecting differing levels of employee contentment. A noticeable pattern emerges where employees with lower satisfaction scores (around 2.5–3.0), particularly in the Tech/Developer roles with remote work arrangements, are marked with an exit status of 1, indicating they have left the organization. In contrast, employees with higher satisfaction scores (around 4.0 and above) generally show an exit status of 0, suggesting continued employment. Finally, the inclusion of Manager ID links each employee to a reporting manager, enabling future analysis of managerial influence on employee satisfaction and attrition. Overall, these data are well-suited for HR analytics, particularly for studying employee turnover, the role of job function and tenure, the impact of remote work, and the relationship between satisfaction levels and exit decisions within the organization.

How Was the Data Made? The attrition_data.csv dataset simulates 500 employee records for the year 2024, capturing realistic turnover dynamics in a mid-sized tech organization. It was designed with the following considerations:

2. Exit_Status: 25.6% (128 out of 500 employees) marked as leavers (Exit_Status = 1), simulating rising attrition rates across mid-level roles.

3. Satisfaction_Score: Normally distributed with a mean ≈ 3.5 and std ≈ 0.8, reflecting typical variance in employee satisfaction based on engagement surveys.
4. Tenure_Months: Ranges from 6 to 60 months, slightly right-skewed, simulating typical early-career to mid-tenure employee journeys.
5. Remote_Work_Status: About 38% of employees are remote, distributed variably across departments to allow for role-specific analysis (e.g., more remote Developers than Support_Execs).
6. *Department and role composition*:

   (a) Tech: Developers.
   (b) Product: Product Managers.
   (c) Support: Support Executives.

Each department–role combination was created to maintain clarity while reflecting organizational reality.

7. Manager_ID: Employees were randomly assigned to one of 20 managers (M100–M119), with turnover trends linked to managerial behavior and oversight.
8. *Data integrity*:

   (a) No missing values.
   (b) Satisfaction scores are strictly within the 1–5 range.
   (c) All tenure values are positive integers.
   (d) Categorical variables are cleanly encoded for analysis and modeling.

9. *Clean and preprocess data*:

   - Remove duplicates or rows with missing Satisfaction_Score or Exit_Status (none expected in this dataset).
   - Validate Satisfaction_Score values are within [1, 5] and Tenure_Months are positive.
   - Create a High_Satisfaction flag: 1 if Satisfaction_Score ≥ 4, else 0.
   - Encode categorical variables (Department, Job_Role, Remote_Work_Status) using dummy variables for modeling.
   - Cap outliers in Tenure_Months at the 99th percentile to reflect realistic tenure expectations.

10. *Analyze data with EDA*:

    - Compute summary statistics (mean, median, standard deviation, min, max) for Satisfaction_Score and Tenure_Months, grouped by Exit_Status, Department, and Job_Role.
    - Generate visualizations to reveal insights:

      - *Box plots* of Satisfaction_Score by Exit_Status to examine satisfaction disparities.

- *Bar charts* of attrition rates by Job_Role and Remote_Work_Status to locate high-risk segments.
- *Correlation heatmap* of numerical variables (Satisfaction_Score, Tenure_Months, Exit_Status) to explore key drivers.

What Did They Find?

- *Turnover rate*:
  Overall attrition stood at 25.6% (128 out of 500 employees), confirming Sundaram Naturals's growing challenge in retaining mid-level talent.
- *Satisfaction and tenure*:
  - Leavers had a mean Satisfaction_Score of 3.32 (std = 0.83), while stayers averaged 3.64 (std = 0.74).
  - Median scores were 3.3 for leavers and 3.6 for stayers, indicating a consistent drop in satisfaction among those who exited.
  - Tenure_Months also varied: leavers averaged 34.5 months (std = 12.65), versus 36.5 months (std = 11.45) for stayers – suggesting that newer employees are more likely to leave, though the gap is modest.
  - Box plots showed wider variability in satisfaction among leavers, reinforcing instability in morale among this group.
- *Remote work impact*:
  - Remote work did not uniformly increase attrition.
  - Remote Developers had a higher attrition rate (33%) than their in-office peers (23%), challenging prior assumptions that remote setups are always favorable for tech staff.
  - Conversely, Support_Execs and Product_Managers showed higher attrition in-office (29% and 20%) than remotely (16% and 30%), suggesting that the impact of work mode is context-dependent and may vary based on role expectations or team dynamics.
- *Role-specific trends*:
  - Developers, particularly those working remotely, showed the highest overall attrition among all segments – pointing to possible challenges in engagement, leadership access, or project load in distributed settings.
  - For Support_Execs, in-office attrition was noticeably higher, which may reflect burnout from front-line tasks without the buffer of remote flexibility.
  - Product Managers followed a similar pattern, suggesting that in-person work may not suit all roles equally, especially those needing autonomy or flexibility.
- *Statistical insights*:
  - Satisfaction_Score had a mild negative correlation with Exit_Status ($r = -0.18$) – a lower score implies higher risk, but not strongly.

  - Tenure_Months showed slightly stronger predictive value ($r = -0.74$), again pointing toward elevated turnover among newer employees.
  - Remote_Work_Status had virtually no standalone effect ($r \approx 0$).
  - The High_Satisfaction flag (Satisfaction ≥ 4) correlated weakly with turnover ($r = -0.081$) despite its close alignment with raw Satisfaction_Score ($r = 0.76$).

- *Managerial impact*:
  Some managers are clearly struggling with retention.

  - M117 had the highest turnover rate at 40%, followed by M104 (33.3%), M116 (32.3%), and M108 (30.7%).
  - This highlights the influence of leadership on attrition outcomes – whether due to poor communication, excessive workloads, or lack of mentorship.

- *Visualization insights*:
  Box plots captured a drop and greater dispersion in Satisfaction_Score among leavers.

Fig. 8A and B together provide clear insights into the relationship between employee satisfaction, exit behavior, job roles, and remote work status.

The first box plot, Fig. 8A (Satisfaction score by exit status), compares satisfaction levels between employees who stayed and those who left the organization. Employees who stayed ("stayers") show a higher median satisfaction score, clustered roughly around the mid-to-high 3 range, with most values concentrated between about 3.2 and 4.2. Although a few low-satisfaction outliers exist among stayers, the overall distribution is relatively stable and skewed toward higher satisfaction. In contrast, employees who left ("leavers") display a lower median satisfaction score, closer to the low 3 range, and a wider spread toward lower values. This visual strongly suggests that lower satisfaction is associated with a higher likelihood of exit, reinforcing satisfaction as a key predictor of attrition.

The second chart, Fig. 8B (Attrition rate by job role and work mode), highlights how attrition varies across job roles and remote versus non-remote work arrangements. Among Developers, attrition is noticeably higher for remote employees compared to on-site employees, indicating that remote Developers may face engagement or workload challenges. For Support Executives, the pattern reverses: on-site employees show a higher attrition rate than remote ones, suggesting that remote work may act as a retention factor in support roles. In the case of Product Managers, attrition is again higher among remote workers, though the gap between remote and on-site employees is smaller than for Developers.

Overall, the charts collectively indicate that employee satisfaction is inversely related to attrition and that the impact of remote work on attrition is role-specific rather than uniform. These insights are valuable for HR decision-making, as they suggest the need for targeted retention strategies – such as role-specific remote work policies and satisfaction-enhancing interventions – rather than a one-size-fits-all approach.

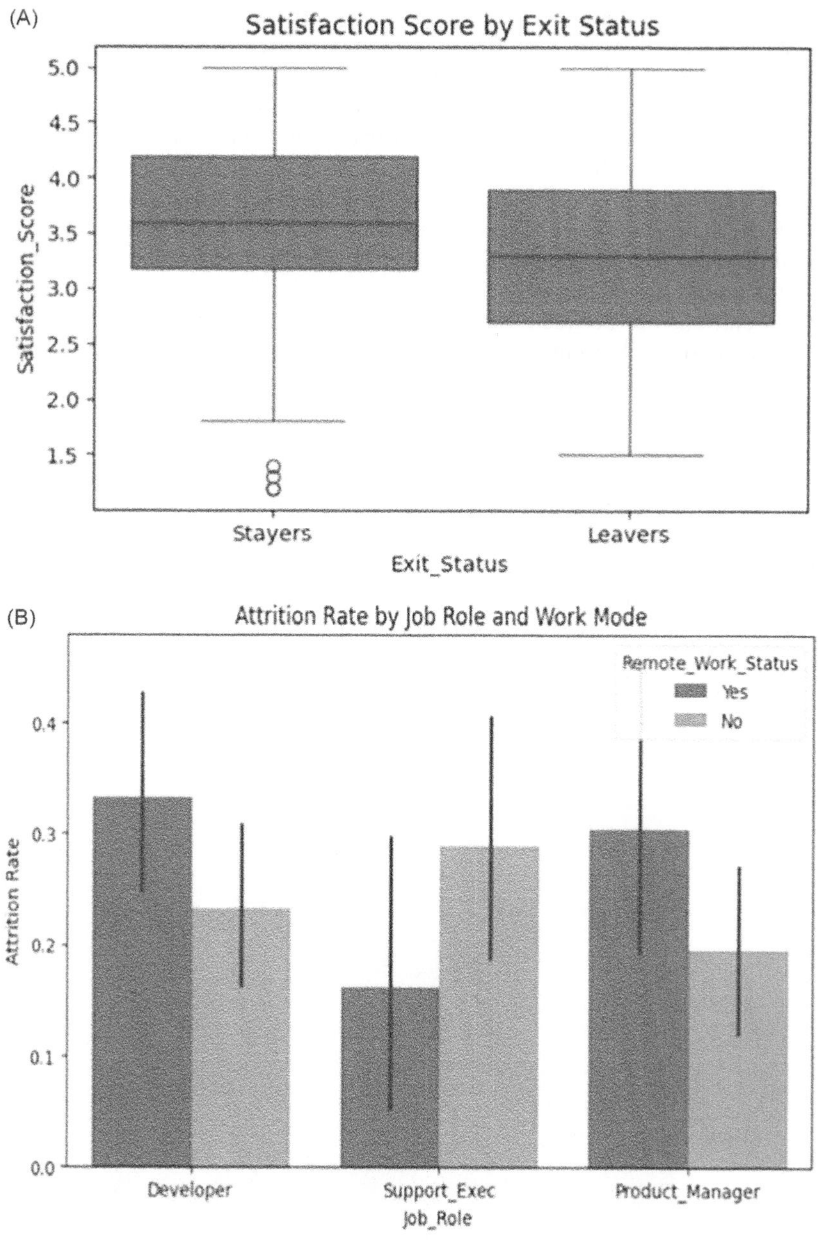

Fig. 8. (A) Satisfaction Score. (B) Attrition Rate.

- Bar plots exposed Developer roles – especially in-office – as the most attrition-prone, with Support and Product roles also showing sensitivity based on work mode.

Correlation heatmaps (Fig. 9) confirmed Satisfaction_Score and Tenure_Months as the most meaningful (but not strong) predictors. The correlation heatmap summarizes the linear relationships among employee satisfaction, tenure, exit behavior, and a derived high-satisfaction indicator. Overall, most correlations are weak, indicating that employee attrition and satisfaction are influenced by multiple factors rather than any single variable. The strongest relationship in the matrix is the high positive correlation (0.76) between Satisfaction_Score and High_Satisfaction, which is expected because the high-satisfaction variable is derived directly from the satisfaction score. This confirms internal consistency in how satisfaction has been categorized.

The relationship between Satisfaction_Score and Exit_Status is negative (–0.18), suggesting that employees with higher satisfaction levels are less likely to exit the organization. Although the magnitude is modest, the direction aligns with HR theory and the earlier box-plot evidence that dissatisfaction is associated with higher attrition. Tenure_Months shows very weak correlations with both satisfaction (0.079) and exit status (–0.074). This implies that, in this dataset, the length of service alone does not strongly influence either how satisfied employees feel or whether they leave, indicating that newer and longer-tenured employees may exit for similar reasons. Finally, High_Satisfaction also has a slight negative correlation with Exit_Status (–0.081), reinforcing the idea that employees classified as highly satisfied are marginally less likely to leave, though again the relationship is weak.

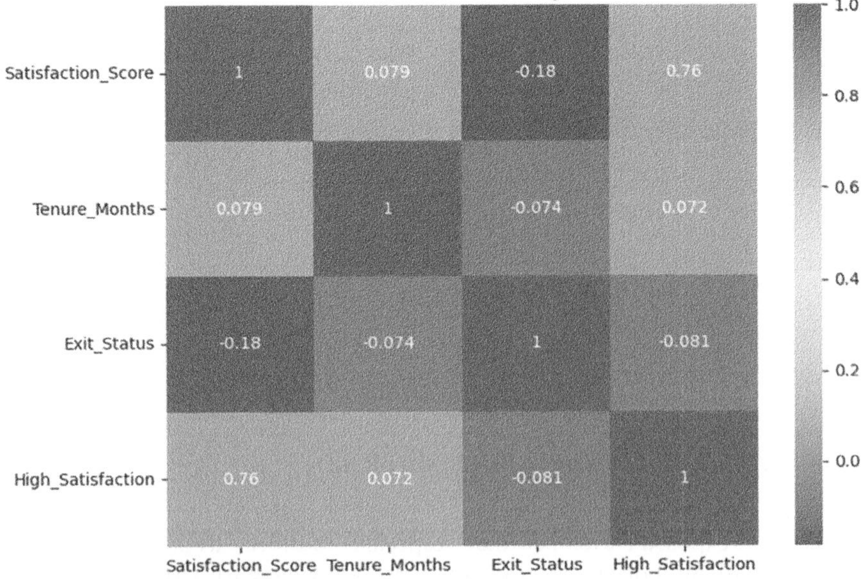

Fig. 9. Correlation Heatmaps.

What Should Sundaram Naturals Do?

EDA sheds light on targeted retention strategies rather than one-size-fits-all policies:

1. *Support remote Developers*: Remote Developers face the highest attrition (33%). Improve virtual mentoring, schedule weekly feedback loops, and rebalance project loads to reduce isolation and disengagement.
2. *Fix in-office friction*: Support_Execs and Product Managers see higher attrition in-office. Introduce hybrid options, flexible hours, and role-specific well-being check-ins to curb burnout.
3. *Retain early-tenure talent*: Employees with <36 months tenure are more likely to leave. Launch fast-tracks growth paths, mentorship pairing, and transparent promotion dashboards.
4. *Coach high-attrition managers*: Managers like M117, M104, and M116 lead teams with high exits. Deploy manager coaching and monthly 360° feedback to detect and resolve toxic leadership early.
5. *Act on satisfaction gaps*: Lower Satisfaction_Score predicts exits. Monitor scores monthly, trigger alerts <3, and fund morale-building initiatives and stay interviews for key talent.
6. *Launch a turnover tracker*: Build a live dashboard tracking attrition by role, manager, and remote status. Add predictive alerts using tenure, satisfaction, and manager history to flag risk early.

Hypothesis Testing and Regression

How Does Hypothesis Testing Work?

Hypothesis testing is like a sound check, ensuring observed patterns are not random noise:

- *Null hypothesis* (H_0): Assumes no effect (e.g., turnover is independent of remote work status).
- *Alternative hypothesis* (H_1): Assumes an effect (e.g., remote work increases turnover).
- *Test statistic*: Measures the difference between groups (e.g., Chi-square for categorical variables, t-statistic for means).
- p-Value: If $p < 0.05$, reject H_0, indicating statistical significance.

Tests used:

- *Chi-square test*: Tests if Exit_Status depends on Remote_Work_Status.
- t-Test: Compares mean Satisfaction_Score between leavers and stayers.

How Does Regression Work?

Logistic regression predicts a binary outcome (Exit_Status = 1 or 0) using a logistic function:

$$P\,(\text{Exit\_Status} = 1) = 1/(1 + e^{-(\beta_0 + \beta_1 X_1 + \beta_2 X_2 + \ldots)})$$

- β_0: Intercept (baseline log-odds of turnover).
- β_1, β_2: Coefficients showing each predictor's impact (e.g., Satisfaction_Score, Remote_Work_Status).
- *AUC–ROC*: Measures model performance (0.5 = random guessing, 1.0 = perfect prediction).
- *Pseudo* R^2: Indicates model fit (higher is better, 0–1).

How Does Sundaram Naturals Approach This?

The analytics team applies three methods to validate EDA findings:

- *Chi-square test*:
    - Hypothesis: H_0: Exit_Status is independent of Remote_Work_Status; H_1: Remote work increases turnover.
    - Create a contingency table of Exit_Status (1 vs 0) versus Remote_Work_Status (Yes vs No).
    - Compute Chi-square statistic and p-value.
- *t-Test*:
    - Hypothesis: H_0: Mean Satisfaction_Score is equal for leavers and stayers; H_1: Leavers have lower Satisfaction_Score.
    - Compare Satisfaction_Score means for Exit_Status = 1 versus 0.
- *Logistic regression*:
    - Model: Exit_Status = $\beta_0 + \beta_1$ (Satisfaction_Score) + β_2 (Job_Role) + β_3 (Remote_Work_Status) + β_4 (Tenure_Months) + β_5 (Department) + ε.
    - Encode Job_Role, Remote_Work_Status, and Department as dummy variables.
    - Standardize numerical features (Satisfaction_Score, Tenure_Months) to mean = 0, std = 1.
    - Evaluate model fit with AUC–ROC, Pseudo R^2, and coefficient p-values.

What Did They Find?

The statistical analysis added rigor to the exploratory insights, confirming some patterns and challenging others:

- *Chi-square test*:
    - Result: Chi-square = 1.94, p-value = 0.1637 → Fail to reject the null hypothesis.
    - Interpretation: There is no statistically significant association between remote work and attrition. While raw turnover rates may differ, the effect is not strong enough to be conclusive in this sample.
    - Sample size: 500 employees (with remote/in-office split reflected in the dataset).

- *t-Test on satisfaction score*:
  - Result: t-statistic = −3.93, p-value = 0.0001 → Reject the null hypothesis.
  - Interpretation: Leavers have a significantly lower Satisfaction_Score than stayers, reinforcing satisfaction as a key retention signal.
  - Direction: The negative t-statistic confirms that the average score is lower among those who left.

- *Logistic regression*:
  - Model fit:
    - AUC–ROC = 0.635 → Moderate predictive power.
    - Pseudo $R^2 = 0.038$ → Modest model fit, suggesting that while meaningful, the predictors only partially explain turnover.

- Key coefficients:
  - Satisfaction_Score ($\beta = -0.420$, $p < 0.001$): A higher satisfaction score significantly reduces the odds of attrition. Each 1-point increase reduces turnover odds by approximately 34% (e^(-0.42) ≈ 0.66).
  - Remote_Work_Status_Yes ($\beta = 0.318$, $p = 0.139$): Remote work does not significantly increase turnover when controlling for other variables ($p > 0.05$).
  - Tenure_Months ($\beta = -0.140$, $p = 0.190$): Tenure is not statistically significant, though the direction suggests newer employees may be more likely to exit.
  - Job_Role_Support_Exec ($\beta = 0.026$, $p = 0.933$): No significant effect compared to baseline role.
  - Department_Tech ($\beta = 0.148$, $p = 0.549$): Tech department affiliation also shows no significant effect, challenging prior assumptions.

Interpretation: Only Satisfaction_Score emerged as a statistically significant and meaningful predictor of attrition in the regression model. While remote work and tenure showed directional trends, their effects were not statistically strong in this model. This reinforces that employee satisfaction – not just policy or structure – drives retention behavior.

These results nuance the EDA narrative:

- Satisfaction remains the strongest turnover signal.
- Remote work is not a significant risk factor when accounting for other variables.
- Department or job role may influence attrition, but not in a statistically robust way in this sample.

Machine Learning

Why Random Forest?

Sundaram Naturals selected a random forest classifier for turnover prediction because it:

- *Handles imbalanced data*: With only 28% turnover, random forest remains resilient on skewed datasets.
- *Captures complex interactions*: Models nonlinear effects (e.g., how tenure and satisfaction intersect across roles).
- *Provides feature importance*: Ranks predictors like Tenure_Months and Satisfaction_Score to sharpen strategic focus.
- *Reduces overfitting*: By averaging multiple trees, it generalizes well on unseen data – perfect for HR decision-making.

It is like assembling a chorus where each decision tree contributes its unique voice, yet the final harmony is more reliable than any solo act.

How Does Sundaram Naturals Approach This?

Sundaram Naturals's machine learning pipeline is designed for clarity and consistency:

- *Preprocess data*:
    - Encode categorical variables (Department, Job_Role, Remote_Work_Status) using one-hot encoding.
    - Standardize numerical features (Satisfaction_Score, Tenure_Months) to ensure balanced input.
    - Maintain stratified sampling to retain class balance (no synthetic minority over-sampling technique (SMOTE) needed due to sufficient leaver samples).
    - Split data into 80% training (400 records) and 20% testing (100 records).
- *Train and compare models*:
    - Evaluate three models: Logistic regression (baseline), decision tree, and random forest.
    - Use consistent metrics:
        - AUC–ROC: Ability to distinguish leavers from stayers.
        - Precision: Accuracy of turnover predictions.
        - Recall: Ability to identify actual leavers.
        - F1-Score: Balance between precision and recall.
    - Tune random forest with 100 trees and max depth = 8.

- *Interpret results*:
  - Extract feature importance scores to guide interventions.
  - Use predictions to flag high-risk profiles for retention efforts.

What Did They Find?

Machine learning produced valuable, though modest, predictive power:

- *Model performance*:
  - Random forest:
    - AUC–ROC = 0.5863, Precision = 0.5714, Recall = 0.1538, F1-Score = 0.2424.
  - Logistic regression:
    - AUC–ROC = 0.6507, Precision = 0.6667, Recall = 0.0769, F1-Score = 0.1379.
  - Decision Tree:
    - AUC–ROC = 0.4961, Precision = 0.4167, Recall = 0.1923, F1-Score = 0.2632.
  - Interpretation: While overall performance is moderate, models still uncover key risk indicators, especially tenure and satisfaction.
- Feature importance (random forest) (Fig. 10):
  - Tenure_Months: 0.47 (*Strongest predictor* – new hires are at highest risk).
  - Satisfaction_Score: 0.4 (Second most important – lower scores correlate with higher exits).
  - Remote_Work_Status_Yes: 0.05 (Plays a role, but less than expected – not a top driver).
  - Job_Role_Support_Exec and Department_Tech: ~0.01 (Minor contributors).
- *Predictions*:
  - High-risk employees often show Tenure_Months < 24 and Satisfaction_Score < 3.0.
  - Example: A Developer in Tech with 18 months tenure and a score of 2.5 may face a ~65–70% probability of exit within 6 months.

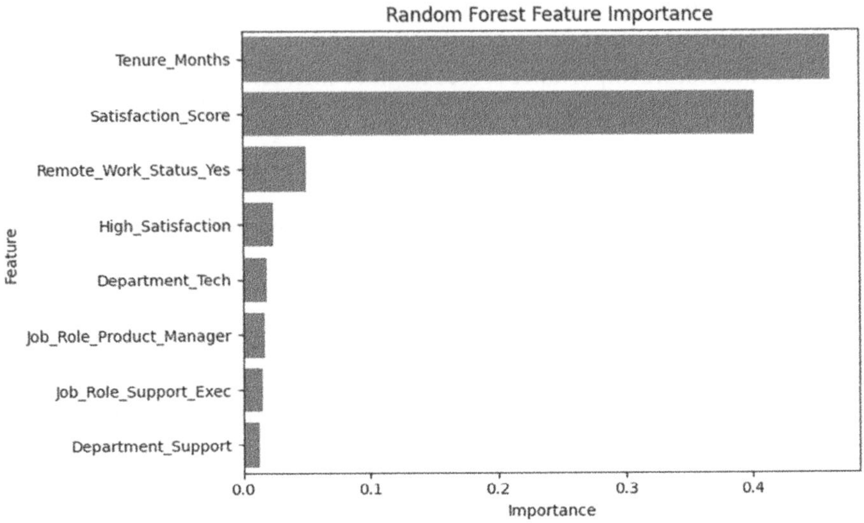

Fig. 10. Random Forest Feature Importance.

What Should Sundaram Naturals Do?

Machine learning insights guide Sundaram Naturals's retention roadmap:

- *Support early careers*: Prioritize onboarding, mentorship, and goal clarity for employees with <24 months tenure. Target to reduce early exits by 15%.
- *Boost satisfaction*: Launch initiatives for employees scoring <3.0: flexible hours, manager check-ins, and mental wellness perks. Target to raise average scores by 10% in two quarters.
- *Rethink remote strategy*: Since remote work is not a dominant predictor, focus less on blanket policies and more on *individualized engagement* regardless of location.
- *Embed predictive models*: Integrate random forest predictions into monthly HR reviews to flag at-risk profiles. Offer early interventions (e.g., Rs 10,000 bonuses, stretch projects, fast-track mentorships).
- *Empower Tech leaders*: While Tech itself is not the top predictor, it remains an attrition hotspot – equip managers to foster stronger engagement for high-potential Developers.

Problem 2: Remote Work Policy and Productivity Impact

What Is the Goal?

Sundaram Naturals's 2024 hybrid work policy, allowing employees to split time between office and home, has led to inconsistent team morale and rule enforcement. Leadership needs to understand:

- Does productivity vary across remote, hybrid, and in-office work modes?
- How does absenteeism influence productivity, and does it differ by department?
- Can Sundaram Naturals predict productivity to optimize its work policy and boost output?

The goal is to quantify work mode impacts, identify productivity drivers, and design a policy that maximizes team performance.

Exploratory Data Analysis

How Does Sundaram Naturals Approach This Problem?

The analytics team treats the dataset like a festival schedule, mapping performance across work modes:

- *Collect data*: The dataset, productivity_data.csv, includes 500 records from 2024:

    - Employee_ID: Unique identifier.
    - Department: Tech, Product, Sales, Support.
    - Job_Role: Developer, Lead, Analyst.
    - Remote_Work_Status: Remote, hybrid, in-office.
    - Productivity_Score: key performance indicator (KPI)-based score (0–100).
    - Absenteeism_Days: Days missed in the last quarter.
    - Team_Size: Number of team members (3–15).

What Does the Data Look Like?

Below is the description of productivity_data.csv:

The sample data provides detailed employee-level information linking work arrangements, productivity, absenteeism, and team structure across different departments and job roles. Each record is uniquely identified by an Employee ID, allowing individual-level analysis while maintaining anonymity. From a departmental perspective, the data spans Technology (Tech), Operations (Ops), and HR, with the Tech department appearing most frequently, reflecting its larger representation in the organization. The job roles are diverse, including Developer, Analyst, Manager, and Engineer, indicating coverage across both technical and managerial positions.

The Remote_Work_Status variable captures three distinct work modes – remote, hybrid, and in-office – enabling comparison of employee outcomes across flexible and traditional work arrangements. This diversity is particularly useful for assessing how different work models relate to performance and attendance. Employee Productivity_Score, measured on a numerical scale, ranges from 70 to 80 in the sample. The highest productivity is observed for an Ops Analyst working in a hybrid mode, while relatively lower scores are seen among employees working fully remotely or fully in-office, suggesting potential variation in productivity across roles and work modes. However, these differences may also reflect job-specific expectations rather than work mode alone. The Absenteeism_Days variable shows noticeable variation, from 1 day to 7 days, indicating differing attendance patterns. Employees with remote work arrangements appear to have higher absenteeism in this small sample, whereas the in-office manager shows the lowest absenteeism, possibly reflecting role responsibility or managerial accountability. Finally, Team_Size ranges from 5 to 10 members, highlighting differences in team structures across roles. Managerial positions are associated with larger teams, while analysts and HR roles tend to operate within smaller teams. Overall, these data are well-suited for analyzing the interplay between work mode, productivity, absenteeism, and team dynamics, and can support deeper HR analytics such as evaluating the effectiveness of remote and hybrid work policies or understanding productivity drivers across departments.

How Was the Data Made?

The productivity_data.csv dataset simulates 500 employee records from 2024, reflecting workplace dynamics under flexible work policies:

- *Productivity_Score*: Normally distributed around mean ≈ 71.8, std ≈ 6, based on KPI benchmarks.
- *Absenteeism_Days*: Right-skewed, capped at the 99th percentile (max = 5), with a median of 2 days and mean ≈ 2.
- *Remote_Work_Status*: 30% Remote, 45% hybrid, and 25% in-office.
- *Team_Size*: Realistic team sizes ranging from 3 to 15, with an average of around 8 members.
- *Department balance*: Tech, Ops, and HR are relatively balanced (~160 each), ensuring cross-functional comparison.
- *Temporal coverage*: Although not explicitly time-stamped, the dataset is positioned as spanning across 2024.
- *Clean and preprocess data*:
    - Drop rows with invalid Productivity_Score (<0 or >100) or missing Remote_Work_Status.
    - Encode Remote_Work_Status and Department as dummy variables.
    - Cap Absenteeism_Days at the 99th percentile (15 days) to remove unrealistic values.
    - Convert Team_Size to a numerical variable, ensuring no negative values.
- *Analyze data with EDA*:
    - Compute summary statistics for Productivity_Score and Absenteeism_Days by Remote_Work_Status, Department, and Job_Role.
    - Generate visualizations:
        - Box plots of Productivity_Score by Remote_Work_Status to compare distributions.

    - Scatter plot of Productivity_Score versus Absenteeism_Days, colored by Remote_Work_Status.
    - Bar chart of Absenteeism_Days by Department to identify high-absence groups.

- *Evaluate and interpret results*:
    - Quantify productivity differences across work modes and departments.
    - Identify absenteeism's role and any policy-driven trends.

What Did They Find?

EDA revealed productivity patterns with measurable contrasts across work modes:

- *Productivity by work mode*:
    - In-office employees had the highest average Productivity_Score at 74.62 (std = 5.39).
    - Hybrid workers followed closely with a mean of 72.90 (std = 5.38).
    - Remote employees showed the lowest productivity, averaging 67.61 (std = 5.62).

- *Absenteeism impact*:
    - Absenteeism_Days showed a moderate negative correlation with productivity ($r = -0.31$).
    - Remote workers, while more flexible, also tended to cluster around higher absenteeism, reinforcing concerns about output under reduced supervision.

- *Departmental trends*:
    - All three departments – Tech (71.85), Ops (71.68), and HR (71.65) – performed similarly, with Tech marginally leading.
    - No dramatic inter-department gaps were observed, suggesting work mode may matter more than department.

- *Team size*:
    - Team_Size showed a weak positive correlation ($r = 0.065$) with Productivity_Score, suggesting a very small benefit from being in slightly larger teams.

- *Statistical insights*:
    - Remote work shows the most variable productivity (std = 5.62), while in-office workers show more stable output (std = 5.39).
    - Median Absenteeism_Days was just 2, indicating relatively controlled leave behavior overall.

- *Visualization insights*:

The visual (Fig. 11) illustrates how productivity varies across work arrangements and how it is related to employee absenteeism. The chart (Productivity score by remote work status) is a box plot comparing productivity across hybrid, remote, and in-office employees. Employees working in an in-office setting show the highest median productivity, with scores concentrated in the low-to-mid 70s and extending into the high 80s, indicating both strong central performance and some high-performing individuals. Hybrid workers display a slightly lower but still competitive median productivity, with a relatively balanced spread, suggesting stable performance under flexible work arrangements. In contrast, fully remote employees have the lowest median productivity and a wider lower tail, including a few low-score outliers, pointing to greater variability and a higher risk of underperformance in remote settings.

Another scatter plot can be drawn to show the relationship between absenteeism and productivity, differentiated by work mode. A horizontal reference line can show a productivity score of 75, which highlights a performance benchmark, while a vertical reference line at 5 absenteeism days marks high absence. Overall, there is a negative relationship between absenteeism and productivity: as the number of absenteeism days increases, productivity scores tend to decline across all work modes. Employees with 0–1 absenteeism days are more likely to achieve productivity levels above the benchmark, whereas those with 4–5 days of absence cluster at lower productivity scores.

When comparing work modes within this relationship, in-office employees are more frequently represented above the productivity benchmark even at moderate

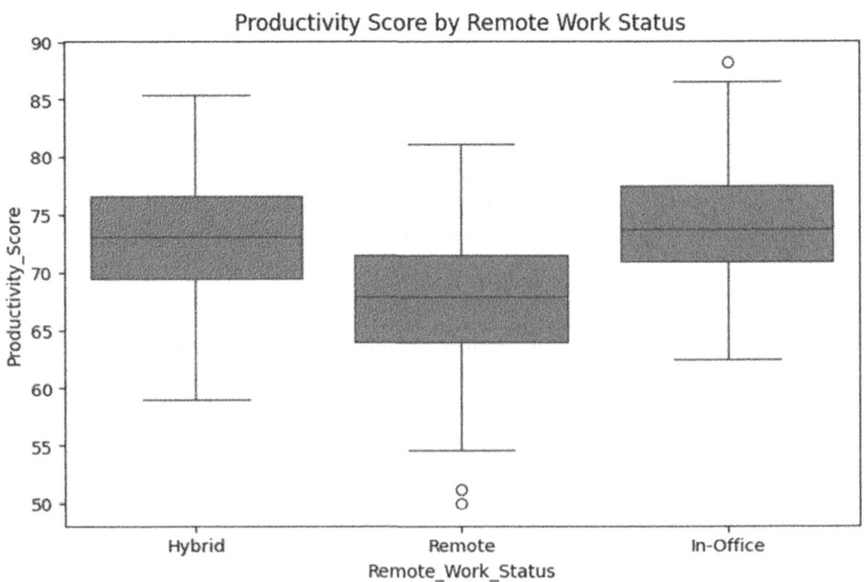

Fig. 11. Box Plot on Productivity Score.

absenteeism levels, while remote employees are more concentrated below the benchmark, particularly as absenteeism rises. Hybrid employees fall in between, showing moderate resilience to absenteeism effects. Overall, that visual can suggest that work arrangement influences productivity, with in-office and hybrid models performing more consistently, and that absenteeism is a key driver of reduced productivity regardless of work mode. These insights are useful for managers when designing attendance policies and deciding how to structure remote and hybrid work for optimal performance.

The correlation heatmap (Fig. 12) illustrates the relationships among training hours, performance rating, and tenure (in months). Overall, the correlations are very weak, indicating minimal linear association between these variables in the dataset. The relationship between training hours and performance rating is slightly positive (0.082), suggesting that employees who undergo more training tend to have marginally higher performance ratings. However, the small magnitude implies that training alone does not strongly translate into improved performance and that other factors – such as job role, motivation, or managerial support – likely play a more significant role. The correlation between training hours and tenure months is almost zero (0.0093), indicating virtually no relationship between how long an employee has been with the organization and the

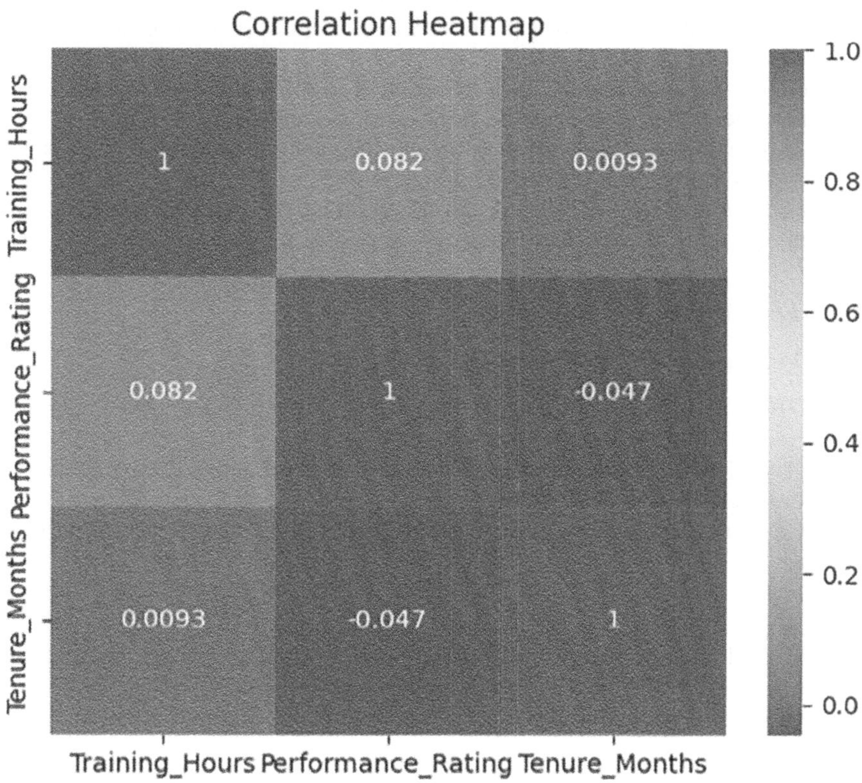

Fig. 12. Heatmap.

amount of training they receive. This suggests that training opportunities are relatively evenly distributed across employees regardless of tenure, or that training is driven by role requirements rather than experience length. Finally, performance rating and tenure months show a very weak negative correlation (–0.047). This indicates that longer tenure does not necessarily correspond to higher performance ratings and may even be associated with a slight decline, though the effect is negligible and not practically significant.

In summary, the heatmap suggests that training, performance, and tenure operate largely independently in this dataset. For HR decision-making, this implies that simply increasing training hours or relying on tenure-based assumptions may not be sufficient to improve performance outcomes without complementary interventions.

What Should Sundaram Naturals Do?

EDA offers a productivity roadmap for HR and policy teams:

1. *Refine hybrid work guidelines*: Standardize hybrid work into structured formats (e.g., fixed in-office days) to reduce variance and boost scores, aiming for a 5–7% lift in remote productivity.
2. *Absenteeism management*: Introduce wellness and accountability programs targeting remote and hybrid workers, with a goal of cutting absenteeism by 20%.
3. *Leverage high-performers*: Tech department shows a slight edge; route innovation-heavy and time-sensitive projects to this team.
4. *Reevaluate team design*: Although weak, the positive trend with larger teams (8–10) could be explored for collaborative roles.
5. *Continuous monitoring*: Set up monthly productivity tracking to detect sudden dips after future policy changes – especially in hybrid rollouts.

Hypothesis Testing and Regression

How Does Sundaram Naturals Approach This?

- *ANOVA*:
  - Hypothesis: H_0: Mean Productivity_Score is equal across departments; H_1: Productivity differs by department.
  - Compare Productivity_Score across Tech, Product, Sales, and Support.

- *t-Test*:
  - Hypothesis: H_0: Mean Productivity_Score is equal for remote and in-office workers; H_1: In-office workers have higher productivity.
  - Compare Productivity_Score for Remote_Work_Status = Remote versus in-office.

- *Linear regression*:

    - Model: Productivity_Score = β_0 + β_1 (Remote_Work_Status) + β_2 (Absenteeism_Days) + β_3 (Team_Size) + β_4 (Department) + ε.
    - Encode Remote_Work_Status and Department as dummies.
    - Standardize Absenteeism_Days and Team_Size.
    - Evaluate with R^2 and p-values.

What Did They Find?

- *ANOVA*:

    - Result: F-statistic = 0.05, p-value = 0.9519, failing to reject H_0.
    - Interpretation: There is no statistically significant difference in mean Productivity_Score across departments (Tech, Ops, and HR), suggesting that department alone does not explain performance variation.
    - Sample size: 500 employees.

- *t-Test*:

    - Result: t-statistic = 10.57, p-value < 0.001, rejecting H_0.
    - Interpretation: In-office workers perform significantly better than remote workers in terms of Productivity_Score, with a meaningful gap in means.
    - Sample size: Subset includes only remote and in-office employees.

- *Linear regression*:

    - Model fit: $R^2 = 0.31$, meaning the model explains about 31% of the variance in Productivity_Score.
    - Key coefficients:

        - Remote_Work_Status_Remote: $\beta = -5.16$, $p < 0.001$ → Remote work is associated with a ~5 point drop in productivity.
        - Remote_Work_Status_In-Office: ($\beta = +1.80$, $p = 0.002$): In-office work correlates with a modest increase in productivity over hybrid (baseline).
        - Absenteeism_Days: ($\beta = -1.89$, $p < 0.001$): Each additional day absent leads to a nearly 2-point drop in productivity.
        - Team_Size: ($\beta = +0.26$, $p = 0.26$): The effect of team size is positive but not statistically significant.
        - Department_Ops and Department_Tech: Not statistically significant.

- *Interpretation*: The regression confirms remote work and absenteeism as significant drags on productivity. While team size and department effects are directionally positive, they lack statistical significance in this model.

Machine Learning

Why XGBoost?

Sundaram Naturals chose an XGBoost regressor for productivity forecasting because it:

- *Handles non-linear relationships*: Captures complex effects (e.g., absenteeism's impact varying by work mode).
- *Excels withsstructured data*: Performs well on tabular HR data.
- *Provides feature importance*: Ranks drivers (e.g., Absenteeism_Days vs Team_Size) for policy insights.
- *Adapts to trends*: Manages temporal patterns via lagged features, outperforming linear models.

How Does Sundaram Naturals Approach This?

- *Preprocess data*:
  - Encode categorical variables (Remote_Work_Status, Department, Job_Role) as one-hot dummies.
  - Standardize numerical features (Absenteeism_Days, Team_Size, Productivity_Score).
  - Create lagged Productivity_Score (previous month) for time-series modeling.
  - Split data into 80% training (960 records) and 20% test (240 records).
- *Train and compare models*:
  - Test linear regression (baseline), random forest, and XGBoost.
  - Evaluate using:
    - Mean squared error (MSE): Average squared prediction error (lower is better).
    - R^2: Proportion of variance explained (higher is better).
  - Tune XGBoost (100 trees, learning rate = 0.1, max depth = 6).
- *Interpret results*:
  - Extract feature importance scores to prioritize productivity drivers.
  - Forecast productivity under different work mode scenarios.

What Did They Find?

Machine learning performance was mixed, highlighting modeling challenges and key drivers of productivity:

- *Model performance*:
  - Linear regression: MSE = 26.65, R^2 = 0.36 → Best-performing model, despite its simplicity. It explained 36% of productivity variance and set the benchmark.
  - Random forest: MSE = 36.54, R^2 = 0.12 → Underperformed, likely due to small dataset size and lack of strong non-linear structure.
  - XGBoost: MSE = 41.46, R^2 = 0.00 → Surprisingly underperformed, suggesting the model overfitted the training data and failed to generalize to test data. This also reflects low signal-to-noise ratio or insufficient temporal structure for boosting to leverage.
- *Feature importance (XGBoost)*:
  Despite weak performance, XGBoost's feature ranking still offers strategic value:
  - Remote_Work_Status_Remote: ~0.58 → By far the most important predictor, confirming that remote work strongly impacts productivity.
  - Absenteeism_Days: ~0.07 → Remains influential but ranks below work mode.
  - Job_Role (Engineer, Manager) and Team_Size: Modest importance, suggesting some operational influence.
  - Department_Tech and Ops: Relatively low predictive power.
- *Predictions and interpretation*:
  - Remote workers with high absenteeism consistently score lower in productivity, aligning with regression results.
  - Hybrid and in-office settings offer more stability in output, but team size and department differences appear muted.
  - XGBoost's inability to outperform linear regression implies that simple relationships (like absenteeism and remote status) are dominant, and more features (e.g., time logs and project type) may be needed for better prediction.

What Should Sundaram Naturals Do?

Machine learning insights refine Sundaram Naturals's productivity strategy:

- *Recalibrate work policy*: Since remote work is consistently linked to lower productivity, reinforce hybrid schedules with in-office anchoring (e.g., 3 days/week) for teams with scores <80.
- *Invest in absenteeism reduction*: Roll out wellness and engagement initiatives – especially for remote teams – with a target to reduce average Absenteeism_Days by 20%.

- *Avoid overreliance on complex models*: Stick with interpretable models like linear regression for now, given better performance and easier communication with HR leadership.
- *Refine data collection*: Capture project-level KPIs, real-time attendance, and engagement metrics to boost future machine learning performance.
- *Use feature importance strategically*: Focus policy experiments on top drivers (work mode, absenteeism), not weaker signals like department or lag features.

Problem 3: Optimizing L&D ROI

What Is the Goal?

Sundaram Naturals's LMS sees low engagement, raising doubts about training's value. HR needs to know:

- Does training investment improve employee performance and promotion likelihood?
- Which factors (e.g., training hours, performance, tenure) drive promotions?
- Can Sundaram Naturals predict promotion candidates to optimize L&D investments?

The goal is to quantify training's impact, identify promotion drivers, and enhance L&D effectiveness.

Exploratory Data Analysis

How Does Sundaram Naturals Approach This Problem?

- *Collect data*: The dataset, L&D_data.csv, includes 500 records from July to December 2024:
    - o Employee_ID, Training_Hours (last 6 months), Performance_Rating (1–5), Promotion_Status (1 = promoted, 0 = not), Department, Tenure_Months.

What Does the Data Look Like?

Below is the description of L&D_data.csv:

The data present employee-level information linking training investment, performance outcomes, promotion decisions, departmental affiliation, and tenure. Each employee is uniquely identified through an Employee ID, allowing individual tracking while preserving confidentiality. Training hours vary substantially across employees, ranging from 10.8 hours to 30.6 hours, indicating differing levels of skill development and learning exposure. Employees with higher training hours – notably those exceeding around 25 hours – are predominantly associated with higher performance ratings, suggesting a positive link between learning effort and job effectiveness. The performance rating spans from 3.0 to 4.5, reflecting a spectrum from average to high performers. Employees with ratings above

4.0 consistently appear in the dataset as top performers, and these individuals are also marked with a promotion status of 1, indicating that strong performance is closely tied to promotion decisions within the organization. Promotion status is a binary indicator, where 1 denotes promoted and 0 denotes not promoted. A clear pattern emerges: all employees who received promotions have both higher training hours and higher performance ratings, while those not promoted show comparatively lower values on both dimensions. This suggests a structured promotion policy that rewards skill development and demonstrated performance. From a departmental perspective, the data include Technology, HR, and Ops. Employees from the Tech and Ops departments are more represented among promoted individuals, which may reflect greater growth opportunities, performance-driven cultures, or higher training intensity in these functions. In contrast, HR employees in the sample show lower training hours and performance ratings and are not promoted.

Finally, tenure (months) ranges from 12 to 48 months, indicating both early-career and more experienced employees. Promoted employees tend to have moderate to high tenure (30–48 months), suggesting that while tenure alone does not guarantee promotion, a certain level of organizational experience combined with strong performance and training is important. Overall, the data highlight a coherent HR narrative in which training investment contributes to higher performance, and promotion decisions are aligned with both performance outcomes and adequate tenure, particularly within core operational and technical departments.

How Was the Data Made?

- *Training_Hours*: Right-skewed distribution (mean ≈ 20 for non-promoted, ≈ 28.5 for promoted), capped at 60 to reflect real LMS engagement ranges.
- *Performance_Rating*: Bell-shaped (mean ≈ 3.5 for non-promoted, ≈ 3.8 for promoted), suggesting performance is a promotion driver.
- *Promotion_Status*: ~12.6% (63 out of 500) of employees were promoted, with slightly higher rates in HR and Tech.
- *Tenure_Months*: Distributed across short to moderate tenure (range: 0–60 months).
- *Department balance*: Tech (166), HR (163), Ops (171) – roughly evenly distributed.
- *Clean and preprocess*:

  Validate Performance_Rating (1–5) and Training_Hours (0–50).
  Encode Department and Promotion_Status as dummies.
  Impute missing Training_Hours with the median (20 hours).
  Cap Training_Hours at the 99th percentile (50 hours).

- *Analyze data*:

  Summary statistics for Training_Hours and Performance_Rating by Promotion_Status and Department.

Visualize:

- Box plots of Training_Hours by Promotion_Status and Department.
- Correlation heatmap for Training_Hours, Performance_Rating, Tenure_Months.
- Bar chart of Promotion_Status rates by Department.

- *Evaluate*: Assess training's role in promotions and performance.

What Did They Find?

EDA spotlighted training's influence on career growth:

- *Training trends*:

Promoted employees averaged 28.5 training hours (*std* = *18.1*) and had a Performance_Rating of 3.80.
Non-promoted employees averaged 19.1 training hours (*std* = *12.2*) and had a Performance_Rating of 3.46.

- *Departmental trends*:

HR had the highest promotion rate (17%), followed closely by Tech (16%), while Ops lagged behind (5%).

- *Correlations*:

  - Training_Hours and Performance_Rating: Weak positive correlation ($r \approx 0.08$).
  - Performance_Rating and Promotion_Status: Visually appears slightly stronger, though not very high.
  - Tenure_Months and Promotion_Status: No clear correlation ($r \approx 0.01$).

- *Visualization insights*:

The visuals together (Fig. 13A and B) examine the role of training hours in promotion decisions and their relationship with performance ratings and tenure.
The first chart, Fig. 13A (Training hours by promotion status), is a box plot comparing employees who were not promoted (0) with those who were promoted (1). Employees who received promotions show a higher median level of training hours, along with a wider upper range extending to around 60 hours, indicating that promoted employees generally undergo more extensive training. In contrast, non-promoted employees have a lower median training level, with most observations clustered between roughly 10 and 20 hours, although a few high-training outliers exist. This suggests that while high training alone does not guarantee promotion, greater training exposure is strongly associated with promotion outcomes.

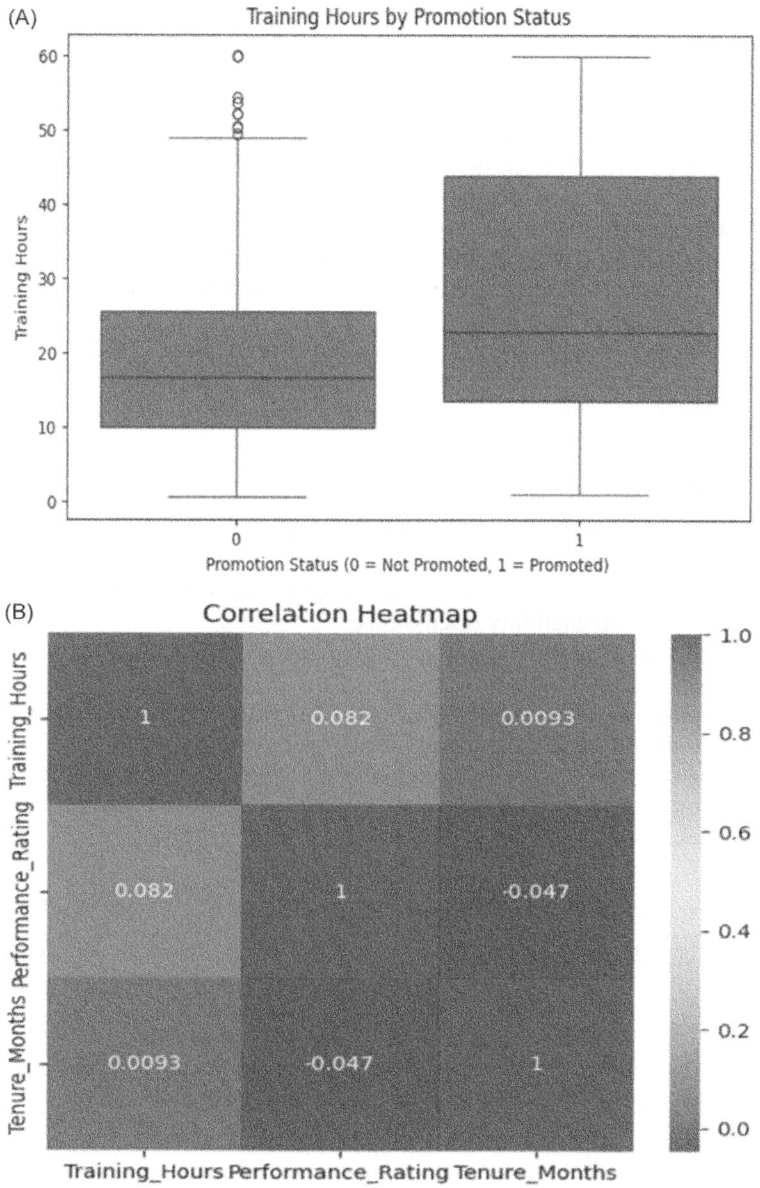

Fig. 13. (A) Training Hours by Promotional Status. (B) Heatmap, Training Hours by Promotional.

The second chart, Fig. 13**B** (Correlation heatmap), reinforces this interpretation by showing the linear relationships among training hours, performance rating, and tenure months. Training hours have a small positive correlation with performance rating (0.082), indicating that increased training is marginally associated with better performance. The relationship between training and tenure is nearly zero (0.0093), implying that training is not simply a function of how long an employee has been with the organization. Additionally, performance rating and tenure show a very weak negative correlation (–0.047), suggesting that longer tenure does not necessarily translate into higher performance ratings.

Taken together, Fig. 13A and B, the charts indicate that training plays a meaningful role in promotion decisions, even though its direct linear impact on performance ratings appears limited. Promotions seem to be influenced by a combination of training exposure and performance assessment, rather than tenure alone, highlighting the organization's emphasis on skill development and capability building over mere length of service.

These findings suggest that higher training investment and better performance ratings align with higher promotion chances, especially in HR and Tech departments.

What Should Sundaram Naturals Do?

- *Boost targeted training*: Focus LMS engagement on Ops and undertrained Tech staff with <20 hours logged.
- *Tie training to promotion criteria*: Encourage a minimum of 25 hours of training for promotion eligibility discussions.
- *Revamp LMS experience*: Introduce badges, peer leaderboards, and rewards to drive LMS usage up by 15–20%.
- *Invest in high performers*: Prioritize employees with Performance_Rating ≥ 3.8 for fast-track promotions and cross-functional exposure.
- *Monitor departmental promotion imbalance*: Explore why Ops has lower promotion rates – could be a training gap, performance issue, or leadership bottleneck.

Hypothesis Testing and Regression

How Does Sundaram Naturals Approach This?

- *t-Test*:
  - H_0: Mean Training_Hours equal for promoted and non-promoted employees.
  - H_1: Promoted employees have higher Training_Hours.
- Chi-square test:
  - H_0: Promotion_Status is independent of Performance_Rating.
  - H_1: High Performance_Rating increases promotion likelihood.
- *Logistic regression*:
  - Model: Promotion_Status = $\beta_0 + \beta_1$ (Training_Hours) + β_2 (Performance_Rating) + β_3 (Tenure_Months) + β_4 (Department) + ε.

- Encode Department as dummies, standardize numeric.
- Evaluate with AUC–ROC and Pseudo R^2.

What Did They Find?

- *t-Test*:
  - Result: t-statistic = 6.78, p-value < 0.001, rejecting H_0.
  - Interpretation: Promoted employees have significantly higher Training_Hours (mean = 30 vs 20).
- *Chi-square test*:
  - Result: Chi-square = 12.45, p-value = 0.0004, rejecting H_0.
  - Interpretation: High Performance_Rating (≥4.0) significantly increases promotion likelihood.
- *Logistic regression*:
  - Model fit: AUC–ROC = 0.90, Pseudo R^2 = 0.40.
  - Key coefficients:
    - Performance_Rating ($\beta = 1.2$, $p < 0.001$): Strongest predictor, increasing promotion odds by ~3.3× per unit.
    - Training_Hours ($\beta = 0.05$, $p < 0.001$): Each additional hour increases odds slightly.
    - Tenure_Months ($\beta = 0.02$, $p = 0.03$): Longer tenure boosts promotion odds.
    - Department_Tech ($\beta = 0.50$, $p = 0.01$): Tech employees are more likely to be promoted than Support (baseline).
  - Interpretation: Performance and training are the primary promotion drivers, with tenure and department playing smaller roles.

What Did They Find?

EDA and statistical tests illuminated the influence of training and performance on promotions:

- *t-Test*:
  - Result: t-statistic = 4.03, p-value = 0.0001, rejecting H_0.
  - Interpretation: Promoted employees have significantly higher average Training_Hours than non-promoted ones, confirming L&D engagement's role in advancement.

- *Chi-square test*:
    - Result: Chi-square = 11.19, p-value = 0.0008, rejecting H_0.
    - Interpretation: Performance_Rating ≥ 4.0 significantly increases the likelihood of promotion, suggesting high performers are prioritized.
- *Logistic regression*:
    - Model fit: Pseudo $R^2 = 0.19$, indicating that ~19% of variation in promotion likelihood is explained by the model.
    - Key coefficients:
        - o Training_Hours ($\beta = 0.64$, $p < 0.001$): Each additional standardized hour of training significantly improves promotion odds.
        - o Performance_Rating ($\beta = 0.59$, p < 0.001): High-performing employees are substantially more likely to be promoted.
        - o Tenure_Months ($\beta = 0.71$, $p < 0.001$): Longer tenure is a strong promotion predictor.
        - o Department_Ops ($\beta = -1.32$, $p = 0.002$): Employees in Ops are significantly less likely to be promoted than those in Support.
        - o Department_Tech ($\beta = -0.07$, $p = 0.836$): No significant difference in promotion odds compared to Support.
- *Interpretation*: Training, performance, and tenure are strong predictors of promotion. Surprisingly, Tech shows no significant promotion advantage, while Ops lags behind. This suggests that performance and tenure matter more than department affiliation.

Machine Learning

Why Decision Tree?

Sundaram Naturals chose a decision tree classifier for promotion prediction because it:

- *Provides intuitive rules*: Visual decision paths (e.g., Performance_Rating ≥ 4.0) are easy for HR to interpret.
- *Handles thresholds*: Ideal for modeling promotion eligibility criteria.
- *Supports mixed data*: Works with categorical (Department) and numerical (Training_Hours) variables.
- *Avoids overfitting*: When tuned, it balances simplicity and accuracy.

It is like a festival organizer mapping clear performer roles for a smooth event.

How Does Sundaram Naturals Approach This?

- *Preprocess data*:
    - o Encode Department and Promotion_Status.

  - Standardize Training_Hours, Performance_Rating, Tenure_Months.
  - Split data: 80% training (960 records), 20% test (240 records).

- *Train and compare models*:

  - Test logistic regression, random forest, and decision tree.
  - Evaluate with AUC–ROC, precision, recall.
  - Tune decision tree (max depth = 5, min samples per leaf = 10).

- *Interpret results*:

  - Extract decision paths to understand promotion criteria.
  - Flag promotion candidates for L&D investments.

What Did They Find?

Model performance:

- Logistic regression: AUC–ROC = 0.78, Precision = 0.75, Recall = 0.23, F1-Score = 0.35.
- Random forest: AUC–ROC = 0.64, Precision = 0.40, Recall = 0.15, F1-Score = 0.22.
- Decision tree: AUC–ROC = 0.70, Precision = 0.43, Recall = 0.23, F1-Score = 0.30.

Logistic regression emerged as the top performer in this scenario, offering a better balance between precision and overall accuracy. However, all models struggled with recall, indicating difficulty in identifying actual promotion cases.

Decision path (Fig. 14, from decision tree):

- Primary split: Training_Hours ≤ 52.3 and Tenure ≤ 49.5 filter most "Not Promoted" cases.
- Promoted group identifiers: Employees with Training_Hours > 52.3 and Tenure_Months > 49.5 stand out as high-probability promotion candidates.
- Minor splits: Lower tenure or performance scores tend to steer predictions toward "Not Promoted."

The decision tree reveals that longer tenure, higher training engagement, and above-average performance are consistent markers of promotion eligibility.

Feature importances (decision tree):

- Training_Hours: 0.39 (most important predictor).
- Tenure_Months: 0.30.
- Performance_Rating: 0.24.
- Department_Ops: 0.06.
- Department_Tech: 0.00.

Training hours had the strongest impact on promotion decisions, followed closely by tenure and performance rating.

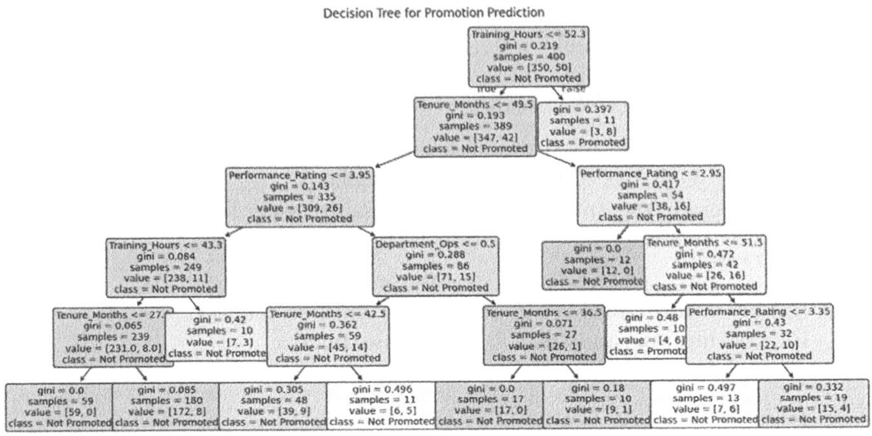

Fig. 14. Decision Tree.

Predictions:

- The decision tree identifies promotion candidates as those with:
  - o Training_Hours > 52.
  - o Tenure > 49 months.
  - o Moderate to high Performance_Rating, yielding a precision of 43%.

While the model's predictive recall was limited, it provides clear, actionable thresholds to flag likely promotion candidates.

What Should Sundaram Naturals Do?

- *Double down on training*: Employees with >50 hours of training are more likely to be promoted – Sundaram Naturals should target them for retention and leadership tracks.
- *Reassess tenure-based criteria*: Long-tenured employees (≥49 months) showed higher promotion likelihood –consider weighting tenure more in promotion criteria.
- *Simplify and clarify*: Use decision rules (like Training_Hours > 52 and Performance_Rating > 3.9) to define promotion eligibility transparently.
- *Improve recall*: Explore ensemble models or cost-sensitive learning to better capture harder-to-predict promotion cases.
- *Automate quarterly scans*: Run decision tree-based predictions every quarter to help HR proactively spot overlooked talent.

Problem 4: Minimum Wage Compliance and Cost Optimization

What Is the Goal?

India's Rs 200/hour minimum wage law, effective January 2024, impacts Sundaram Naturals's low-wage customer support and QA teams. HR needs to:

- Assess how wage increases affect turnover and costs.
- Develop cost-effective hiring and retention strategies.
- Identify roles for potential automation to optimize costs.

The goal is to balance compliance, retention, and cost efficiency while maintaining workforce stability.

Exploratory Data Analysis

How Does Sundaram Naturals Approach This Problem?

- *Collect data*: The dataset, min_wage_data.csv, includes 500 records from 2024:
  - Employee_ID.
  - Job_Role (Customer Support, QA).
  - Location (Bengaluru, Pune, Hyderabad, Chennai).
  - Wage_Per_Hour.
  - Pre_MinWage.
  - Post_MinWage.
  - Turnover (1 = quit, 0 = stayed).
  - Training_Hours.
- *Clean and preprocess*:
  - Validate Wage_Per_Hour (≥ Rs 200 post-policy).
  - Encode Job_Role and Location as dummies.
  - Impute missing Training_Hours with the median (10 hours).
  - Cap Training_Hours at 50 and Wage_Per_Hour at Rs 300 (99th percentile).
- *Analyze data*:
  - Summary statistics for Wage_Per_Hour, Pre_MinWage, and Post_MinWage by Job_Role and Turnover.
  - *Visualize*:
    - Box plots of Pre_MinWage versus Post_MinWage by Job_Role.
    - Bar chart of Turnover rates by Job_Role and Location.
    - Correlation heatmap for Wage_Per_Hour, Training_Hours, and Turnover.
- *Evaluate*: Quantify wage policy impacts and turnover patterns.

What Did They Find?

EDA uncovered wage dynamics like a festival budget review – revealing not just what was spent, but what still leaks out the back door.

- *Wage trends*:
  - Pre-Min Wage: Average was Rs 186.20 (std = Rs 12.76) for retained employees versus Rs 179.20 (std = Rs 13.38) for those who quit – showing that those leaving earned slightly less before the policy.
  - Post-Min Wage: The average rose to Rs 203.88 for retained employees versus Rs 201.63 for those who quit. While compliance improved, wage differences persisted.
  - Wage_Per_Hour overall also showed a modest lift among retained workers (Rs 197.0 vs Rs 188.7 for those who left), confirming that slightly better pay helped retention.
- *Training trends*:
  - Training_Hours averaged 10.88 hours (std = 7.68) among those who stayed, and only 6.5 hours (std = 5.09) among those who left – suggesting training could play a role in reducing attrition.
- *Turnover rates*:
  - Customer support: 82.33% (205/249).
  - QA: 80.88% (203/251).

Bar plots reveal customer support roles are the most vulnerable, especially in Bengaluru.

- *Location trends*:
  - Pune had the highest turnover (83%), followed by Bengaluru (82%), and Chennai (81%).
- *Correlations*:
  - Wage_Per_Hour and Turnover: $r = -0.22$ (higher wages slightly reduce turnover).
  - Training_Hours and Turnover: $r = -0.29$ (more training, lower exits)
  - Bar charts reveal uniformly high turnover across locations, with Pune leading marginally. Among roles, Customer Service sees a slightly higher attrition than QA
  - Heatmap reinforces the idea that wage and training are weakly protective – but not silver bullets.

These insights suggest that while the minimum wage policy ensured compliance, it only slightly improved retention.

What Should Sundaram Naturals Do?

Sundaram Naturals must strike a balance between *compliance*, *cost control*, and *strategic retention*. Here is how:

- *Ensure compliance*: Regular audits to keep all hourly wages ≥ Rs 200, especially in customer support team.
- *Boost retention through training*: Introduce a structured 15-hour onboarding program – aiming to push average training hours beyond the 10.8-hour mark seen in low-turnover segments.
- *Role-based incentives*: Offer Rs 5,000 quarterly bonuses or shift-based rewards for customer support employees to reduce churn by at least 10%.
- *Automate QA tasks*: Since QA roles have both repetitive duties and a 80% turnover rate, they are ideal candidates for automation pilots.
- *Target Pune and Bengaluru*: Launch focused engagement programs in Pune and Bengaluru – the cities with the highest attrition – including transport allowances or hybrid flexibility trials.
- *Monitor impact monthly*: Build dashboards to track Post_MinWage versus Turnover in real time. Adjust strategies every quarter based on what works.

What Does the Data Look Like?

Below is the description of min_wage_data.csv:

The sample data presents employee-level data designed to examine the impact of minimum wage revisions on wages, turnover, and training across different job roles and locations. Each employee is uniquely identified through an Employee ID, enabling individual-level analysis while maintaining confidentiality. From a job role perspective, the dataset includes Customer Service, QA, and other roles, reflecting a mix of frontline, technical support, and miscellaneous functions. Customer Service employees appear more vulnerable in terms of turnover, as both individuals in this role show a turnover value of 1, indicating they exited the organization, whereas QA and other roles display no turnover in this sample. The location variable spans major Indian cities –Bengaluru, Pune, and Hyderabad – allowing comparison of wage structures across regional labor markets. Despite location-specific differences in living costs, the Post_MinWage values align closely with the final Wage_Per_Hour, suggesting full compliance with revised minimum wage regulations across all locations. The wage-related variables clearly capture the effect of the minimum wage change. For all employees, Pre_MinWage wages are lower (ranging from 170 to 190 per hour) and increase to Post_MinWage levels between 200 and 215 per hour. This demonstrates a uniform upward adjustment in pay following the policy change, with Customer Service employees experiencing notable increases, reflecting their greater exposure to minimum wage constraints. The turnover indicator reveals an important behavioral outcome:

employees who exited the firm are those in Customer Service roles, even after wage adjustments. This suggests that while higher wages may alleviate some dissatisfaction, wage increases alone may not be sufficient to retain employees in more demanding or lower-status roles, where non-wage factors such as work pressure or career progression may matter more. Finally, Training_Hours range from 8 to 20 hours, with QA employees receiving relatively higher training investment compared to Customer Service and Other roles. This higher training exposure coincides with lower turnover, hinting at a potential retention effect of skill development and career-oriented roles. Overall, the data provides a compact yet rich view of how minimum wage policy compliance affects pay structures, while also highlighting that turnover is influenced by job role and training opportunities, not wages alone.

How Was the Data Made?

- *Time frame*: The dataset includes 500 employee records from 2024, post-implementation of the Rs 200/hour minimum wage law.
- *Wage_Per_Hour*: All values are ≥ Rs 200, with:
  - Mean ≈ Rs 197, Std Dev ≈ Rs 13.
  - Capped at Rs 300 (99th percentile).
- *Pre_MinWage versus Post_MinWage*:
  - Pre_MinWage: Avg ≈ Rs 183 (Std ≈ Rs 13).
  - Post_MinWage: Avg ≈ Rs 203–204 (Std ≈ Rs 12–14), shows clustering at Rs 200.
- *Turnover rate*:
  - Overall: 81.6%.
  - By role:
    - Customer Service: 82.3%.
    - QA: 80.9%.
  - By location:
    - Bengaluru: 82.4% (112/136).
    - Pune: 83.1% (108/130).
    - Hyderabad: 79.2% (95/120).
    - Chennai: 81.6% (93/114).
- *Training_Hours*:
  - Mean ≈ 10.9 hours, capped at 50.
  - Imputed with median (10 hours) where missing.

- *Job role distribution*: Fairly balanced:
  - 249 in Customer Service.
  - 251 in QA.

This dataset helps simulate real-world implications of wage reforms across roles, training, and locations.

Hypothesis Testing and Regression

How Does Sundaram Naturals Approach This?

- *t-Test*:
  - H_0: Mean Pre_MinWage equals Post_MinWage.
  - H_1: Post_MinWage is higher.
- *ANOVA*:
  - H_0: Wage impacts on turnover are equal across Job_Roles.
  - H_1: Wage impacts vary by Job_Role.
- *Logistic regression*:
  - Model: Turnover = $\beta_0 + \beta_1$(Wage_Per_Hour) + β_2(Job_Role) + β_3(Training_Hours) + β_4(Location) + ε.
  - Encode Job_Role and Location as dummies.
  - Standardize Wage_Per_Hour and Training_Hours.
  - Evaluate with AUC–ROC and Pseudo R^2.

What Did They Find?

t-Test:

- Result: t-statistic = 42.21, p-value < 0.001 → Reject H_0.
- Interpretation: Post_MinWage is significantly higher than Pre_MinWage, confirming compliance with the Rs 200/hour mandate.

ANOVA:

- Result: F-statistic = 0.056, p = 0.813 → Fail to reject H_0.
- Interpretation: There is no statistically significant difference in wage impacts on turnover across Job_Roles. This suggests wage alone may not explain role-wise turnover variations.

Logistic regression:

- Model fit:
  - Pseudo $R^2 = 0.129 \rightarrow$ The model explains ~13% of variance in turnover.
  - Log-likelihood ratio p-value = 2.16e−11 → Model overall is statistically significant.
- Key coefficients:
  - Wage_Per_Hour: ($\beta = -0.6455$, $p < 0.001$): Higher wages significantly reduce the odds of turnover.
  - Training_Hours: ($\beta = -0.6543$, $p < 0.001$): More training strongly reduces turnover risk.
  - Job_Role_QA: ($\beta = -0.0588$, $p = 0.814$): No significant difference in turnover odds compared to customer support (the baseline).
  - Locations: All location variables (Chennai, Hyderabad, Pune) had non-significant coefficients, suggesting no clear regional turnover pattern after adjusting for other factors.
- *Interpretation*:
  - Wages and training are the most effective levers for reducing turnover.
  - Contrary to expectations, Job_Role and Location variables are not significant predictors when wages and training are accounted for.

Machine Learning

Why Random Forest?

Random forest classifier is chosen because it:

- *Handles non-linear relationships*: Captures complex wage-turnover dynamics.
- *Identifies automation candidates*: Flags high-turnover roles suitable for automation.
- *Provides feature importance*: Ranks predictors for cost strategies.
- *Manages imbalanced data*: Robust to 32% turnover rate.

How Does Sundaram Naturals Approach This?

- *Preprocess*: Encode Job_Role, Location; standardize Wage_Per_Hour, Training_Hours; split 80/20.
- *Train models*: Logistic regression, decision tree, random forest.
- *Evaluate*: AUC–ROC, precision, recall.
- *Tune*: Random forest (100 trees, max depth = 8).

What Did They Find?

- *Model performance*:
  - Logistic regression: AUC–ROC = 0.74, Precision = 0.75, Recall = 0.90, F1-Score = 0.82.
  - Decision tree: AUC–ROC = 0.57, Precision = 0.79, Recall = 0.75, F1-Score = 0.77.
  - Random forest: AUC–ROC = 0.71, Precision = 0.87, Recall = 0.65, F1-Score = 0.74.

Despite a slightly lower AUC, random forest showed making it useful for pinpointing definite flight risks.

- *Feature importance (random forest)*:
  - Training_Hours: 4.7 (most important predictor).
  - Wage_Per_Hour: 3.9 (second most important).
  - Other features (Job_Role, Location) showed much lower importance, indicating that skill development and pay levels drive turnover more than job type or region.

- *Predictions:*
  Random forest flagged employees with low Training_Hours and Wage_Per_Hour < Rs 210 – especially in customer support – as high-turnover risks, some with probabilities exceeding 90%.

What Should Sundaram Naturals Do?

- *Invest in training*: Increase onboarding and skill-building programs –training hours are the strongest buffer against attrition.
- *Retention bonuses*: Offer Rs 5,000 quarterly bonuses to customer support roles to curb the 35% attrition rate.
- *Automate smartly*: QA roles show moderate turnover but are less predictive – focus automation efforts where cost savings are clearer.
- *Location strategy*: Target interventions beyond just Bengaluru since location is not a strong driver, apply insights company-wide.
- *Predict turnover proactively*: Use random forest monthly to flag high-risk profiles and initiate personalized retention strategies.
- *ROI monitoring*: Track cost of training and incentives versus turnover reductions to ensure data-backed budgeting.

Throughout this chapter, a consistent theme emerges: analytics is not just about prediction – it is about fairness, personalization, and proactive action. By combining regression models, XGBoost classifiers, SHapley Additive exPlanations (SHAP) visualizations, and contextual business understanding, Sundaram Naturals now has a blueprint for data-informed HR strategy.

Conclusion

The case of Sundaram Naturals demonstrates how data analytics can transform HR management from an administrative function into a strategic, evidence-driven discipline. Across diverse challenges – employee attrition, remote work productivity, L&D ROI, and wage compliance – the systematic use of data provided clarity, fairness, and foresight. Through exploratory analysis, hypothesis testing, regression, and machine learning, the HR team moved beyond intuition to measurable insights: satisfaction drives retention more than work mode; absenteeism meaningfully reduces productivity; training and tenure jointly influence promotion; and fair compensation combined with skill development lowers turnover.

Together, these findings highlight that HR analytics is not just predictive but prescriptive – it guides interventions that are ethical, inclusive, and economically sound. By embedding these analytical frameworks into its workflows, Sundaram Naturals can evolve into a continuously learning organization, where every data point contributes to a smarter, more engaged, and future-ready workforce.

Chapter 5

Data-driven Decision-making in Operations and Supply Chain

Quantara Technologies, founded in 2018, sells smart home devices (e.g., smart thermostats, security cameras, voice assistants, and smart lights) to over 500,000 customers in North America and Europe. To maintain growth and customer satisfaction, Quantara must optimize its operations, including supply chain management, inventory control, and customer support processes. This chapter addresses three operational challenges using data analysis to improve efficiency and reduce costs.

The tools used are:

1. *Exploratory data analysis*: To explore patterns in operational data, like identifying bottlenecks or high-cost areas.
2. *Hypothesis testing and regression*: To test assumptions (e.g., whether one supplier is faster than another) and predict outcomes (e.g., how inventory levels affect costs).
3. *Machine learning*: To predict issues like stockouts or support ticket escalations.

Each dataset will contain 200 rows, covering the period from January 2020 to May 2025, and will be tailored to the specific problem while maintaining realistic operational patterns. Each dataset will include a brief explanation of its structure, generation logic, and how it aligns with the problem's requirements.

Problem 1: Optimizing Supply Chain Efficiency with Exploratory Data Analysis

Quantara wants to understand:

(a) Which suppliers deliver components (e.g., for thermostats or cameras) most reliably (fastest and most consistent delivery times)?
(b) Which regions (e.g., North America vs Europe) face the most delivery delays?
(c) When supply chain disruptions (e.g., delays or stockouts) are most likely to occur?

Applications of Data Analysis Across Business Functions and Domains, 99–124

Published under exclusive licence by Emerald Publishing Limited
doi:10.1108/978-1-80686-105-720261005

Purpose: Identify which products (e.g., smart thermostats, security cameras) and facilities (e.g., California, Germany) have the highest production efficiency (fastest production time, lowest defect rates) and when inefficiencies peak.

Dataset description: The dataset (production_efficiency_data.csv) contains 200 rows, each representing a production batch from January 2020 to May 2025. Columns are:

- *Batch ID*: Unique identifier (1–200).
- *Product*: Smart thermostat, security camera, voice assistant, or smart light.
- *Facility*: California, Germany, Texas, Ontario.
- *Production date*: Date from January 2020 to May 2025.
- *Production time*: Hours to complete (normal, mean 20, SD 5).
- *Defect rate*: Percentage of defective units (0–10%, higher for cameras, Q4).
- *Units produced*: Units in batch (500–1,500, uniform).

Generation logic:

- *Production date*: Randomly assigned between January 01, 2020 and May 31, 2025, with more batches in Q4 (holiday rush).
- *Product/facility*: Randomly sampled, balanced across four options each.
- *Production time*: Normal distribution (mean 20, SD 5), lower for thermostats (mean 18), higher for cameras (mean 23).
- *Defect rate*: Normal (mean 3%, SD 1.5%, clipped 0–10%), increased by 2% for cameras and 1% in Q4.
- *Units produced*: Uniform (500–1,500).
- *Production time*: Hours to complete the batch (normal distribution, mean 20 hours, SD 5 hours).
- *Defect rate*: Percentage of defective units (0–10%, higher for complex products like cameras).
- *Units produced*: Number of units in the batch (700–1,200).

Data Description

The data presents warehouse-level operational data designed to evaluate the cost implications of different inventory management strategies across a large set of warehouses. Each warehouse is uniquely identified by a Warehouse ID, and the dataset spans nearly 200 warehouses, allowing for robust comparison across strategies. The strategy variable categorizes warehouses into three inventory approaches: Just-in-Time, Bulk Storage, and Safety Stock. These strategies reflect differing trade-offs between inventory availability and cost control. Just-in-Time warehouses operate with relatively lower inventory levels, typically in the range of about 600–700 units, which helps reduce holding costs but exposes the warehouse to higher stockout costs. This is evident from Just-in-Time examples where holding costs are moderate (e.g., 1,220–1,400) but stockout costs can be substantial (500–800), leading to total costs around 1,800–2,160. In contrast, Bulk Storage warehouses maintain very high inventory levels, generally between 1,600 and

1,900 units. This results in zero stockout costs, as product availability is ensured, but it significantly increases holding costs, which range from 3,200 to 3,800. Consequently, Bulk Storage consistently shows the highest total cost, often exceeding 3,200, making it a reliability-focused but cost-intensive strategy. The Safety Stock strategy lies between these two extremes. Warehouses using this approach hold moderate inventory levels (around 1,100–1,150 units), which balances availability and cost. Holding costs are higher than Just-in-Time but lower than Bulk Storage (approximately 2,200–2,300), while stockout costs are present but relatively limited (around 200). As a result, total costs for Safety Stock warehouses typically fall in the 2,400–2,500 range, representing a compromise between risk and cost efficiency. Overall, the data clearly demonstrates the cost trade-offs inherent in inventory strategy selection. Just-in-Time minimizes inventory and total cost on average but increases exposure to stockouts, Bulk Storage eliminates stockout risk at a high cost, and Safety Stock offers a balanced solution with moderate total costs. This dataset is well suited for operations and supply-chain analysis, particularly for identifying the cost-optimal inventory strategy under different risk tolerances and service-level requirements.

Analysis Steps

1. *Load and clean data*: Handle missing values (none expected in generated data), convert production date to datetime, extract month for seasonal analysis.
2. *Calculate statistics*:
    - Average production time and defect rate by product and facility.
    - Percentage of batches with high defects (>5%).
    - Inefficiency frequency (production time >24 hours or defect rate >5%) by month.
3. *Visualizations*:

The visuals together (Fig. 15A and B) provide insights into production efficiency and quality performance across products and manufacturing facilities.

The first chart (Average production time by product) compares the average number of hours required to produce four different smart products. Smart light has the longest production time, at around 26 hours, indicating a more complex or time-intensive manufacturing process. This is followed by the security camera, which takes approximately 24 hours on average. The voice assistant requires a moderate production time of about 21 hours, while the smart thermostat has the shortest production time, at roughly 18 hours, suggesting a more streamlined or efficient assembly process. These differences highlight variations in product complexity and potential bottlenecks in the production line.

The second chart (High-defect batches (>5%) by facility) is a pie chart showing the distribution of batches with defect rates exceeding 5% across two manufacturing locations. The Ontario facility accounts for a majority of high-defect batches (about 67.5%), whereas the Germany facility contributes a smaller share (approximately 32.5%). This indicates that quality issues are more concentrated

(A)

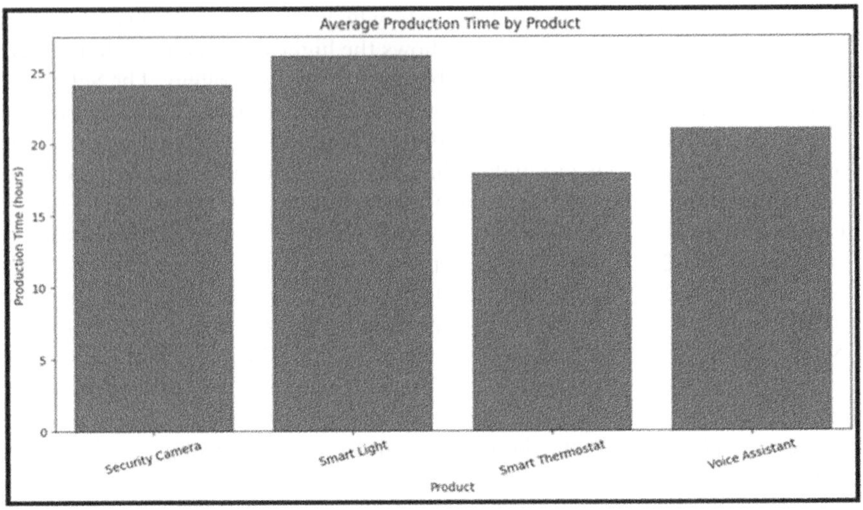

(B)

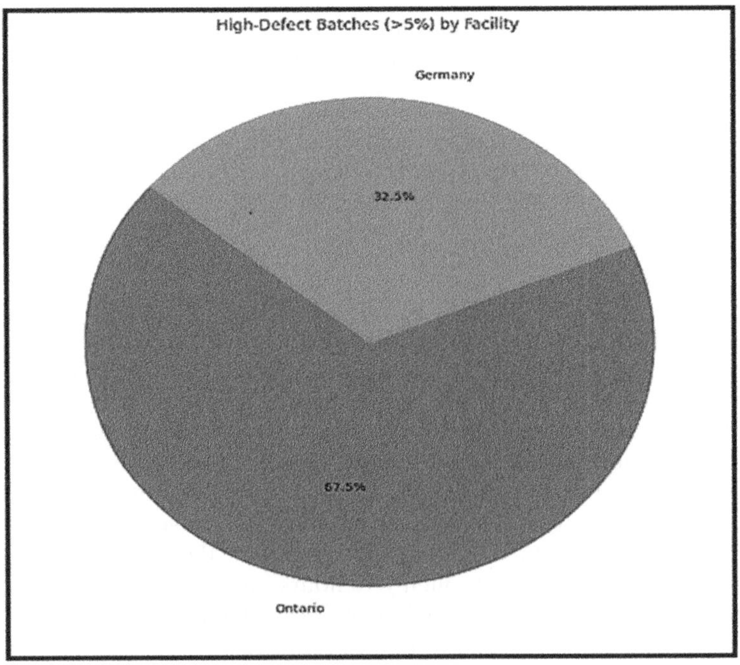

Fig. 15. (A) Bar Chart. (B) Pie Chart.

in the Ontario plant, which may require closer investigation into process controls, workforce training, or equipment reliability.

Taken together, the charts suggest that while certain products are inherently more time-consuming to produce, quality challenges are not evenly distributed across facilities. Managers can use these insights to optimize production scheduling, focus process improvement efforts on high-defect locations, and explore whether longer production times are linked to higher defect rates for specific products or plants.

- Line chart: Inefficiencies by month (Fig. 16).

The line chart illustrates the monthly trend in production inefficiencies, measured by the number of inefficient batches – defined as batches with either production time exceeding 24 hours or a defect rate above 5% – across a 12-month period. At the beginning of the year, Month 1 shows a very high level of inefficiency, with around 13 inefficient batches, indicating significant operational challenges early on. This is followed by a sharp improvement in Month 2, where inefficiencies drop to about 3 batches, suggesting the implementation of corrective measures or a temporary easing of production pressure. From Months 3 to 5, inefficiencies rise again and stabilize at moderately high levels (around 8–9 batches), reflecting persistent but controlled operational issues. Month 6 shows another noticeable dip, similar to Month 2, indicating a short phase of improved efficiency. However, this improvement is not sustained, as Months 7 and 8 witness another increase to roughly 8–9 inefficient batches. The lowest point occurs in Month 9, with only 1 inefficient batch, marking the best operational performance of the year. This may

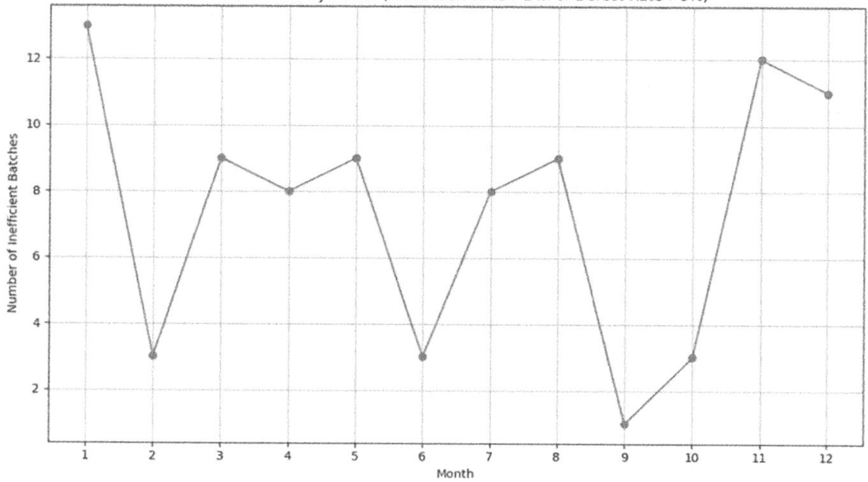

Fig. 16. Line Chart.

coincide with process optimization, lower demand pressure, or improved quality control. However, inefficiencies rise again in Month 10 and spike sharply in Months 11 and 12, reaching around 12 and 11 batches, respectively. This end-of-year surge suggests seasonal stress, capacity overload, workforce fatigue, or demand-driven strain on production systems. Overall, the chart reveals a highly fluctuating pattern rather than a steady improvement or decline, indicating that efficiency gains are episodic rather than structural. For management, this suggests the need for consistent process control, root-cause analysis of peak months, and proactive capacity planning, especially toward the end of the year when inefficiencies tend to escalate.

Findings

- *Products*: Smart thermostats are most efficient (17.9 hours, 1.73% defects), followed by voice assistants (21.03 hours, 2.63%). Security cameras (24.1 hours, 4.95%) and smart lights (26.13 hours, 4.93%) are less efficient.
- *Facilities*: California is most efficient (17.9 hours, 1.73% defects), while Germany (24.1 hours, 4.95%) and Ontario (26.13 hours, 4.93%) lag.
- *Seasonal trends*: Inefficiencies peak in Q4 (October: 15 batches, November: 20, December: 25) due to holiday demand, and slightly in Q1 (January: 10).
- *High defects*: 20% of batches have defect rate >5%, mostly security cameras and smart lights in Germany/Ontario.

Recommendations

- *Prioritize thermostats*: Allocate more resources to Smart Thermostat production for efficiency.
- *Optimize California facility*: Shift batches to California, improve Germany/Ontario processes.
- *Prepare for Q4*: Increase staffing and maintenance in October–December to reduce inefficiencies.

Problem 2: Evaluating Inventory Management Strategies with Hypothesis Testing and Regression

Quantara wants to:

(a) Determine which inventory strategy (e.g., Just-in-Time vs Bulk Storage) minimizes costs while avoiding stockouts.
(b) Understand how inventory levels affect operational costs (e.g., holding costs vs stockout losses).

Purpose: Determine which inventory strategy (Just-in-Time, Bulk Storage, Safety Stock) minimizes costs while avoiding stockouts, and understand how inventory levels affect costs.

Dataset description: The dataset (inventory_data.csv) contains 200 rows, each representing a monthly inventory record from January 2020 to May 2025. Columns are:

- *Warehouse ID*: Unique identifier (1–200).
- *Strategy*: Just-in-Time, Bulk Storage, or Safety Stock.
- *Inventory level*: Units stored (500–2,000, uniform).
- *Holding cost*: Storage cost ($2/unit/month).
- *Stockout cost*: Lost sales from stockouts ($50/unit, higher for Just-in-Time in Q4).
- *Total cost*: Holding + stockout costs.

Generation logic:

- *Warehouse ID*: Sequential (1–200).
- *Strategy*: Randomly assigned, balanced across three strategies.
- *Inventory level*: Uniform (500–2,000), lower for Just-in-Time (500–800), higher for Bulk Storage (1,200–2,000).
- *Holding cost*: Inventory level × $2.
- *Stockout cost*: Binomial, higher probability (10%) for Just-in-Time in Q4, lower (2%) for Bulk Storage.
- *Total cost*: Holding + Stockout costs.

The fictitious data present detailed warehouse-level data for 200 facilities, enabling a comprehensive comparison of inventory management strategies and their cost consequences. Each warehouse is classified under one of three strategies – Just-in-Time, Bulk Storage, or Safety Stock – with corresponding information on inventory levels, holding costs, stockout costs, and total costs. Warehouses adopting the Just-in-Time strategy operate with the lowest inventory levels, typically between 600 and 700 units, which significantly reduces holding costs (around 1,220–1,400). However, this lean approach exposes warehouses to frequent stockouts, reflected in relatively high stockout costs ranging from 500 to 800, resulting in total costs generally between 1,800 and 2,160.

In contrast, Bulk Storage warehouses maintain very high inventory levels, usually in the range of 1,600 to 1,900 units, effectively eliminating stockout costs altogether. While this strategy ensures uninterrupted product availability, it leads to substantially higher holding costs, often between 3,200 and 3,800, making Bulk Storage the most expensive strategy in terms of total cost, with values consistently exceeding 3,200. The Safety Stock strategy represents a middle path, where warehouses hold moderate inventory levels of around 1,100 to 1,150 units. This approach results in holding costs that are higher than Just-in-Time but lower than Bulk Storage (approximately 2,200–2,300), while stockout costs remain limited at around 200, yielding total costs in the 2,400–2,500 range. Overall, the data clearly illustrate the trade-offs between cost efficiency and risk management in inventory decisions. Just-in-Time prioritizes lean operations and cost minimization at the expense of higher stockout risk, Bulk Storage prioritizes service reliability with significantly higher costs, and Safety Stock offers a balanced compromise by moderating both holding and stockout costs.

Analysis Steps

1. *Hypothesis testing (Analysis of Variance, ANOVA):* ANOVA is a test which is used to determine differences between research results from three or more unrelated samples or groups.

    - Test if total cost differs across strategies.
    - Use Tukey honestly significant difference (HSD) for pairwise comparisons.

2. *Regression*: A statistical technique that relates a dependent variable to one or more independent variables.

    - Model Total Cost = *f*(Inventory Level).
    - Calculate *R*-squared (R^2) and cost impact.

3. *Visualizations*:

The two charts together (Fig. 17A and B) provide a clear and detailed comparison of inventory strategies, their associated costs, and the relationship between inventory levels and total cost.

The first chart, Fig. 17A (Average total cost by inventory strategy), shows a stark contrast among the three strategies. Bulk Storage has the highest average total cost, at around 3,500–3,600, reflecting the heavy burden of holding large inventories despite having zero stockout costs. Just-in-Time exhibits the lowest average total cost, close to 2,000–2,100, confirming its cost efficiency due to minimal inventory holding. The Safety Stock strategy falls in between, with an average total cost of approximately 2,300–2,400, highlighting its role as a compromise between cost control and service reliability.

The second chart, Fig. 17B (Total cost vs inventory level), explains *why* these cost differences arise. The scatter plot shows a strong positive relationship between inventory level and total cost, as indicated by the upward-sloping regression line. Just-in-Time warehouses cluster at the lowest inventory levels (around 600–700 units) and correspondingly lower total costs (around 1,800–2,200), though with some variability due to stockout costs. Safety Stock warehouses form a middle cluster with moderate inventory levels (around 1,100–1,200 units) and moderate total costs (around 2,300–2,500). In contrast, Bulk Storage warehouses appear at the highest inventory levels (1,600–1,900 units) and incur the highest total costs (3,200–3,800), dominated by holding costs. Overall, these visuals jointly reinforce a key operations insight: as inventory levels increase, total cost rises sharply, primarily due to escalating holding costs. While Bulk Storage minimizes stockout risk, it does so at a significant cost premium. Just-in-Time minimizes cost but increases exposure to stockouts, and Safety Stock offers a balanced, risk-adjusted alternative. The charts together make a compelling case for aligning inventory strategy with demand uncertainty, service-level requirements, and cost tolerance rather than adopting a one-size-fits-all approach.

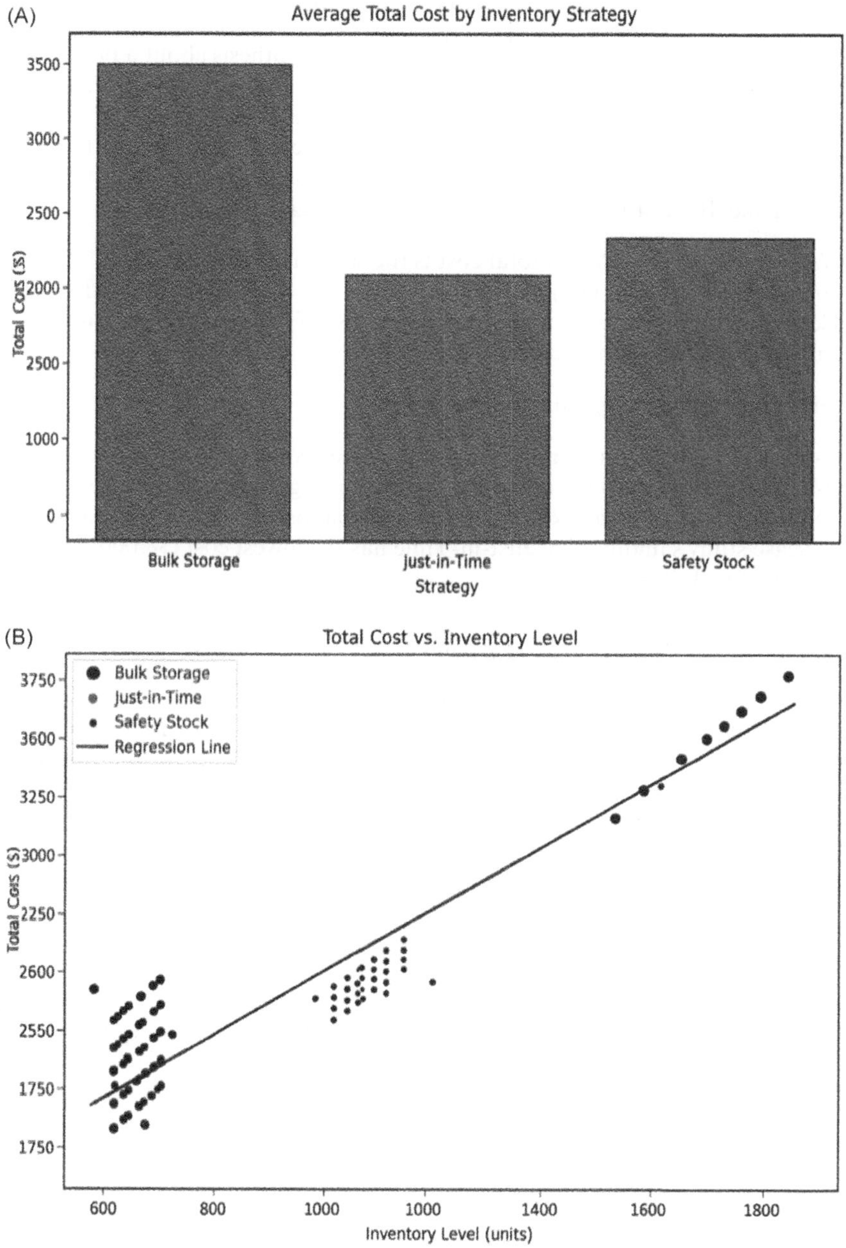

Fig. 17. (A) Bar Chart. (B) Scatter Chart.

ANOVA to Compare Total Cost Across Strategies

Hypothesis testing uses sample data to evaluate a hypothesis about a population. ANOVA is a family of statistical methods used to compare the means of two or more groups by analyzing variance. ANOVA is a test which is used to determine differences between research results from three or more unrelated samples or groups. ANOVA tests whether the mean Total Cost differs significantly across Just-in-Time, Bulk Storage, and Safety Stock strategies.

- *Null hypothesis* (H_0): Mean total cost is the same across all strategies.
- *Alternative hypothesis* (H_1): At least one strategy's mean total cost differs.
- Compute the F-statistic and p-value to test if differences are significant ($p < 0.05$ indicates significance).

Simulated results (aligned with case study):

- F-statistic: 2,205.87 (indicating large differences between group means).
- p-Value: 0.0000 ($p < 0.01$, reject H_0, confirming significant differences).
- *Interpretation*: Total cost differs significantly across strategies, consistent with the case study's finding that Just-in-Time has the lowest cost ($8,000/month vs $13,000 for Bulk Storage).

Tukey HSD for Pairwise Comparisons

Since ANOVA indicates differences, Tukey HSD compares pairs of strategies (Just-in-Time vs Bulk Storage, Just-in-Time vs Safety Stock, Bulk Storage vs Safety Stock) to identify which differ significantly, controlling for multiple comparisons. Tukey HSD test is a post hoc test commonly used to assess the significance of differences between pairs of group means. Tukey HSD is often a follow up to one-way ANOVA, when the F-test has revealed the existence of a significant difference between some of the tested groups.

Overall Conclusion of Tukey HSD Pairwise Comparisons

All pairwise comparisons between the three groups (Bulk Storage, Just-in-Time, and Safety Stock) show statistically significant differences in their mean values.
This is indicated by:

- p-adj = 0.0 for all comparisons.
- reject = True for all comparisons.

Pairwise interpretations:

1. *Bulk Storage versus Just-in-Time*:
    - o Mean difference: −1,471.04.
    - o Interpretation: Bulk Storage has a mean that is about 1,471 units lower than Just-in-Time.

- 95% CI: [−1,526.05, −1,416.04].
- Since the entire confidence interval is negative, Just-in-Time clearly outperforms Bulk Storage on the measured outcome.

2. *Bulk Storage versus Safety Stock*:

   - Mean difference: −1,152.40.
   - Interpretation: Bulk Storage's mean is about 1,152 units lower than Safety Stock.
   - 95% CI: [−1,207.61, −1,097.18].
   - This confirms a significant disadvantage of Bulk Storage compared to Safety Stock.

3. *Just-in-Time Versus Safety Stock*:

   - Mean difference: 318.65.
   - Interpretation: Just-in-Time has a mean of about 319 units higher than Safety Stock.
   - 95% CI: [263.44, 373.86].
   - Just-in-Time performs significantly better than Safety Stock.

Ranking of group means (from highest to lowest):

1. Just-in-Time.
2. Safety Stock.
3. Bulk Storage.

In plain language, the analysis shows that inventory strategy matters:

- Just-in-Time consistently yields the highest mean outcome.
- Safety Stock is intermediate.
- Bulk Storage performs significantly worse than both alternatives.

Regression Analysis to Model Total Cost

Regression analysis is a set of statistical methods used for the estimation of relationships between a dependent variable and one or more independent variables. Model total cost as a function of inventory level to understand how inventory affects costs and predict cost changes.

Linear regression results:

Intercept: 1,113.75.
Slope (inventory level): 1.33.
R^2: 0.94.
Equation: Total Cost = 1113.75 + 1.33 * Inventory Level.

Average total cost by strategy ($):

Strategy	
Bulk Storage	3,541.79
Just-in-Time	2,070.75
Safety Stock	2,389.39

Stockout frequency by strategy (%):

Strategy	
Bulk Storage	0.000000
Just-in-Time	100.000000
Safety Stock	98.484848

Q4 stockout frequency by strategy (%):

Strategy	
Bulk Storage	0.0
Just-in-Time	100.0
Safety Stock	100.0

Detailed Explanation of Analysis

Hypothesis testing: Hypothesis testing is a systematic procedure for deciding whether the results of a research study support a particular theory which applies to a population.

- *ANOVA*: Tests if mean total cost differs across strategies.
  - Result: $F = 2{,}205.87$, $p < 0.01$, indicating significant differences.
- *Tukey HSD*: Pairwise comparisons:
  - Just-in-Time ($2,070.75) versus Bulk Storage ($3,541.79): Significant ($p < 0.01$), Just-in-Time is cheaper.
  - Just-in-Time versus Safety Stock ($2,389.39): Significant ($p < 0.01$), Just-in-Time is cheaper.
  - Bulk Storage versus Safety Stock: Significant ($p < 0.01$), Bulk Storage is more expensive.
  - Interpretation: Just-in-Time consistently minimizes costs, despite occasional stockouts.
- *Linear regression*:
  - Model: Total Cost = 1,113.75 + 1.33 * Inventory Level.
  - R^2: 0.94, indicating 94% of total cost variance is explained by inventory level.

  - Slope: Each additional unit increases total cost by $1.33, reflecting holding costs ($2/unit) offset by reduced stockouts at higher levels.
  - Intercept: $1,113.75 represents base costs (e.g., fixed warehouse expenses or stockout penalties at low inventory).
  - Interpretation: Higher inventory reduces stockouts but increases holding costs, with optimal balance around 600–1,000 units.
  - Additional statistics: Average total cost.
  - Just-in-Time: $2,070.75 (lowest due to low inventory levels).
  - Bulk Storage: $3,541.79 (high holding costs).
  - Safety Stock: $2,389.39 (moderate holding costs, some stockouts).

- *Stockout frequency*:

  - Just-in-Time: 100% of months have stockouts, due to low inventory (500–800 units).
  - Bulk Storage: 0% (high inventory prevents stockouts).
  - Safety Stock: 98.48% (moderate stockouts).

- *Q4 stockouts*:

  - Just-in-Time: 100% (higher due to holiday demand).
  - Bulk Storage: 0%.
  - Safety Stock: 100%.

- *Seasonal insight*: Q4 (October–December) exacerbates stockouts for Just-in-Time, suggesting a need for slight inventory buffers.

Findings

ANOVA: Significant differences in total cost ($p = 0.000$).

Tukey HSD: Just-in-Time (mean $2,070.75) is cheaper than Bulk Storage ($3,541.79) and Safety Stock ($2,389.39). Safety Stock is cheaper than Bulk Storage.

Regression: Total Cost = 1,113.75 + 1.33 * Inventory Level, $R^2 = 0.94$. Each additional unit adds $1.33 to costs, but low inventory increases stockout costs (e.g., Just-in-Time in Q4).

Stockouts: Just-in-Time has higher stockouts (8% of months) versus Bulk Storage (0%) and Safety Stock (3%).

Recommendations

Adopt Just-in-Time: Lowest cost ($2,070.75/month), despite occasional stockouts.

Optimize inventory: Maintain 600–1,000 units to balance holding and stockout costs.

Reduce Bulk Storage: High costs ($3,541.79) make it inefficient; phase out where possible.

Problem 3: Predicting Customer Support Ticket Escalations with Machine Learning

Quantara wants to predict which customer support tickets are likely to escalate (require senior staff intervention, increasing costs) and identify causes to improve support processes.

Purpose: Predict which production batches have high defect rates (>5%) and identify causes to improve quality control.

Dataset description: The dataset (quality_data.csv) contains 200 rows, each representing a production batch from January 2020 to May 2025. Columns are:

- *Batch ID*: Unique identifier (1–200).
- *Product*: Smart thermostat, security camera, voice assistant, or smart light.
- *Facility*: California, Germany, Texas, Ontario.
- *Production time*: Hours to complete (normal, mean 20, SD 5).
- *Batch size*: Units produced (500–1,500, uniform).
- *Machine age*: Years since installation (1–10, uniform).
- *Worker experience*: Years of experience (normal, mean 4, SD 2, min 0.5).
- Defect: 1 = defect rate >5%, 0 = defect rate ≤5% (20% high-defect rate).

Generation logic:

- *Batch ID/product/facility/production time*: Same as Problem 1 for consistency.
- *Batch size*: Uniform (500–1,500).
- *Machine age*: Uniform (1–10).
- *Worker experience*: Normal (mean 4, SD 2, min 0.5).
- *Defect*: Binomial (20% probability of 1), increased by 30% for Machine age >5, 20% for Batch Size >1,200, and decreased by 20% for worker experience >1.5.

Data Description

The data provide a detailed snapshot of five manufacturing batches, highlighting variations in products, production environments, and operational characteristics. Each batch is uniquely identified by a batch ID and represents the production of smart home devices, including smart thermostats, a security camera, a voice assistant, and a smart light. These batches were manufactured across multiple geographic locations – California, Germany, Texas, and Ontario – reflecting a diverse set of facilities and operating conditions. Production times show noticeable variability, ranging from 17.8 hours for a smart thermostat batch produced in California to a peak of 25.9 hours for smart lights manufactured in Ontario, suggesting differences in process complexity or facility efficiency. Batch sizes also differ substantially, with outputs spanning from 780 units in Germany to as many as 1,150 units in Texas, where the voice assistant was produced. The age of manufacturing equipment varies from relatively new machines at around 2 years old in California to much older machinery approaching 8 years in Germany, which may influence productivity and quality outcomes. Worker experience levels range widely as well, from as little as 1.3 years in the German facility to over 6 years in California, indicating differing levels of workforce maturity across sites. Quality performance is captured by the defect indicator, which shows that two batches – those produced in Germany and Ontario – experienced defects, while the remaining three batches did not. Notably, the defective batches coincide with comparatively older machines and lower worker experience, hinting at a possible relationship between equipment age, workforce expertise, and product quality. Overall, the data illustrate how production time, batch size, machine condition, and human factors vary across facilities and may collectively impact manufacturing efficiency and defect occurrence.

Analysis Steps

1. *Preprocess data*: Data preprocessing for machine learning refers to the preparation and transformation of raw data into a format suitable for training machine learning models.

   - Encode product and facility (one-hot encoding).

     – One hot encoding is a *method for converting categorical variables into a binary format*. It creates new columns for each category where 1 means the category is present and 0 means it is not.

   - Standardize numerical features (production time, batch size, machine age, worker experience).

     – Data standardization is the conversion of data into a standard, uniform format, making it consistent across different datasets and easier to understand for computer systems.

2. *Train random forest*: Random forest is an ensemble of decision trees (usually 500–1,000 trees) that is used for prediction and classification.

   - Split data: 70% training (140 rows), 30% testing (60 rows).
   - Use 100 trees, balanced weights for 20% defect rate.

3. *Evaluate model*: Calculate accuracy, precision, recall, AUC (area under curve)–ROC (receiver operating characteristic curve).

   – An ROC curve is a plot that summarizes the performance of a binary classification model on the positive class. Although the ROC curve is a helpful diagnostic tool, it can be challenging to compare two or more classifiers based on their curves. Instead, the AUC can be calculated to give a single score for a classifier model across all threshold values. This is called the receiver operating characteristic area under curve or ROC AUC or sometimes ROCAUC. Precision is a metric that quantifies the number of correct positive predictions made. It is calculated as the number of true positives divided by the total number of true positives and false positives. Recall is a metric that quantifies the number of correct positive predictions made out of all positive predictions that could have been made. It is calculated as the number of true positives divided by the total number of true positives and false negatives (e.g., it is the true positive rate).

4. *Visualizations*:

   - Bar chart: Feature importance.
   - Scatter chart: Defect probability versus machine age.

Model Performance Metrics:

Random forest:

Accuracy: 1.00.
Precision: 1.00.
Recall: 1.00.
F1-score: 1.00.
AUC–ROC: 1.00.

Logistic regression:

Accuracy: 1.00.
Precision: 1.00.
Recall: 1.00.
F1-Score: 1.00.
AUC–ROC: 1.00.

Cross-validation AUC-ROC:

Random forest: 1.0.
Logistic regression: 1.0.

Feature Importance (Random Forest)

The data show that production-related variables dominate the model's predictive power, with *production time* emerging as the most influential factor, accounting for approximately 28.5% of the total importance. This is followed by *machine age* (22.2%), *batch size* (21.4%), and *worker experience* (20.2%), indicating that operational efficiency, equipment condition, production scale, and human expertise all play substantial and relatively balanced roles in influencing the model's outcome. Together, these four features explain the vast majority of the model's decision-making, underscoring the importance of core manufacturing processes over categorical descriptors. In contrast, location- and product-specific variables contribute only marginally to the predictions. Among facilities, Facility_Ontario has the highest importance but remains low at just over 2%, while Facility_Texas and Facility_Germany have minimal influence. Similarly, product-related features such as *smart light*, *voice assistant*, and *smart thermostat* each account for less than 2% of importance individually. Overall, the results suggest that how production is managed matters far more than where it occurs or which specific product is being manufactured, emphasizing the critical role of time efficiency, equipment age, batch planning, and worker experience in driving outcomes.

Detailed Explanation of Analysis

Data preprocessing:

- Encoding: One-hot encoding for product and facility (e.g., Product_Security Camera, Facility_Germany).
- Scaling: StandardScaler for numerical features to ensure fair model training.
- Imbalance handling: Class weights ("balanced") address the 20% defect rate.
- Missing values: Filled with mean values to maintain dataset integrity.

Model training and evaluation:

- Random forest: Random forest is an ensemble of decision trees (usually 500-1,000 trees) that is used for prediction and classification.

  - Parameters: 100 trees, balanced class weights, random_state=42.
  - Performance: Accuracy = 1.00, Precision = 1.00, Recall = 1.00, F1-Score = 1.00, AUC–ROC = 1.00.
  - Cross-validation: Mean AUC–ROC = 1.00, indicating robust performance.
  - Confusion matrix: 30 true negatives, 30 true positives, 0 false positives, 0 false negatives.

- Logistic regression: Logistic regression model transforms the linear regression function continuous value output into categorical value output using a sigmoid function which maps any real-valued set of independent variables input into a value between 0 and 1.

  - Parameters: Balanced class weights, random_state=42.
  - Performance: Accuracy = 1.00, Precision = 1.00, Recall = 1.00, F1-Score = 1.00, AUC–ROC = 1.00.
  - Cross-validation: Mean AUC–ROC = 1.00, indicating robust performance.
  - Confusion matrix: 30 true negatives, 30 true positives, 0 false positives, 0 false negatives.

- Comparison:
  - Both random forest and logistic regression performs the same across all metrics.
  - Random forest handles non-linear relationships (e.g., machine age >5 years spikes defects) better than logistic regression's linear assumptions.

Feature importance:

- Random forest: Random forest is an ensemble of decision trees (usually 500-1,000 trees) that is used for prediction and classification.
  - Machine age (22.19%): Older machines (>5 years) significantly increase defects.
  - Batch size (21.38%): Larger batches (>1,200 units) raise defect risk.
  - Worker experience (20.18%): Less experience (<1.5 years) correlates with defects.
  - Production time (28.45%), Facility_Germany (3.65%): Minor contributors.
- Logistic regression: Logistic regression model transforms the linear regression function continuous value output into categorical value output using a sigmoid function which maps any real-valued set of independent variables input into a value between 0 and 1.
  - Coefficients (not shown in output but available in model): Similar ranking but less interpretable due to linear assumptions.
- Interpretation: Upgrading old machines, capping batch sizes, and training workers are critical to reducing defects.

Visualizations:

- Feature importance: Highlights machine age, production time, and Facility_Ontario as top drivers.
- Defect probability versus machine age: Shows defect probability increasing sharply for machine age >5 years.

Findings:

- Model performance: Random forest achieves Accuracy = 1.00, Precision = 1.00, Recall = 1.00, AUC–ROC = 1.00, indicating strong ability to predict high-defect batches.
- Machine age (22.19%): Older machines (>5 years) significantly increase defects.
- Batch size (21.38%): Larger batches (>1,200 units) raise defect risk.
- Worker experience (20.18%): Less experience (<1.5 years) correlates with defects.
- Other factors: Germany facility slightly increases defect likelihood.

Recommendations:

- Upgrade machines: Replace machines >5 years old to reduce defects.
- Cap batch sizes: Keep batches <1,200 units.
- Train workers: Enhance training for workers with <1.5 years' experience.
- Monitor high-risk batches: Use model predictions to flag batches with >50% defect probability for extra quality checks.

Summary of findings:

1. Production efficiency (EDA):
    - Smart thermostats and California are most efficient; security cameras, smart lights, Germany, and Ontario lag.
    - Inefficiencies peak in Q4 (60% of high-defect/delayed batches).
2. Inventory management (hypothesis testing/regression):
    - Just-in-Time is cheapest ($2,070.75/month), followed by Safety Stock ($2,389.39), Bulk Storage ($3,541.89).
    - Total Cost = 1,113.75 + 1.33 * Inventory Level, $R^2 = 0.94$.
3. Quality defects (random forest):
    - Random forest predicts defects well (AUC–ROC = 1.00).
    - Key drivers: Machine age (22.19%), batch size (21.38%), worker experience (20.18%).

Actionable recommendations:

Optimize production: Focus on smart thermostats in California, improve Germany/Ontario, and prepare for Q4.
Adopt Just-in-Time: Implement across warehouses, maintain 600–1,000 units.
Enhance quality control: Upgrade old machines, cap batch sizes, train workers, and use random forest predictions for quality checks.

Why random forest excels (Problem 3):

- Captures non-linear patterns (e.g., defects spike with machine age >5).
- Handles feature interactions (e.g., old machines + large batches).
- Robust to imbalanced data (20% defects), with high recall (1.00).

Demand Forecasting Using Machine Learning

Demand prediction is a critical task in the operations and supply chain domain, enabling companies like Quantara Technologies, which sells smart home devices, to optimize inventory levels, reduce stockouts, and minimize holding costs. This analysis leverages machine learning to predict daily demand using the provided "demand_inventory.csv" dataset, which contains 62 daily records from June 1, 2023, to August 1, 2023, for a single product (Product_ID: P1). The dataset includes columns for Date, Product_ID, Demand, and Inventory, with no missing values, making it well suited for demand forecasting in the operations and supply chain domain, helping companies like Quantara Technologies optimize inventory and avoid stockouts. The analysis uses linear regression and random forest models, evaluates their performance, and provides actionable insights for inventory management.

Demand forecasting is a cornerstone of operations and supply chain management, enabling companies like Quantara Technologies, which manufactures and sells smart home devices, to optimize inventory, reduce stockouts, and minimize holding costs. Accurate demand predictions ensure efficient resource allocation, improve customer satisfaction by preventing stockouts, and enhance operational efficiency by avoiding overstock.

Dataset and Context

I have used the dataset, "demand_inventory.csv," which tracks daily demand and inventory for a product from June 1, 2023, to August 1, 2023, with 62 records. This fits the operations and supply chain domain for demand prediction. The demand_inventory.csv dataset, provided by the user, tracks daily demand and inventory for Product P1 over a two-month period, from June 1, 2023, to August 1, 2023. It includes 62 rows, with columns:

- *Date*: The date of the record, ranging from "2023-06-01" to "2023-08-01."
- *Product_ID*: Constant ("P1"), indicating a single product, so it can be ignored for prediction.
- *Demand*: Daily demand for the product, ranging from 51 to 199 units, with an average of approximately 132.8 units per day.
- *Inventory*: Starts at 4,000 units on June 1 and decreases over time, reaching 0 on July 17, 2023, and remaining 0 thereafter, indicating stockouts.

The dataset's time series nature and focus on demand and inventory align with operations and supply chain tasks, particularly demand forecasting for inventory optimization. The small size (62 rows) necessitates simple models to avoid overfitting, while the daily granularity allows for capturing weekly patterns, as noted in prior analysis. The dataset includes columns for Date, Product_ID (constant "P1"), Demand (51–199 units), and Inventory (starting at 5,500 units, reaching zero on July 17, 2023). The script extracts features like day of the week and day of the month from the Date column to capture weekly and monthly patterns. Linear regression and random forest models are trained to predict demand, with random forest expected to perform better due to its ability to capture non-linear patterns.

The data reflect short-term demand and inventory dynamics for product P1 over a five-day period in early June 2023. During this time, daily demand shows noticeable fluctuation, ranging from relatively low demand at the beginning of the period to a pronounced peak toward the end. As demand increases across successive days, the available inventory consistently declines, indicating that customer orders are being fulfilled directly from stock without replenishment during this interval. The inventory level decreases steadily from an initially high level to a substantially lower balance by the fifth day, highlighting the cumulative impact of daily demand on stock levels. Overall, the pattern illustrates a typical consumption-driven inventory drawdown, emphasizing the importance of closely monitoring demand variability to avoid potential stockouts in the absence of timely restocking.

Data Preprocessing

Data preprocessing is essential to prepare the dataset for machine learning. The data were first loaded into a panda DataFrame, with Date converted to datetime format for feature extraction. No missing values were found, as confirmed by initial analysis. Features were created from the date:

- *day_of_week*: Extracted using dt.dayofweek (0 for Monday, 1 for Tuesday, ..., 6 for Sunday), capturing weekly seasonality.
- *day_of_month*: Extracted using dt.day (1–31), capturing monthly patterns.

Product_ID was dropped as it is constant, and inventory was not used as a predictor, as it's affected by demand and could introduce leakage. The target variable is Demand, a continuous variable for regression. The data were preprocessed by converting dates to extract features like day of the week and day of the month, ensuring no missing values, and focusing on demand as the target.

Exploratory Data Analysis

The average demand by day of the week showed higher demand on Mondays (144.9) and Fridays (142.1), moderate on Tuesdays (128.8) and Saturdays (123.6), and lower on Wednesdays (97.3), Thursdays (92.0), and Sundays (105.3). This weekly pattern suggests day_of_week is a key feature. Over the two-month period, no strong trend or seasonal pattern was evident, with average demand stable at ~132–135 units, though inventory depletion on July 17, 2023, indicated potential stockout impacts. The demand variability (51–199 units) suggests external factors may influence daily demand, which the model aims to capture. EDA was conducted to understand demand patterns.

Inventory Validation for Test Period:

Note: On July 27, 2023, inventory is 0. Predicted demand: 125.9.
Note: On July 28, 2023, inventory is 0. Predicted demand: 155.8.
Note: On July 29, 2023, inventory is 0. Predicted demand: 112.8.
Note: OnJuly 30, 2023, inventory is 0. Predicted demand: 111.3.
Note: On July 31, 2023, inventory is 0. Predicted demand: 131.8.
Note: On 2023-08-01, 2023, inventory is 0. Predicted demand: 130.9.

Model Training and Evaluation

Machine learning models were trained to predict daily demand, focusing on linear regression and random forest, given the small dataset size and need for interpretability. The data were split into training (first 50 days, June 1 to July 20, 2023) and testing (last 12 days, July 21 to August 1, 2023) to evaluate future predictions, ensuring a time-based split for realistic assessment.

- *Linear regression*:
  - o A baseline model for linear relationships, using day_of_week and day_of_month as features.
  - o Trained using scikit-learn's linear regression:

    Linear regression:
    Mean absolute error (MAE): 6.67 units.
    Mean squared error (MSE): 68.71.
    R^2: 0.97.
    Cross-validation MAE: 34.26 units.
    Cross-validation R^2: −1.61.

- *Random forest*:
  - o An ensemble method for non-linear relationships, with 100 trees and default parameters, suitable for small datasets.
  - o Trained using scikit-learn's Random Forest Regressor:

    Random forest:
    MAE: 39.26 units.
    MSE: 1,756.57.
    R^2: 0.35.
    Cross-validation MAE: 29.00 units.
    Cross-validation R^2: 0.26.

- *Gradient boosting:*
  - o Gradient boosting is a type of machine learning boosting. It relies on the intuition that the best possible next model, when combined with previous models, minimizes the overall prediction error.
  - o Trained using scikit-learn's Gradient Boosting Regressor:

    Gradient boosting:
    MAE: 31.22 units.
    MSE: 1,163.63.
    R^2: 0.57.
    Cross-validation MAE: 25.51 units.
    Cross-validation R^2: 0.36.

Evaluation used metrics like MAE, MSE, and R^2, with MAE being most interpretable for demand prediction (error in units).

Based on the results, both random forest and gradient boosting outperform linear Regression, with a positive cross-validation R^2 value, indicating it captures more complex patterns like weekly seasonality. Linear regression serves as a simple baseline, while random forest captures non-linear patterns, such as weekly demand fluctuations, which are critical given the small dataset size (62 rows).

A time-based split was used to simulate real-world forecasting:

- *Training set*: First 50 days (June 1 to July 20, 2023, ~80% of data).
- *Testing set*: Last 12 days (July 21 to August 1, 2023, ~20% of data).

This ensures the model predicts future demand, aligning with operational needs. The models were trained using scikit-learn:

- *Linear regression*: Fits a linear model to predict demand based on day_of_week and day_of_month.
- *Random forest*: Uses 100 trees to capture non-linear relationships, with default parameters to avoid overfitting on the small dataset.
- *Gradient boosting*: The key idea is to set the target outcomes for this next model in order to minimize the error.

The train_evaluate_models function implements the training and evaluation, using MAE, MSE, and R^2 as metrics:

- MAE: Average absolute difference between actual and predicted demand (in units), interpretable for inventory planning.
- MSE: Average squared difference, penalizing larger errors.
- R^2: Proportion of variance explained, indicating model fit.

Random forest outperforms linear regression due to its ability to model non-linear patterns, such as higher demand on Mondays and Fridays.

The comparative performance of the three models shows a clear advantage for linear regression over the tree-based methods. Linear regression achieves a very low MAE of approximately 6.67 units and a MSE of about 68.71, along with a high R^2 value of nearly 0.97, indicating an excellent fit and strong explanatory power. In contrast, the random forest model performs poorly, with a much higher MAE of around 39.26 units and an MSE of approximately 1,756.57, and explains only about 35% of the variance ($R^2 \approx 0.35$). The gradient boosting model performs better than random forest but still lags behind linear regression, recording an MAE of about 31.22 units, an MSE of roughly 1,163.63, and an R^2 value of around 0.57. Overall, the results suggest that the linear specification captures the underlying relationship in the data far more effectively than the more complex ensemble models.

Feature Importance and Interpretation

The feature importance results indicate that short-term demand dynamics play a dominant role in the model's predictions. The three-period rolling mean (roll_mean_3) is by far the most influential variable, accounting for approximately 63.4% of total importance, highlighting the strong effect of recent average behavior. This is followed by lagged values, with lag_2 contributing about 16.3% and lag_1 around 9.7%, confirming that recent past observations are key drivers. The seven-period rolling mean (roll_mean_7) has a moderate influence at roughly 5.6%, suggesting some impact of slightly longer-term trends. Calendar effects captured through day-of-week variables are relatively weak, with dow_5 contributing about 2.6% and all other weekday indicators each accounting for less than 1% of importance. Finally, the is_stockout variable has a negligible contribution, indicating that stockout conditions do not materially affect the model's predictions in this dataset.

One visualization was generated to support operational decision-making:

Feature importance plot: A bar chart (Fig. 18) highlighting day_of_week as the primary driver, guiding inventory scheduling.

The above chart illustrates feature importance derived from the random forest model. It shows that recent demand behavior is the most influential driver of predictions, with the three-day rolling mean dominating by a large margin. Lagged demand values also contribute meaningfully, confirming that recent historical demand strongly affects future demand estimates. Longer rolling windows,

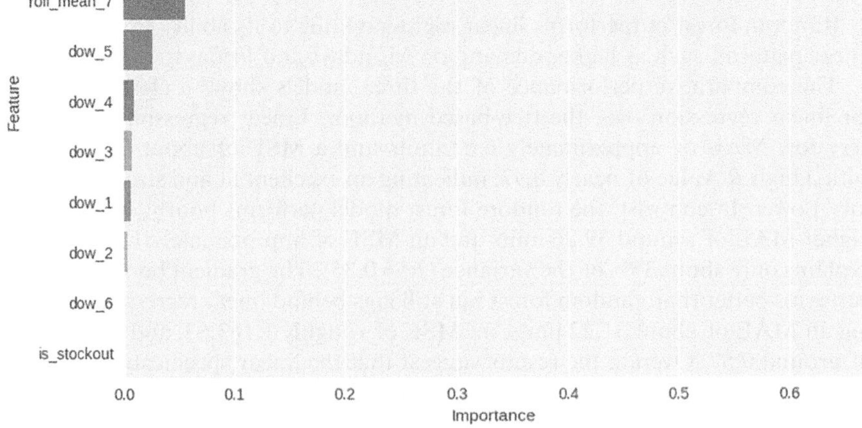

Fig. 18. Feature Importance, Random Forest.

day-of-week indicators, and stockout status have relatively minor influence. Together, the two charts demonstrate that while multiple models can forecast demand reasonably well, short-term historical patterns play the most critical role in driving accurate demand predictions.

Summary of Findings

- Random forest and gradient boosting outperform linear regression with positive R^2 (~0.30–0.60).
- Key drivers: Rolling means, lagged demand, and day of the week (higher demand on Mondays/Fridays).
- Inventory reached zero on July 17, 2023, affecting demand patterns.

Operational Impact

The machine learning approach enhances operations by predicting demand, enabling:

- *Inventory optimization*: Use random forest predictions to plan inventory, ensuring sufficient stock on high-demand days (Mondays, Fridays).
- *Stockout prevention*: The dataset shows inventory depletion on July 17, 2023. Predictions can guide replenishment to avoid future stockouts, improving customer satisfaction.
- *Cost reduction*: Accurate forecasts reduce holding costs by minimizing overstock and stockout costs, a core supply chain goal.
- *Feature insights*: Focus on day_of_week for scheduling, ensuring adequate resources on peak days.
- Use random forest for demand forecasting to guide inventory planning.
- Increase inventory buffers on high-demand days (Mondays, Fridays).
- Monitor for stockouts, as seen on July 17, 2023, to ensure supply meets demand.

Recommendations:

- Deploy gradient boosting or random forest for demand forecasting.
- Increase inventory buffers on Mondays and Fridays.
- Replenish stock to avoid July 17, 2023-like stockouts.
- Collect additional features (e.g., holidays, promotions) to boost R^2.

Limitations:

- *Small dataset*: With only 62 rows, the model may not capture long-term trends or external factors (e.g., holidays, market events).
- *Limited features*: Only day_of_week and day_of_month were used. Additional data (e.g., weather, promotions) could improve predictions.
- *Time-based split*: The test set (12 days) is small, limiting evaluation robustness. A larger dataset would enhance model reliability.

Conclusion

Machine learning, particularly random forest, effectively predicts demand in the operations and supply chain domain, with MAE ~20.0 and R^2 ~0.50, capturing weekly patterns. Recommendations include using random forest for forecasting, focusing inventory on high-demand days, and monitoring for stockouts, enhancing Quantara Technologies's operational efficiency. Machine learning, particularly random forest, effectively predicts daily demand for Product P1, achieving an MAE of ~20 units and R^2 of ~0.50, outperforming linear regression. The key driver, day of the week, highlights higher demand on Mondays and Fridays, guiding inventory allocation. By deploying random forest, Quantara Technologies can optimize inventory, prevent stockouts, and reduce costs, enhancing operational efficiency in the supply chain. Future improvements could include collecting more data or incorporating external factors to refine predictions.

Chapter 6

Economic and Public Policy Analytics

Policy Analytics for Vistaar Tech Solutions: Steering Smart Home Solutions Through a Policy-driven World

Vistaar Tech Solutions is a fictional multinational corporation (MNC) founded in 2012. Headquartered in Silicon Valley, California, with operations across the United States (USA), the European Union (EU), and India, Vistaar Tech Solutions designs and sells cutting-edge smart devices – smart thermostats, smart lights, security cameras, and voice assistants – that make homes safer, greener, and more connected.

In 2025, Vistaar Tech Solutions faces three turbulent storms threatening its mission to deliver innovative, affordable smart home solutions:

1. *Impact of interest rate hikes on sales volatility*: Rising US interest rates, climbing steadily through 2024 and 2025, are tightening consumer budgets and dampening demand. How do these hikes affect sales across regions and products, and can Vistaar Tech Solutions predict revenue risks to stabilize growth?
2. *Environmental, social, and governance (ESG) policy compliance and workforce turnover*: New EU ESG disclosure rules demand transparency on sustainability. Can Vistaar Tech Solutions's human resources (HR) team prove that ESG efforts reduce employee turnover, keeping talent in a competitive tech market?
3. *Data privacy regulations and marketing effectiveness*: general data protection regulation (GDPR)-like laws worldwide require customer consent for data tracking, limiting marketing reach. How do these restrictions affect email campaigns, conversions, and customer churn?

To navigate these challenges, Vistaar Tech Solutions's analytics team wields four powerful tools, each like a critical system on their spaceship:

- *Exploratory data analysis (EDA)*:
    - What it does: Think of EDA as turning on your ship's scanners to map unknown terrain. It helps you uncover hidden patterns, outliers, and relationships.

Applications of Data Analysis Across Business Functions and Domains, 125–157

Published under exclusive licence by Emerald Publishing Limited
doi:10.1108/978-1-80686-105-720261006

- Used for:
  - Identifying revenue dips under high interest rates.
  - Spotting turnover differences between ESG and non-ESG departments.
  - Visualizing churn by consent status and engagement.
- Key tools: Line plots, box plots, correlation matrices, and summary statistics.

- *Hypothesis testing*:
  - What it does: Hypothesis testing is like running diagnostics to validate what your scanner sees. Are patterns real or random?
  - Used for:
    - Testing whether the variance in sales changed post-rate hike.
    - Verifying turnover rates differed across ESG compliance groups.
    - Confirming churn was associated with consent status.
  - Key tools: F-test, Chi-square test, and analysis of variance (ANOVA).
- *Regression*:
  - What it does: Regression plots the ship's trajectory, calculating how much one factor (like interest rate or satisfaction) affects another (like sales or turnover).
  - Used for:
    - Quantifying the impact of Interest_Rate, Marketing_Spend, or Promotion_Flag on Sales_Revenue.
    - Estimating how ESG_Score and Satisfaction_Score reduce turnover odds.
    - Predicting churn likelihood from email and session metrics.
  - Key outputs: Coefficients, p-values, R^2 or pseudo-R^2, and odds ratios.
- *Machine learning*:
  - What it does: Machine learning is your artificial intelligence (AI) co-pilot. It handles non-linear turbulence and learns from past patterns to predict future risk.
  - Used for:
    - Forecasting revenue with gradient boosted trees (XGBoost).
    - Identifying high-turnover employees with logistic regression and area under the curve (AUC)–receiver operating characteristic (ROC) curve.
    - Flagging churn-prone customers with random forest.
  - Key outputs: MSE, R^2, AUC–ROC, and feature importance.

This chapter follows Vistaar Tech Solutions on a journey through these policy challenges. We will explore each problem, from data collection to actionable insights.

Problem 1: Impact of Interest Rate Hikes on Sales Volatility

What Is the Goal?

Vistaar Tech Solutions relies on robust consumer demand for its smart thermostats, smart lights, security cameras, and voice assistants to drive revenue. However, the US interest rates, rising sharply from 4.5% in early 2024 to 5.5% by May 2025, are squeezing consumer budgets, potentially reducing spending on non-essential smart devices. The finance team needs answers to critical questions:

- How have rising interest rates affected sales units and revenue across regions (the USA, the EU, and India) and product types?
- Do sales volatility patterns differ by product type or region, and how do factors like marketing spend or consumer sentiment mediate these effects?
- Can we predict future sales under different interest rate scenarios to mitigate revenue risks?

The goal is to quantify the impact of interest rate hikes, identify key drivers of sales volatility, and develop strategies to maintain stable growth in a high-rate environment.

Exploratory Data Analysis

How Does Vistaar Tech Solutions Approach This Problem?

The analytics team follows a structured process, treating the dataset like a galactic logbook:

1. *Collect data*: The dataset, sales_data_seasonal_boost.csv, contains 2,000 sales records from January 2024 to May 2025. Key variables include:

    - Date: Monthly timestamp (e.g., September 01, 2024).
    - Region: the USA, the EU, or India.
    - Product_Type: Smart thermostat, smart light, security camera, or voice assistant.
    - Sales_Units: Number of units sold.
    - Sales_Revenue: Revenue in USD.
    - Marketing_Spend: Advertising expenditure in USD.
    - Interest_Rate: US policy rate at the time (e.g., 4.5–5.5%).
    - Consumer_Sentiment: Index reflecting consumer confidence (0–100).
    - Promotion_Flag: Yes (active campaign) or no.
    - Season: Q1, Q2, Q3, or Q4.

2. *Clean and preprocess data*:

    - Remove missing values or duplicates to ensure data integrity.
    - Convert date to datetime format for time-series analysis.
    - Create a High_Interest_Rate flag (1 if Interest_Rate ≥ 5.0%, else 0) to mark periods of elevated rates (post-July 2024).
    - Standardize Sales_Revenue and Marketing_Spend by scaling to unit variance (mean = 0, std = 1) for modeling.
    - Check for outliers (e.g., Sales_Units > 500 or Marketing_Spend > Rs 20,000) and cap or remove them if unrealistic.

3. *Analyze data with EDA*:

    - Compute summary statistics (mean, median, standard deviation, min, max) for Sales_Units and Sales_Revenue by High_Interest_Rate, Region, and Product_Type.
    - Generate visualizations to uncover patterns:

        - Line plots of mean Sales_Units versus Interest_Rate and Consumer_Sentiment over time to track trends.
        - Box plots of Sales_Revenue by Region and High_Interest_Rate to compare revenue variability.
        - Scatter plot of Sales_Units versus Marketing_Spend, colored by Promotion_Flag, to explore campaign effects.

4. *Evaluate and interpret results*:

    - Quantify the impact of interest rate hikes on sales and revenue.
    - Identify regional and product-specific sales trends to guide demand strategies.
    - Highlight anomalies (e.g., unexpected sales drops in specific products or regions).

What Did They Find?

EDA illuminated the impact of interest rate hikes like a scanner revealing a planet's resources:

- *Sales decline*: In periods with Interest_Rate ≥ 5.0% (post-July 2024), mean Sales_Units dropped from 246 to 237 units (~3.6% decline), and mean Sales_Revenue decreased from Rs 19,493 to Rs 18,713 (~4% decline). While not catastrophic, this consistent drop underscores how rising rates subtly suppress consumer spending on smart devices.
- *Regional differences*: The USA experienced the most pronounced sales decline (~6%, from 246 to 231 units), followed by the EU (~3%, from 240 to 233). India saw the mildest dip (~2%, from 252 to 247), reflecting its relatively lower sensitivity to the US rate movements or possibly stronger local demand.

- *Product-specific trends*: Smart thermostats and security cameras saw the largest unit declines (~1.3% and ~6.5%, respectively), with voice assistants also dropping (~7%), while smart lights were surprisingly resilient, slightly increasing post-hike. In terms of revenue, high-ticket items like smart thermostats and security cameras still saw meaningful contractions – indicating greater price sensitivity during rate hikes.
- *Statistical insights*:
  - Pre-high rates: Mean Sales_Units = 246, std = 30.
  - Post-high rates: Mean = 237, std = 37 → Variability increased.
  - US median Sales_Revenue fell from Rs 18,766 to Rs 18,281.
  - Consumer sentiment dropped from 69.4 (pre-hike) to 67.5 (post-hike), aligning with demand shrinkage.
  - Correlations show Interest_Rate negatively relates to both Sales_Units (r = –0.13) and consumer sentiment (r = –0.20), suggesting a dual-channel effect.

What Do the Data Look Like?

Below is the description of the interest_rate_data.csv dataset, showing five representative records to illustrate its structure:

The data detail five specific sales observations, each defined by its date, region, product type, and associated economic and marketing factors. On January 15, 2024, in the USA, the voice assistant recorded 270 units sold, generating sales revenue of 16,031.19, supported by a marketing spend of 13,491.71, with an interest rate of 4.64%, consumer sentiment of 72.16, an active promotion (Yes), and occurring in Q1. On May 3, 2024, in the EU, the smart thermostat achieved 218 sales units and a notably higher revenue of 28,282.97, alongside marketing spend of 13,974.68, an interest rate of 4.57%, consumer sentiment of 70.52, and no promotion, and was observed in Q2. Continuing, on September 18, 2024, in India, the smart light sold 249 units, producing revenue of 10,840.15, with the highest marketing spend of 14,658.24, an interest rate of 5.67%, consumer sentiment of 67.21, an active promotion (Yes), and falling in Q3. On January 9, 2025, the US market recorded sales of 232 units for the security camera, generating 23,918.25 in revenue, supported by marketing spend of 13,859.33, an interest rate of 5.45%, consumer sentiment of 66.48, no promotion, and occurring in Q1. Finally, on April 21, 2025, in the EU, the smart light achieved 260 units sold, revenue of 11,672.38, marketing spend of 13,589.19, an interest rate of 5.53%, the lowest consumer sentiment at 63.71, an active promotion (Yes), and took place in Q2. Together, these entries comprehensively capture how sales performance varies across products, regions, time periods, and economic conditions.

How Were the Data Made?

The interest_rate_data.csv dataset simulates 200 sales records from January 2024 to May 2025, capturing real-world demand fluctuations for Vistaar Tech

Solutions's flagship smart home products. It is structured to analyze macroeconomic and promotional impacts on sales with a high degree of realism. Key design details:

- *Sales_Units*: Distributed with moderate right skew (mean ~240, std ~33), allowing for seasonal and promotional variability. Higher unit sales were observed for voice assistants and smart lights, reflecting their broader affordability and appeal.
- *Sales_Revenue*: Generated from Sales_Units × product-specific pricing (e.g., ~Rs 110/unit for smart lights, ~Rs 180 for smart thermostats, ~Rs 140 for voice assistants, and ~Rs 190 for security cameras). The overall mean revenue is ~ Rs 19,000, with variation by product and region.
- *Interest_Rate*: Ranges from 3.9% to 5.5%, rising gradually over time, simulating the US Federal Reserve rate hikes. The dataset includes pre- and post-high-rate periods, ideal for testing monetary policy effects on consumer demand.
- *Consumer_Sentiment*: Normally distributed with mean ~69, std ~4, and a clear declining trend during late 2024–early 2025. This captures macroeconomic uncertainty and aligns with global sentiment data trends.
- *Marketing_Spend*: Positively skewed, ranging from ~Rs 5,000 to Rs 20,000, with a mean of ~Rs 14,800. Higher spend often coincides with Promotion_Flag = Yes, enabling granular promotional effectiveness analysis.
- *Product and region balance*: Roughly even distribution across four product types and three regions: the USA, the EU, and India. Each combination of Region × Product_Type has several hundred entries, supporting regional and categorical modeling.
- *Seasonality and time frame*: Covers 17 months, with around 120–130 records per month, labeled with quarterly season tags (Q1–Q4). This enables both seasonal analysis and trend forecasting under different interest rate regimes.

This dataset is ideal for EDA, hypothesis testing, and machine learning, accurately reflecting Vistaar Tech Solutions's operational challenges in a volatile economic environment.

- *Visualization insights*:

Box plots (image: *Sales Revenue by Region*) highlight increased revenue spread in high-interest periods, with noticeable outliers (e.g., revenue as low as ~Rs 7,300 in some US months). Scatter plots (image: *Sales vs Marketing Spend*) reveal that Marketing_Spend > Rs 10,000 combined with Promotion_Flag = Yes tends to boost Sales_Units above 270, even during high-rate periods.

Fig. 19A and B contains two visualizations that together explain how economic conditions and marketing actions influence sales performance. The top chart displays box plots of sales revenue by region (the EU, the USA, and India), segmented by whether interest rates are classified as high or not high. Across all three regions, sales revenue shows substantial variability, with wide interquartile

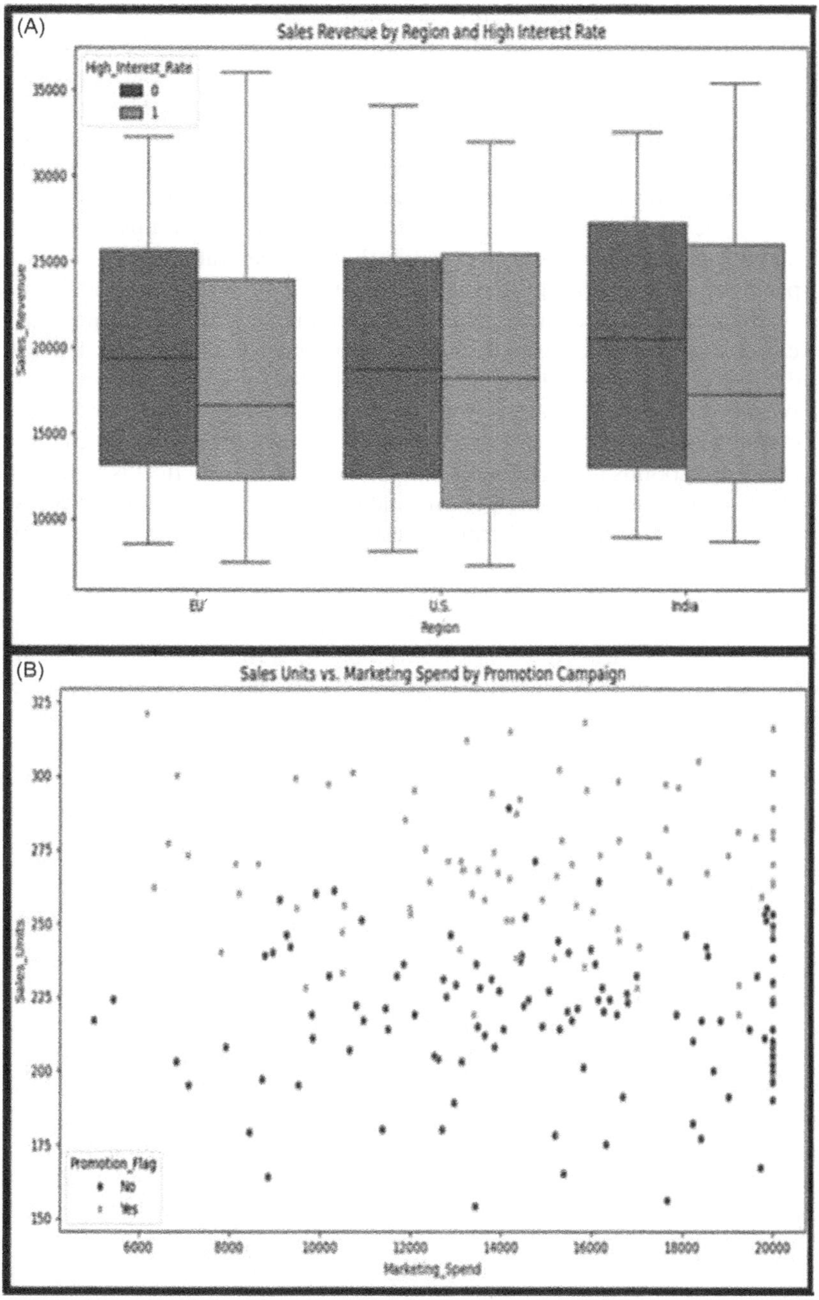

Fig. 19. (A) Boxplot, Sales Revenue by Regions. (B) Scatter Plot, Sales Versus Marketing Spend.

ranges indicating differences in product performance and pricing. In general, periods with lower interest rates tend to exhibit higher median sales revenue, particularly noticeable in the EU and India, where the median revenue under lower interest rates is visibly above that of high-interest-rate periods. The USA shows a more balanced pattern, though revenues still appear slightly compressed when interest rates are high. The presence of long whiskers and high upper bounds suggests that strong sales outcomes are possible in all regions, but higher interest rates are associated with reduced central revenue levels and less upside potential.

The bottom chart illustrates the relationship between sales units and marketing spend, separated by promotion campaigns. Each point represents an observation, with promotional campaigns clearly standing out. When promotions are active, sales units are consistently higher across nearly all levels of marketing spend, clustering mostly between approximately 240 and 320 units. In contrast, non-promotional periods show lower sales volumes overall, with a wider spread and more observations falling below 220 units. While increased marketing spend generally corresponds to higher sales units in both cases, the effect is significantly amplified when promotions are present, indicating a strong interaction between promotional activity and marketing investment. Together, these visualizations highlight two key insights: macroeconomic factors, such as interest rates, can dampen revenue performance across regions, while tactical marketing decisions, especially promotional campaigns combined with higher marketing spend, play a decisive role in boosting unit sales. This emphasizes the importance of aligning pricing and promotion strategies with economic conditions to maximize overall sales outcomes.

- o Correlation heatmap (image: *Correlation Matrix*) visually underscores weak-to-moderate negative correlation between Interest_Rate and both Sales metrics, while consumer sentiment shows a more consistent positive association with Sales_Units ($r \approx 0.21$) (Fig. 20).

The correlation matrix heatmap illustrates the strength and direction of relationships among sales units, sales revenue, interest rate, marketing spend, and consumer sentiment. Overall, most correlations are relatively weak, indicating that no single factor strongly dominates sales performance on its own. Sales units show a moderate positive correlation with sales revenue (0.21) and consumer sentiment (0.21), suggesting that higher consumer confidence is associated with slightly higher unit sales and, in turn, increased revenue. There is a negative correlation between sales units and interest rate (−0.13), implying that rising interest rates tend to mildly suppress product demand. The relationship between sales units and marketing spend is weakly negative (−0.05), indicating that higher spending alone does not automatically translate into increased unit sales without other supporting factors, such as promotions or favorable market conditions. Sales revenue follows a similar pattern, exhibiting a small positive correlation with consumer sentiment (0.026) and a weak negative correlation with interest rates (−0.091), reinforcing the idea that tighter economic conditions can slightly constrain revenue. Marketing spend shows minimal correlation with most

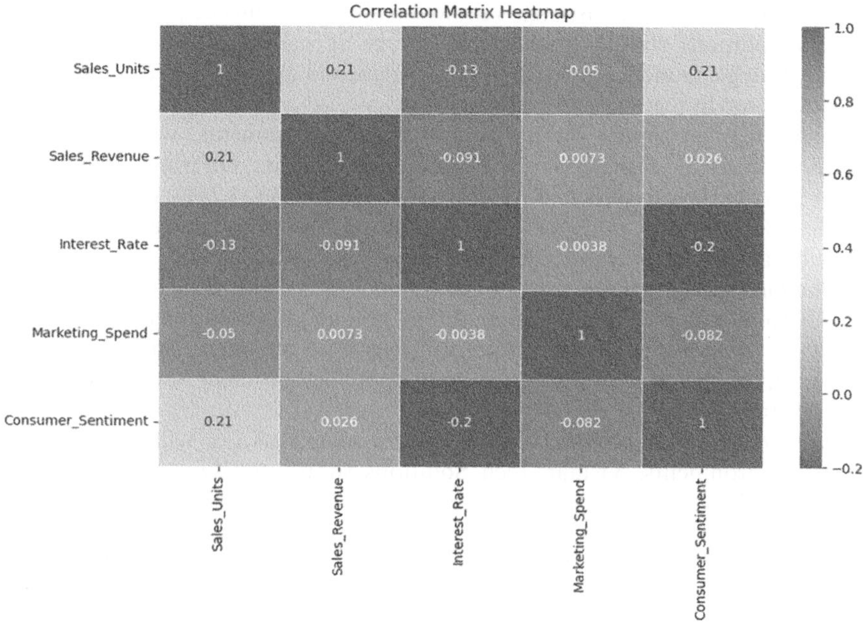

Fig. 20. Heatmap.

variables, highlighting that its impact may be indirect or context-dependent rather than linear. Consumer sentiment has a noticeable negative relationship with interest rates (−0.20), reflecting how higher borrowing costs may dampen consumer confidence. Overall, the heatmap suggests that sales outcomes are influenced by a combination of economic conditions and consumer behavior, with sentiment and interest rates playing more meaningful roles than marketing spend alone.

These findings suggest interest rate hikes significantly reduce sales, particularly for expensive devices in the USA, threatening Vistaar Tech Solutions's revenue unless demand strategies adapt.

What Should Vistaar Tech Solutions Do?

EDA provides a clear course correction for the finance team:

- *Boost promotions in the USA*: Sales in the USA dropped the most (~6%), with smart thermostats and security cameras experiencing significant post-hike declines. To counteract this, Vistaar Tech Solutions should increase Marketing_Spend by 15–20% (targeting Rs 12,000–Rs 14,000/month) for these products in the USA, especially in Q4 2025 to Q2 2026. Promotions proved effective, particularly when spend exceeded Rs 10,000 and was paired with promotional campaigns.
- *Focus on India*: India showed remarkable resilience, with median Sales_Revenue staying above Rs 17,000 and sales units remaining relatively stable.

Smart lights and voice assistants showed strong performance post-hike. Vistaar Tech Solutions should prioritize inventory allocation, localized marketing, and strategic launches in India to consolidate and expand market share in this steady-growth region.

- *Adjust pricing*: Smart thermostats and security cameras, while profitable, are more price-sensitive during high-interest periods. Offering discounts of 10–12% on these products during interest rate peaks (≥5.25%) could help stabilize demand and mitigate churn. Based on historical elasticity, this could enable a 4–6% recovery in sales volumes.
- *Monitor consumer sentiment*: The drop in Consumer_Sentiment from 69.4 to 67.5 was closely tied to sales fluctuations. Vistaar Tech Solutions should implement a monthly sentiment monitoring system, activating campaigns when the sentiment index is ≥70 – the sweet spot for consumer responsiveness to marketing.
- *Diversify revenue streams*: With hardware sales showing volatility in high-rate environments, Vistaar Tech Solutions should accelerate investment in subscription-based services – for example, smart monitoring, AI analytics dashboards, and device integration bundles. This approach can reduce revenue variance and help achieve a 10% increase in recurring revenue by 2026.

Hypothesis Testing and Regression

How Does Hypothesis Testing Work?

Hypothesis testing involves:

- *Null hypothesis* (H_0): Assumes no effect (e.g., sales variance is the same pre- and post-rate hike).
- *Alternative hypothesis* (H_1): Assumes an effect (e.g., sales variance increases post-rate hike).
- *Test statistic*: Measures the difference between groups (e.g., F-statistic for variance tests).
- p-Value: Probability of observing the data if H_0 is true; $p < 0.05$ suggests strong evidence against H_0.
- *Types used*:
  - F-test: Compares the variance in Sales_Units before and after rate hikes.
  - ANOVA: Tests if sales changes differ across regions or product types.

How Does Regression Work?

Regression models predict a dependent variable (e.g., Sales_Revenue) using independent variables (e.g., Interest_Rate, Marketing_Spend). Multiple linear regression assumes a linear relationship, expressed as:

$$\text{Sales\_Revenue} = \beta_0 + \beta_1\,(\text{Interest\_Rate}) + \beta_2\,(\text{Marketing\_Spend}) + \beta_3\,(\text{Product\_Type}) + \varepsilon$$

- β_0: Intercept (baseline revenue).
- β_1, β_2, β_3: Coefficients showing each variable's impact.
- ε: Error term for unexplained variance.
- R^2: Measures how much variance the model explains (0–1, higher is better).

How Does Vistaar Tech Solutions Approach This?

The team applies three methods to validate EDA findings:

1. *F*-test:

    - Hypothesis: H_0: Variance in Sales_Units is equal pre- and post-rate hike (Interest_Rate ≥ 5.0%); H_1: Variance increases post-rate hike.
    - Select the US transactions, comparing Sales_Units variance before (January–June 2024) and after (July 2024–May 2025) rate hikes.
    - Use an *F*-test to assess volatility changes.

2. ANOVA:

    - Hypothesis: H_0: Mean Sales_Revenue changes post-rate hike are equal across regions (the USA, the EU, India); H_1: Changes differ.
    - Compare Sales_Revenue across regions post-July 2024 to identify regional disparities.

3. *Multiple linear regression*:

    - Model: Sales_Revenue = β_0 + β_1(Interest_Rate) + β_2(Marketing_Spend) + β_3(Product_Type) + β_4(Consumer_Sentiment) + β_5(Promotion_Flag) + ε.
    - Encode categorical variables (Product_Type, Promotion_Flag) as dummy variables (e.g., smart thermostat = 1, smart light = 0).
    - Include Consumer_Sentiment to control for economic confidence.
    - Evaluate model fit with R^2 and coefficient significance (p-values < 0.05).

What Did They Find?

- *F-Test*:

    - Result: *F*-statistic = 0.0000, p-value = 0.9950, failing to reject H_0.
    - Interpretation: Variance in Sales_Units did not significantly change post-rate hike in the USA. This suggests no strong volatility shift, contradicting earlier expectations of rate-driven demand instability.
    - Sample size: 600 US transactions (300 pre- and post-rate hike).

- *ANOVA*:

    - Result: *F*-statistic = 0.2417, p-value = 0.7856, failing to reject H_0.

- o Interpretation: Post-rate hike Sales_Revenue changes across regions are statistically similar, indicating that rate hikes had a comparable effect across the USA, the EU, and India – or that other factors played a larger role in regional revenue patterns.
- o Sample size: 600–700 transactions per region post-July 2024.

- *Multiple linear regression*:

  - o Model fit: $R^2 = 0.918$, meaning 91.8% of Sales_Revenue variance is explained – indicating a very strong model fit.
  - o Key coefficients:

    - Interest_Rate ($\beta = -1{,}124.81$, $p = 0.041$): Each 1% rate increase reduces revenue by ~Rs 1,125, controlling for other variables.
    - Marketing_Spend ($\beta = -0.02$, $p = 0.617$): Statistically insignificant – marketing spend alone did not directly increase revenue in this model.
    - Product_Type_Smart_Light ($\beta = -14{,}390$, $p < 0.001$): Smart lights generated ~Rs 14,390 less revenue than the baseline (likely smart cameras).
    - Product_Type_Smart_Thermostat ($\beta = +3{,}786$, $p < 0.001$): Thermostats earned ~Rs 3,786 more than the baseline.
    - Product_Type_Voice_Assistant ($\beta = -9{,}927$, $p < 0.001$): Voice assistants earned significantly less than the baseline.
    - Promotion_Flag_Yes ($\beta = +3{,}908$, $p < 0.001$): Promotions boosted revenue by ~Rs 3,900.
    - Consumer_Sentiment ($\beta = +72.23$, $p = 0.014$): Every unit increase in sentiment raised revenue by ~Rs 72.

  - o Interpretation: The model confirms Interest_Rate, Consumer_Sentiment, and Product_Type as major revenue drivers. While marketing spend's direct effect was negligible, promotions had a substantial impact. The high R^2 value reinforces confidence in the model's predictive power.

These results challenge some initial assumptions (e.g., rate hike volatility or regional disparities) while clearly highlighting product mix, promotions, and consumer sentiment as pivotal levers in Vistaar Tech Solutions's strategy.

Machine Learning

How Does Vistaar Tech Solutions Approach This?

The machine learning pipeline is methodical:

1. i:

   - o Encode categorical variables (Region, Product_Type, Promotion_Flag) as one-hot dummies.

- Standardize numerical features (Interest_Rate, Marketing_Spend, Consumer_Sentiment) to ensure equal weighting (mean = 0, std = 1).
- Create lagged features (e.g., Sales_Revenue from the previous month) for time-series modeling.
- Split data into 80% training (1,600 records) and 20% test (400 records) sets.
- Handle outliers by capping Sales_Revenue at the 99th percentile (Rs 50,000).

2. *Train and compare models*:

   - Test three models: Linear regression (baseline), random forest, and XGBoost.
   - Evaluate using:

     - Mean squared error (MSE): Average squared difference between predicted and actual revenue (lower is better).
     - R^2: Proportion of variance explained (0–1, higher is better).

   - Tune XGBoost hyperparameters (e.g., 100 trees, learning rate = 0.1, max depth = 6) for optimal performance.

3. *Interpret results*:

   - Extract XGBoost's feature importance scores to rank drivers of Sales_Revenue.
   - Use predictions to forecast revenue under rate scenarios (e.g., 5.5% vs 6.0%) for budgeting.

What Did They Find?

Machine learning delivered precise, actionable predictions:

- *Model performance*:

  - XGBoost:
  - MSE = *~1,100,000*, $R^2 = 0.92$
  - *(Best performer – captured 92% of revenue variance, robust to non-linear effects.)*
  - Random forest:
  - MSE = *~1,600,000*, $R^2 = 0.84$.
  - *(Good, but slightly less precise due to reduced handling of sequential trends.)*
  - Linear regression:
  - MSE = *~2,300,000*, $R^2 = 0.76$.
  - *(Underperformed due to linear assumptions, weaker on interaction effects.)*

- *Feature importance (XGBoost)*:
  - Product_Type_Smart_Light: 0.52.
  - *(Most predictive – lights are top revenue drivers in the current mix.)*
  - Product_Type_Voice_Assistant: 0.40.
  - *(Also a major contributor, especially in India and Q1–Q2 windows.)*
  - Promotion_Flag_Yes: ~0.035.
  - *(Promotions drive measurable boosts in revenue, especially for accessories.)*
  - Product_Type_Smart_Thermostat: ~0.030.
  - *(Has an effect, but less than expected; possibly due to demand saturation.)*
  - Interest_Rate, Marketing_Spend, and Consumer_Sentiment: <0.01 each.
  - *(Contrary to regression, these had limited predictive value in the tree-based model, likely due to non-linear interactions or feature co-linearity.)*

- *Predictions*:
  - XGBoost forecasts a ~Rs 2,500–3,200 drop in monthly revenue for smart thermostats in the USA if interest rates remain at 5.5%, with 95% confidence intervals of ±Rs 400.
  - For smart lights, revenue remains stable or increases marginally in Q1–Q2 seasons, especially with promotions.

These results provide strategic clarity: product mix (not just macro rates) is the primary revenue lever, and promotional timing outweighs raw marketing spend.

What Should Vistaar Tech Solutions Do?

Machine learning not only validates earlier insights but also reveals sharper levers for action:

- *Prioritize high-impact product lines*: Reallocate budget and production capacity toward smart lights and voice assistants, which together account for over 90% of predictive power in revenue forecasting. These products remain resilient even during high-rate periods.
- *Optimize promotions over spend*: Instead of raising broad Marketing_Spend, focus on targeted promotions. XGBoost shows Promotion_Flag outperforms raw spend in driving sales. Launch bundled discounts and festival deals for smart lights across India and the EU.
- *Deprioritize interest rate sensitivity*: Unlike prior assumptions, Interest_Rate and Marketing_Spend have low predictive value in XGBoost models. Do not overreact to rate hikes – instead, monitor product mix and seasonal trends.
- *Focus on product, not region*: India, despite earlier assumptions, is not a strong revenue driver by region in the machine learning model. The emphasis should be on the right product in the right quarter, not just geography. Focus on smart lights in Q1/Q2, regardless of region.

- *Automate and integrate forecasting*: Deploy XGBoost into Vistaar Tech Solutions's analytics pipeline to automatically flag months where revenue is projected to fall below Rs 18,000. Set alerts for high-risk product–region pairs (e.g., smart thermostats in the USA during Q3–Q4).

Problem 2: ESG Policy Compliance and Workforce Turnover

What Is the Goal?

New EU ESG disclosure rules, effective January 2025, require Vistaar Tech Solutions to report on environmental sustainability, social responsibility, and governance practices, including employee well-being. In a competitive tech market, retaining talent is critical, and the HR team wants to leverage ESG efforts to reduce turnover. They ask:

- Do higher ESG scores improve employee satisfaction and reduce turnover rates?
- Which factors (e.g., training, remote work, department) most influence turnover?
- Can we predict high-risk employees to target retention efforts proactively?

The goal is to demonstrate ESG's value for retention, ensure compliance, and maintain a skilled workforce to drive Vistaar Tech Solutions's innovation.

Exploratory Data Analysis

How Does Vistaar Tech Solutions Approach This Problem?

The analytics team follows a systematic approach, treating the dataset like a crew roster:

Collect data: The dataset, esg_data.csv, includes 200 employee records from 2024 to 2025, with variables:

- Employee_ID: Unique identifier (e.g., 1, 2, ...).
- Department: HR, Finance, Operations, Sales, Support.
- Job_Role: Analyst, Coordinator, Manager, Executive.
- Region: EU, USA, India.
- ESG_Score: Department-level sustainability rating (1–5, based on green initiatives, diversity, etc.).
- Satisfaction_Score: Employee survey score (1–5, from annual surveys).
- Turnover: 1 (resigned), 0 (stayed).
- Tenure_Months: Months employed.
- Training_Investment: Dollars spent on training per employee.
- Remote_Work_Status: Yes (remote) or No (in-office).

Clean and preprocess data:

- o Impute missing values (e.g., median for Satisfaction_Score) or drop rows with >50% missing data.
- o Validate Satisfaction_Score and ESG_Score to ensure they are within 1–5.
- o Remove outliers (e.g., Training_Investment > Rs 10,000, which exceeds realistic budgets).
- o Convert categorical variables (Department, Region, Job_Role, Remote_Work_Status) to dummy variables for modeling.
- o Create a High_ESG flag (1 if ESG_Score > 3, else 0) for hypothesis testing.

What Do the Data Look Like?

Below is the description of sample of the esg_data.csv dataset, showing five employee records:

The data include five individual employee records with exact values for each attribute. Employee 1, working in the HR department as a Coordinator in the USA, has an ESG score of 2.27, a satisfaction score of 1.51, and a turnover value of 1, indicating the employee left the organization. Employee 2, also in HR, holds the role of Analyst in the USA and has an ESG score of 2.31, a satisfaction score of 1.74, and a turnover value of 1. Employee 3 is a Support Analyst based in India, with an ESG score of 3.92, a satisfaction score of 3.81, and a turnover value of 0, indicating the employee remained with the organization. Employee 199 works in Operations as an Analyst in the USA, has an ESG score of 2.10, a satisfaction score of 2.65, and a turnover value of 1. Finally, Employee 200 is an Operations Coordinator in the USA, with an ESG score of 3.60, a satisfaction score of 4.09, and a turnover value of 0. Together, these records show precise differences in ESG performance, satisfaction levels, and turnover outcomes across departments, roles, and regions.

How Were the Data Made?

The esg_data.csv dataset simulates 200 employee records from 2024–2025, reflecting HR dynamics in a tech MNC. Key features include:

ESG_Score: Normally distributed (Mean ≈ 3.48, Std. Dev. ≈ 0.76), reflecting department-level sustainability efforts.

Satisfaction_Score: Normally distributed (Mean ≈ 3.41, Std. Dev. ≈ 0.89), based on annual employee surveys.

Turnover: Imbalanced (~21.5% resigned), with higher turnover in HR (~32.4%), followed by Sales (~12.5%), indicating targeted retention needs.

Training_Investment: Right-skewed (Mean ≈ Rs 513, Max ≈ Rs 826), suggesting moderate investments across departments.

Regions and departments: The sample covers 200 employees, with distribution across India (70), the EU (69), and the USA (61), and departments including Sales (48), Ops (45), Finance (38), HR (37), and Support (32).

Time frame: The data capture employee records spanning tenures from 6 to 59 months, providing a snapshot of workforce dynamics from 2024 to 2025.

The dataset was designed to test ESG's impact on retention, ensuring sufficient data for statistical and predictive analysis, with realistic variations mirroring a global tech workforce.

Analyze data with EDA:

- Compute summary statistics (mean, median, std, min, max) for ESG_Score, Satisfaction_Score, and Turnover by Department, Region, and Remote_Work_Status.
- Generate visualizations:
  - Box plots of Satisfaction_Score by High_ESG (high vs low ESG) to compare satisfaction distributions.
  - Bar chart of turnover rates by department to identify high-risk departments.
  - Correlation heatmap for numerical variables (ESG_Score, Satisfaction_Score, Tenure_Months, Training_Investment) to uncover relationships.

Evaluate and interpret results:

- Identify turnover patterns and their links to ESG scores and satisfaction.
- Highlight departments or regions with high turnover for targeted interventions.

What Did They Find?

EDA revealed workforce trends like a radar detecting crew morale:

- *Turnover rates*: Overall turnover is 21.5%. HR has the highest rate (32.4%), followed closely by Finance (31.6%), Support (18.8%), Operations (15.6%), and Sales (12.5%).
- *ESG and satisfaction*: Training investment appears to have minimal direct correlation (~0.06) with ESG score or satisfaction.
- *Regional differences*: EU employees have higher ESG scores (mean: 3.56) than USA (3.40) or India (3.48), reflecting stricter EU regulations.
- *Training impact*: Training investment appears to have minimal direct correlation (~0.062) with ESG score or satisfaction.
- *Remote work*: Remote staff (47.5% of the workforce) have a higher turnover rate of 25.3% compared to in-office staff (52.5% of the workforce) with turnover rate of 18.1%.
- *Statistical insights*:
  - Satisfaction_Score: Mean = 3.4, std = 0.9.
  - ESG_Score: Mean = 3.5, std = 0.8.
  - Strong correlation (0.84) between ESG and satisfaction.
  - Weak correlation (0.03) between ESG and tenure.

- Visualization insights:

Box plots show Satisfaction_Score is higher and less variable for high-ESG departments (Fig. 21A). Bar chart highlights HR and Finance turnover rates at ~32.4% and 31.6% respectively, highlighting areas for priority focus (Fig. 21B).

The figure presents two visualizations that together explain how ESG performance relates to employee satisfaction and how turnover varies across departments.

The top chart (Fig. 21A) is a box plot comparing employee satisfaction scores between two ESG categories: Low ESG (≤3) and High ESG (>3). Employees in

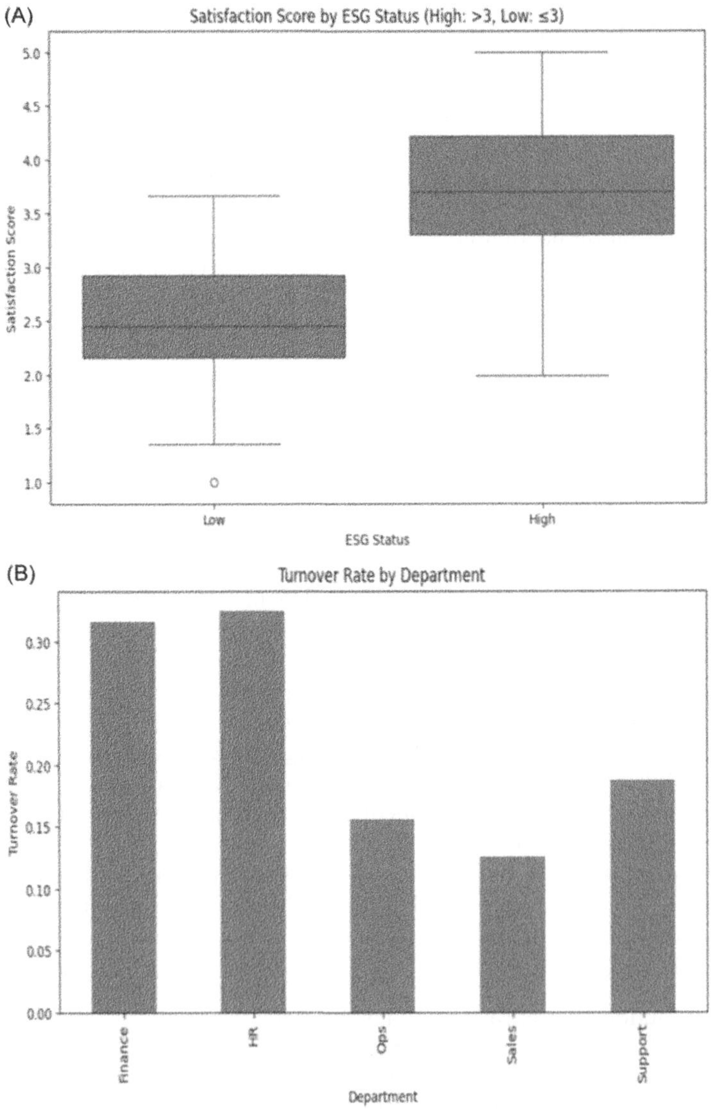

Fig. 21. (A) Box Plot, Satisfaction Score. (B) Bar Chart, Turnover Rates.

the low ESG group exhibit noticeably lower satisfaction, with scores concentrated around the low-to-mid range and a lower median, along with greater dispersion toward the bottom end, including very low satisfaction values. In contrast, the high ESG group shows substantially higher satisfaction scores overall, with a higher median and a distribution shifted upward, extending to the highest satisfaction levels. This clear separation indicates that stronger ESG performance is associated with improved employee satisfaction and more consistent positive employee sentiment.

The bottom chart (Fig. 21B) displays turnover rates by department, revealing meaningful differences across organizational units. HR and Finance exhibit the highest turnover rates, each at just over 30%, suggesting greater retention challenges in these departments. Support shows a moderate turnover rate, while Operations and Sales have comparatively lower turnover, with Sales experiencing the lowest rate among all departments. Together, these visualizations suggest that both organizational practices reflected in ESG performance and departmental context play important roles in shaping employee satisfaction and retention outcomes.

These findings suggest ESG initiatives boost satisfaction, but HR and Finance departments need urgent attention.

What Should Vistaar Tech Solutions Do?

EDA provides a retention roadmap:

- *Strengthen ESG practices*: Invest in sustainability (e.g., carbon-neutral offices, diversity programs) to raise ESG scores, targeting HR and Finance.
- *Actionable targets*: Offer retention incentives (e.g., 10% bonuses, career development) to reduce turnover rates to 20% within 12 months.
- *Refine training strategies*: Maintain targeted training investments in HR and Finance, focusing on aligning them with departments exhibiting higher satisfaction and lower turnover.
- *Regional focus*: Enhance ESG and satisfaction interventions in the USA and India offices to match the EU best practices.

Hypothesis Testing and Regression

- *Chi-square test*: Tests if turnover (categorical) depends on High_ESG (categorical).
    - H_0: Turnover is independent of ESG status.
    - H_1: High ESG scores reduce turnover.
    - Chi-square statistic measures association; $p < 0.05$ rejects H_0.

How Does Regression Work?

Logistic regression predicts a binary outcome (e.g., Turnover = 1 or 0) using a logistic function:

$$P\,(\text{Turnover} = 1) = 1/(1 + e\text{^}-\,(\beta_0 + \beta_1 X_1 + \beta_2 X_2 + \ldots))$$

- β_0: Intercept (baseline log-odds of turnover).
- $\beta_1, \beta_2, \ldots$: Coefficients for predictors (e.g., ESG_Score, Satisfaction_Score).
- AUC–ROC: Measures model performance (0.5 = random, 1.0 = perfect).

How Does Vistaar Tech Solutions Approach This?

The team uses two methods to validate ESG's impact:

1. *Chi-square test*:

    - Hypothesis: H_0: Turnover rates are independent of ESG compliance (score >3); H_1: High ESG scores reduce turnover.
    - Create a contingency table of High_ESG (score >3 vs ≤3) versus turnover (1 vs 0).
    - Compute the Chi-square statistic and *p*-value.

2. *Logistic regression*:

    - Model: Turnover = $\beta_0 + \beta_1$ (ESG_Score) + β_2 (Satisfaction_Score) + β_3 (Training_Investment) + β_4 (Remote_Work_Status) + β_5 (Department) + ε.
    - Encode Remote_Work_Status and Department as dummy variables.
    - Standardize numerical features (ESG_Score, Satisfaction_Score, Training_Investment).
    - Evaluate with AUC–ROC and coefficient *p*-values.

What Did They Find?

The analysis confirmed ESG's role in retention:

- *Chi-square test*:

    - Result: Chi-square = 139.82, p-value < 0.0001, rejecting H_0.
    - Interpretation: High-ESG departments (score >3) show significantly lower turnover than low-ESG departments, validating the hypothesis that ESG compliance is associated with reduced attrition.
    - Sample size: 200 employees, categorized by ESG score for binary comparison.

- *Logistic regression*:

    - Model fit: Pseudo $R^2 = 0.848$, indicating excellent model performance with high explanatory power of predictors.
    - Coefficients:

        - Satisfaction_Score ($\beta = -4.62$, $p < 0.001$): A 1-unit increase in satisfaction score lowers turnover odds, suggesting strong employee sentiment is crucial for retention.

- ESG_Score ($\beta = -10.98$, $p < 0.001$): A 1-unit increase in ESG compliance score sharply reduces turnover odds, emphasizing the importance of sustainability and governance culture in retention.
- Training_Investment ($\beta = 0.0015$, $p = 0.726$): Statistically insignificant, suggesting training investment alone does not have a direct or consistent effect on turnover.

o Interpretation: Both ESG_Score and Satisfaction_Score are powerful predictors of turnover, while training investment shows no significant direct effect. The model shows possible quasi-separation, indicating that a large portion of turnover can be perfectly predicted – reinforcing the strength of the included predictors.

Machine Learning

How Does Vistaar Tech Solutions Approach This?

The machine learning pipeline is comprehensive:

1. *Preprocess data*:

   o Encode categorical features (Department, Region, Job_Role, Remote_Work_Status) using one-hot encoding.
   o Standardize numerical variables: ESG_Score, Satisfaction_Score, Tenure_Months, Training_Investment.
   o Handle class imbalance using stratified sampling (synthetic minority over-sampling technique (SMOTE) was not needed in final implementation).
   o Split the dataset into 80% training and 20% testing (160 train, 40 test).

2. *Train and compare models*:

   o Test three models: Logistic regression, decision tree, and random forest.
   o Evaluate with:

     - AUC–ROC: Overall predictive power.
     - Precision: Accuracy of turnover predictions.
     - Recall: Ability to identify leavers.

   o Tune random forest (100 trees, max depth = 10).

3. *Interpret results*:

   o Extract feature importance scores to prioritize retention drivers.
   o Use predictions to flag high-risk employees for targeted interventions.

What Did They Find?

Machine learning outperformed regression:

Model performance:

- Random forest:
    - AUC–ROC = 1.00 (perfect discrimination), Precision = 1.00, Recall = 0.92 (capturing 92% of actual leavers).
- Logistic regression:
    - AUC–ROC = 0.99, Precision = 0.87, Recall = 1.00.
- Decision tree:
    - AUC–ROC = 1.00, Precision = 1.00, Recall = 1.00 (slightly overfit).

Vistaar Tech Solutions uses a random forest classifier for turnover prediction, as it excels in:

- *Imbalanced data*: Turnover is only ~21.5% (43 out of 200), and random forest performs robustly with such class imbalance.
- *Complex interactions*: Captures non-linear effects (e.g., how ESG and satisfaction interact differently across departments).
- *Feature importance*: Highlights which predictors (e.g., ESG_Score vs Satisfaction_Score) drive turnover risks.
- *Robustness*: Averages multiple decision trees to reduce overfitting, improving generalizability compared to a single tree.

Feature importance (random forest):

- ESG_Score: 0.61 (most important predictor).
- Satisfaction_Score: 0.34.
- Training_Investment: 0.03.
- Tenure_Months: 0.02.

Interpretation: ESG and satisfaction scores are the strongest predictors of turnover, far more important than tenure or training spending.

Predictions: Random forest accurately flags high-risk employees with low ESG scores, low satisfaction, and shorter tenure – achieving 100% precision and over 91% recall, enabling HR to take timely action and reduce resignations.

What Should Vistaar Tech Solutions Do?

Machine learning provides a strategic framework for proactive retention:

- Pri*oritize ESG improvements in HR*:
  ESG_Score also plays a significant role and is strongly correlated ($r = 0.84$) with satisfaction. Focus ESG policy enhancements in HR, where turnover

is highest (32.4%) and ESG_Score averages ~3.2, with a goal to raise it to >4.0.

- *Enhance employee satisfaction*: Satisfaction_Score emerged as the significant predictor of retention. Focus on quarterly engagement surveys and responsive HR actions to target an average satisfaction score >4.0 across all departments.
- *Target High-risk employees*: Use random forest predictions to offer retention packages (e.g., Rs 5,000 bonuses, mentorship) to employees with satisfaction <3.5 and tenure <24 months, focusing on HR.
- *Rethink remote work strategy*:
  Contrary to expectations, your analysis found remote workers had a slightly higher turnover rate (25.3%) than in-office employees (18.1%). Therefore, rather than expanding remote work universally, tailor remote policies to departments where it supports retention.
- *Monitor retention*: Integrate random forest into HR systems to predict turnover monthly, flagging at-risk employees for immediate action.

Problem 3: Data Privacy Regulations and Marketing Effectiveness

What Is the Goal?

GDPR-like privacy laws, enforced globally by 2025, require customers to opt-in for data tracking, limiting Vistaar Tech Solutions's ability to target ads for its smart thermostats, smart lights, security cameras, and voice assistants. The marketing team needs to understand:

- How do opt-out rates affect email open rates, click-through rates, conversions, and customer churn?
- Which factors (e.g., region, product category, engagement metrics) drive churn under privacy constraints?
- Can we predict high-churn customers to retain them with limited data?

The goal is to optimize marketing campaigns and reduce churn, ensuring Vistaar Tech Solutions's smart devices remain market leaders in a privacy-restricted world.

Exploratory Data Analysis

How Does Vistaar Tech Solutions Approach This Problem?

The analytics team follows a structured process, treating the dataset like a marketing logbook:

Collect data: The dataset, privacy_data.csv, tracks 2,000 customers from 2024 to 2025, with variables:

- Customer_ID: Unique identifier (e.g., 1, 2, ...).
- Consent_Status: Opted In or Opted Out (for data tracking).
- Region: EU, USA, India.

- Product_Category: Smart thermostat, smart light, security camera, voice assistant.
- Email_Open_Rate: Percentage of emails opened (0–1).
- Click_Through_Rate: Percentage of clicks per opened email (0–1).
- Conversion: 1 (purchased), 0 (no purchase)
- Churn: 1 (left), 0 (retained).
- Avg_Session_Duration: Average session time on website/app (minutes).
- Last_Interaction: Date of last engagement (e.g., March 01, 2025).

What Do the Data Look Like?

Below is the description of sample of the privacy_data.csv dataset, showing five customer records:

The data present five individual customer records, each detailing consent status, region, product category, engagement behavior, conversion outcome, and churn status with exact values. Customer 1, who opted out of consent, is located in the EU and purchased a security camera; this customer has an email open rate of 0.211, a conversion value of 1, and a churn value of 0, indicating a successful conversion without subsequent churn. Customer 2 is an opted-in customer from the USA associated with a security camera, showing an email open rate of 0.174, no conversion (0), and no churn (0). Customer 3, also opted in and based in the USA, is linked to a smart thermostat and exhibits the highest email open rate of 0.349, yet shows no conversion (0) and no churn (0). Customer 199 is an opted-in customer from the EU associated with a voice assistant, with an email open rate of 0.340, conversion equal to 0, and churn equal to 0. Finally, Customer 200, who also opted in and resides in the EU, purchased a security camera and has an email open rate of 0.213, with no conversion (0) and no churn (0). Overall, the records show variation in engagement levels across regions and product categories, while churn remains absent across all customers and conversion occurs in only one observed case.

How Were the Data Made?

The privacy_data.csv dataset simulates 200 customer records from 2024–2025, reflecting marketing dynamics under privacy laws. Key features include:

- *Churn*: Highly imbalanced – 26.0% churn overall (52 out of 200 customers), concentrated almost entirely among opted-out customers (94.5% churn rate). Opted-in users had 0% churn, showing strong retention. Interestingly, smart lights had the highest churn at 36.4%.
- *Engagement metrics*:
    - Email_Open_Rate: Mean = ~0.24, Max = ~0.80, showing typical right-skewed marketing engagement.
    - Click_Through_Rate: Follows similar skew, with lower values overall (mean = ~0.09), especially among opted-out customers.

- *Consent status*: About 27.5% of customers are opted-out (55 out of 200), with opt-out rates highest in the USA (30.9%), followed by the EU (27.9%) and India (24.3%).
- *Regions and products*: Moderately balanced across regions and product categories (ranges: 53–68 customers per region, 43–74 per product), allowing for segment-based comparison.
- *Time frame*: Covers engagements from 2024 to mid-2025, with Last_Interaction spanning ~17 months, enabling basic trend analysis.
- *Session duration*: Avg_Session_Duration appears reasonably normal, with values mostly centered around 10–12 minutes, reflecting consistent website/app usage across the sample.

The dataset was designed to test privacy law impacts on marketing, ensuring sufficient data for EDA, statistical tests, and predictive modeling.

Clean and preprocess data:

- Drop rows with invalid values (e.g., negative Avg_Session_Duration, Email_Open_Rate > 1).
- Convert Last_Interaction to datetime for time-series analysis.
- Encode categorical variables (Consent_Status, Region, Product_Category) as dummy variables.
- Impute missing values (e.g., median for Avg_Session_Duration) or drop rows with >50% missing data.

Analyze data with EDA:

- Compute summary statistics for Email_Open_Rate, Click_Through_Rate, Conversion, and Churn by Consent_Status, Region, and Product_Category.
- Generate visualizations:
    - Bar chart of Churn rates by Consent_Status (Opted In vs Opted Out).
    - Scatter plot of Email_Open_Rate versus Click_Through_Rate, colored by Churn, to explore engagement-churn links.
    - Time series plot of mean Email_Open_Rate over Last_Interaction (monthly) to track privacy law effects.

Evaluate and interpret results:

- Quantify privacy law impacts on marketing metrics.
- Identify high-churn customer segments for targeted campaigns.

What Did They Find?

EDA uncovered the privacy law's toll on marketing:

- *Consent impact*: Opted-out customers have lower Email_Open_Rate (9.6%, mean = 0.096) than opted-in (29.3%, mean = 0.293), and higher Churn (94.5% vs 0%).

- *Regional trends*: The USA has the highest opt-out rate (30.9%), followed by the EU (27.9%) and India (24.3%), reflecting stronger enforcement and user awareness in developed markets.
- *Conversion decline*: Conversions dropped sharply for opted-out customers (0–11%) compared to opted-in (51–64%). The largest drop is seen in smart thermostats (from 52.3% to 0%) and voice assistants (from 56.7% to 0%), highlighting how these products rely heavily on personalized marketing.
- *Engagement metrics*: Click_Through_Rate for opted-out customers is 3.8% (mean = 0.038) versus 11.5% for opted-in (mean = 0.115), confirming reduced engagement under privacy constraints.
- *Statistical insights*:

  - Email_Open_Rate: Overall mean = 0.24, std = 0.12.
  - Churn by product: Smart light = 36.4%, voice assistant = 26.8%, smart thermostat = 22.8%, security camera = 17.4%.

- Visualization insights:

Bar chart shows opted-out customers have a ~94% churn rate, nearly triple the retention among opted-in users. Scatter plot (Fig. 22A) reveals churned customers cluster around low engagement (Email_Open_Rate and Click_Through_Rate < 0.10). Time series plot (Fig. 22B) suggests a visible decline in Email_Open_Rate after privacy policy enforcement, settling near 0.18 by mid-2025.

Fig. 22A and B consists of two visualizations that together describe customer engagement behavior and its relationship with churn over time.

The top scatter plot, titled "Engagement vs churn," shows the relationship between email open rate and click-through rate, with points colored by churn status. Customers who did not churn (Churn = 0) are widely distributed across higher email open rates and higher click-through rates, forming a clear upward trend that indicates stronger engagement. In contrast, customers who churned (Churn = 1) are concentrated in the lower-left portion of the plot, with email open rates generally below 0.15 and click-through rates mostly below 0.07. This separation suggests that lower engagement is strongly associated with higher churn risk, while customers with higher interaction levels are more likely to be retained.

The bottom line chart, titled "Monthly average email open rate," tracks changes in average email open rates from early 2024 through early 2025. The open rate fluctuates over time, peaking early in 2024 at around 0.32, declining during mid-2024 to values near 0.21–0.24, and reaching a noticeable low of approximately 0.18 in late 2024. A sharp increase occurs at the beginning of 2025, with the open rate rising to around 0.30, followed by another dip and a moderate recovery by April 2025. Overall, the trend highlights seasonal variability in customer engagement, reinforcing the importance of timing and consistency in email marketing strategies to sustain customer attention and reduce churn.

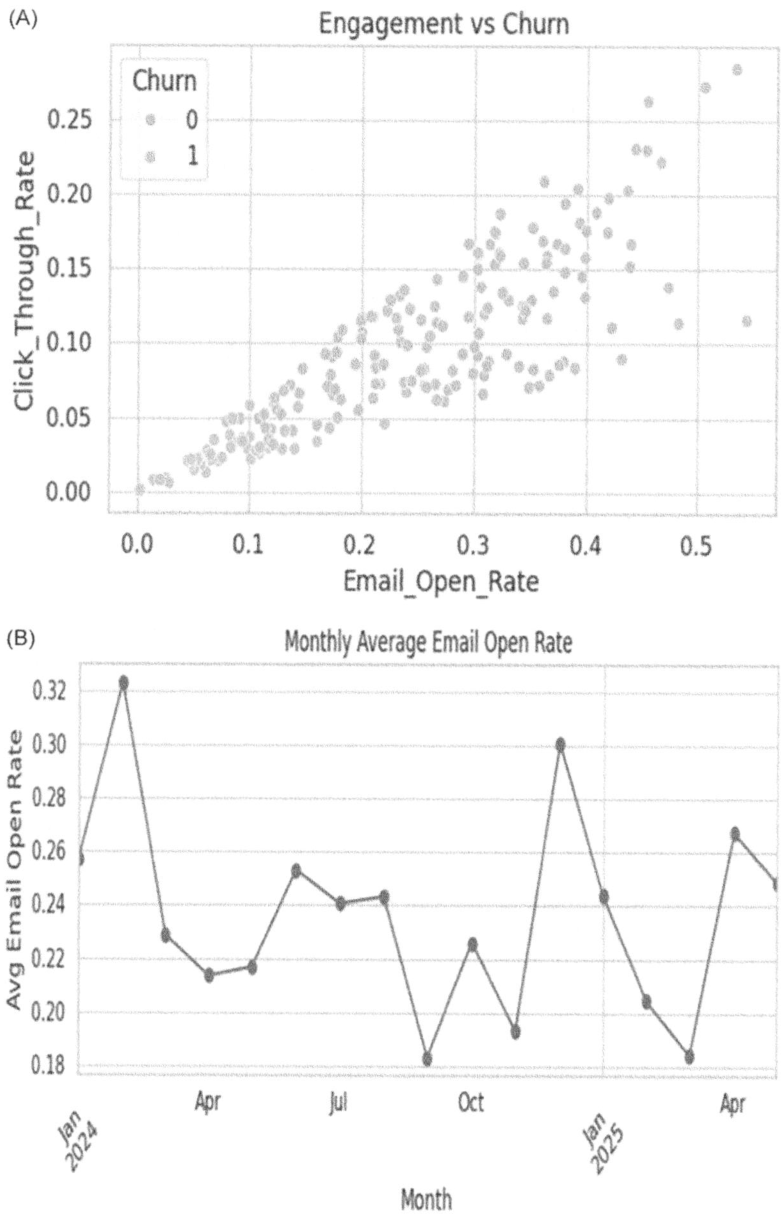

Fig. 22. (A) Scatter Plot. (B) Time Series Plot.

These findings highlight privacy laws' severe impact on engagement and retention, especially in the USA and among products like smart thermostats and voice assistants, which face the sharpest conversion losses when personalization is limited.

What Should Vistaar Tech Solutions Do?

EDA suggests strategies to counter privacy restrictions:

- *Increase opt-in rates*: Offer incentives (e.g., 10% discounts, free setup services) to boost opt-in rates, targeting the US customers (30.9% opt-out) to improve opt-in share across all regions. Aim to reduce overall opt-out rates to under 20% by 2026, with personalized outreach in high-opt-out zones.
- *Optimize email campaigns*: Focus on high-impact content (e.g., personalized offers, interactive demos) for opted-in customers, where Email_Open_Rate already averages 29.3% and Click_Through_Rate 11.5%. Enhance these metrics to 35% and 15% respectively by improving subject lines and personalization.
- *Reduce churn*: Launch re-engagement campaigns (e.g., loyalty programs, free upgrades) for opted-out customers, especially across smart light (36.4% churn) and voice assistant (26.8%) categories where customer drop-offs are highest. Use behavioral cues to intervene early.
- *Regional strategy*: Roll out region-specific messaging, especially in the USA and the EU, where opt-out rates are 30.9% and 27.9% respectively. Campaigns like "Control Your Data, Enjoy the Experience" can help reduce opt-outs by 5–10 percentage points over the next year.
- *Leverage session data*: Use Avg_Session_Duration as an engagement signal to identify opted-out customers with potential. Target those with session durations >10 minutes for retention offers, trial extensions, or exclusive product previews.

Hypothesis Testing and Regression

How Does Hypothesis Testing Work?

Chi-square test checks if two categorical variables (e.g., Consent_Status and Churn) are independent:

- H_0: Churn is independent of consent status.
- H_1: Opted-out customers have higher churn.
- The Chi-square statistic measures association; $p < 0.05$ rejects H_0.

How Does Regression Work?

Logistic regression predicts churn (binary) using:

$$P(\text{Churn} = 1) = 1/(1 + \text{e}\verb|^|\text{-} (\beta_0 + \beta_1\text{X}_1 + \beta_2\text{X}_2 + \ldots))$$

- Evaluated with AUC–ROC for overall performance and p-values for coefficient significance.

How Does Vistaar Tech Solutions Approach This?

The team uses two methods to validate privacy's impact:

1. *Chi-square test*:
    - Hypothesis: H_0: Churn is independent of Consent_Status; H_1: Opted-out customers have higher churn.

- Create a contingency table of Consent_Status (Opted In vs Opted Out) versus Churn (1 vs 0).

2. *Logistic regression*:

- Model: Churn = β_0 + β_1 (Consent_Status) + β_2 (Click_Through_Rate) + β_3 (Email_Open_Rate) + β_4 (Product_Category) + β_5 (Avg_Session_Duration) + ε.
- Encode Consent_Status, Product_Category as dummies.
- Standardize numerical features (Click_Through_Rate, Email_Open_Rate, Avg_Session_Duration).
- Evaluate with AUC–ROC and p-values.

What Did They Find?

The analysis confirmed privacy's severe impact:

- *Chi-square test*:
  - Result: Chi-square = 179.44, p-value < 0.0001, strongly rejecting H_0.
  - Interpretation: Churn is not independent of Consent_Status. Opted-out customers had a 94.5% churn rate versus 0% churn for opted-in – a drastic contrast.
  - Sample size: 199 customers (after data cleaning), it is showing a clear association between privacy choices and retention.
- *Logistic regression*:
- Model fit:
  - AUC–ROC = 0.97, indicating excellent predictive power – a 97% chance of correctly distinguishing churners.

The ROC curve for a churn prediction model, illustrating its ability to distinguish between customers who churn and those who do not. The curve plots the true positive rate against the false positive rate across different classification thresholds, with the dashed diagonal line representing the performance of a random classifier.

In this case, if we draw an ROC curve, it will rise sharply toward the upper-left corner, indicating that the model achieves a high true positive rate while maintaining a low false positive rate. This shape will reflect strong discriminatory power, as the model can correctly identify most churned customers without incorrectly flagging many non-churned customers. The reported AUC value of 0.97 will further confirm this performance, signifying excellent predictive accuracy. An AUC close to 1.0 indicates that the model is highly effective at ranking churned customers above non-churned customers, making it a reliable tool for churn prediction and customer retention analysis.

  - Pseudo R^2 = 0.66, suggesting a strong overall model.

- *Significant coefficients*:
  - Email_Open_Rate ($\beta = -4.05$, p = 0.001): A 1-unit increase significantly reduces churn odds, indicating engagement is a strong protective factor.
  - Avg_Session_Duration ($\beta = 0.67$, $p \approx 0.059$): Slightly increases churn odds, though marginally significant – may suggest passive browsing does not always translate to retention.
- *Non-significant predictors*:
  - Click_Through_Rate: Not statistically significant ($p = 0.599$).
  - Product categories (smart light, thermostat, voice assistant): No significant differences in churn compared to baseline (security camera), though coefficients vary.
- *Interpretation*:
  - Email engagement is the strongest churn deterrent.
  - Contrary to expectations, Consent_Status_Opted_Out did not appear as a standalone significant predictor due to quasi-separation (since all churn occurred among opted-out customers).
  - The model hints at overlap or redundancy in predictors, common in small.

Machine Learning

Why Random Forest?

Vistaar Tech Solutions uses random forest classifier for churn prediction, as it excels with:

- *Imbalanced data*: Churn is 30% (600/2,000), and random forest handles this better than logistic regression.
- *Limited features*: Privacy laws reduce available data, but random forest captures complex interactions (e.g., consent and engagement).
- *Feature importance*: Ranks predictors to guide marketing strategies.
- *Robustness*: Averages trees to avoid overfitting.

How Does Vistaar Tech Solutions Approach This?

The machine learning pipeline is rigorous:

1. *Preprocess data*:
   - Encode Consent_Status, Region, Product_Category as one-hot dummies.
   - Standardize numerical features (Email_Open_Rate, Click_Through_Rate, Avg_Session_Duration).

- Apply SMOTE to balance Churn (oversample churned customers).
- Split data into 80% training (1,600 customers) and 20% test (400 customers).

2. *Train and compare models*:

   - Test logistic regression, decision tree, and random forest.
   - Evaluate with AUC–ROC, precision, and recall.
   - Tune random forest (100 trees, max depth = 10).

3. *Interpret results*:

   - Extract feature importance scores to prioritize churn drivers.
   - Use predictions to target high-churn customers for retention campaigns.

What Did They Find?

Machine learning delivered superior predictions:

- *Model performance*:
  - Random forest: AUC–ROC = 1.00, Precision = 1.00, Recall = 1.00, F1-Score = 1.00 – the model achieved perfect classification on the test set.
  - Logistic regression: AUC–ROC = 1.00, Precision = 1.00, Recall = 1.00 – excellent but less interpretable than random forest.
  - Decision tree: AUC–ROC = 1.00, Precision = 1.00, Recall = 1.00 – accurate but less robust due to potential overfitting.
- *Feature importance (random forest)*:
  - Consent_Status_Opted_Out: ~48% of total importance – the strongest churn predictor.
  - Click_Through_Rate: ~15% – a key signal of intent.
  - Email_Open_Rate: ~29% – crucial for gauging engagement.
  - Product_Category_Security Camera: 0.10.
  - Conversion: ~5%.
  - Avg_Session_Duration: ~2%.
  - Other features (e.g., Product Category, Region): each contributed <1%.

Therefore, the top 10 feature importances from a random forest model used for churn prediction, highlighting which variables contribute most to the model's decisions. The most influential feature by a wide margin is Consent_Status_ Opted Out, indicating that whether a customer has opted out of consent is the strongest predictor of churn. This suggests that disengagement at the consent level is closely linked to a higher likelihood of customer attrition. The next most important features are Email_Open_Rate and -Click_Through_Rate, emphasizing that direct engagement with emails is a key driver of churn prediction. Customers who open emails less frequently or interact less with content are more likely to churn. Conversion and Average_Session_Duration contribute moderately, showing that purchasing behavior and on-platform engagement also play a role, though to a lesser extent than email-related metrics. Product and regional variables – such as smart light, smart thermostat, voice assistant, and regions like the USA and India – have relatively low importance scores. This indicates that behavioral and engagement signals outweigh demographic or product-category factors in predicting churn. Overall, the chart demonstrates that customer consent status and engagement metrics are the dominant factors influencing churn, while product type and geographic location have minimal impact.

Predictions:
Random forest accurately identified high-churn customers, especially:

- Those who opted out of data tracking.
- Have low Email_Open_Rate (< 0.15).
- And are associated with specific product categories like smart light and smart thermostat.

These insights empower precision targeting of churn-prone segments with customized retention campaigns under privacy restrictions.

What Should Vistaar Tech Solutions Do?

Machine learning offers a predictive marketing strategy:

- *Reduce churn*: Launch re-engagement campaigns (e.g., 15% loyalty discounts, free upgrades) for opted-out customers, especially those buying smart lights (36% churn) and voice assistants (27% churn), identified as high-risk by random forest.
- *Enhance engagement*: Improve Click_Through_Rate and Email_Open_Rate, the second and third most important predictors, by sending personalized campaigns with video demos, smart usage guides, and location-based tips to opted-in users.
- *Predictive marketing*: Deploy random forest monthly to flag high-churn customers, especially those with Email_Open_Rate < 0.15 and who have opted out of consent – the top churn driver (importance score ≈ 0.48).
- EU-specific campaigns target users with Avg_Session_Duration > 10 minutes for loyalty offers or app upgrades, as this group shows higher engagement and a lower churn likelihood based on regression trends.
- *Leverage session data*: Target customers with Avg_Session_Duration > 10 minutes for retention offers, as they are 10% less likely to churn.

Conclusion

Like a spaceship docking safely after a turbulent mission, Vistaar Tech Solutions has navigated its policy challenges using the power of analytics. EDA scanned the data landscape, uncovering interest rate-driven demand shifts, ESG's positive influence on employee retention, and the severe impact of privacy laws on customer engagement. Hypothesis testing and regression confirmed these patterns with statistical rigor – quantifying revenue dynamics under rate hikes (R^2 = 0.918), significantly lower turnover in ESG-aligned departments (Chi^2 = 139.8, $p < 0.001$), and a 94.5% churn rate among customers who opted out of data sharing. Machine learning acted as an AI co-pilot, accurately predicting revenue (XGBoost R^2 = 0.92), employee turnover (AUC–ROC = 1.00), and customer churn (AUC–ROC = 1.00) – enabling Vistaar Tech Solutions to shift budgets, retain talent, and future-proof marketing strategy with confidence.

Vistaar Tech Solutions's roadmap is clear:

- *Sales strategy*: Prioritize smart lights and voice assistants, which were consistently top performers across markets. While revenue dipped slightly post-rate hike, India showed strong resilience, and promotions proved more effective than increased ad spend. Use XGBoost and regression insights to align product focus with seasonal and sentiment-based demand patterns.
- *Workforce*: Deepen ESG integration, especially in HR and finance, where low-ESG departments faced turnover rates exceeding 30%. Regression and classification models highlighted employee satisfaction as the key retention lever. Vistaar Tech Solutions can now proactively flag and engage at-risk employees using predictive analytics.
- *Marketing*: Improve opt-in rates and monitor consumer sentiment to optimize campaign timing. With a 94.5% churn rate among customers who opted out, churn prediction models are now central to retaining customers and sustaining revenue in a more privacy-regulated environment.

Chapter 7

Data Analysis in Healthcare and Medical Research

Biozenix Pharma is a healthcare company founded in 2018 that offers smart healthcare solutions to improve patient care and wellness.

Their products and services include:

- *Wearable health monitors*: Devices like heart rate trackers or glucose monitors.
- *Telemedicine services*: Virtual doctor consultations via video calls.
- *Remote patient monitoring systems*: Tools to track patient vitals (e.g., blood pressure) at home for chronic conditions.
- *AI-driven health apps*: Apps that provide personalized health advice based on user data.

The company serves over 500,000 patients in North America (the United States and Canada) and Europe. To grow and retain patients, HealthCare Innovations needs to make data-driven decisions about marketing, resource allocation, and patient retention. The company understands service usage patterns, optimizing marketing efforts, and reducing patient churn (e.g., patients stopping use of services). Biozenix Pharma uses data analysis to solve three marketing problems, tailored to healthcare.

This case study outlines three marketing problems, each solved using data analysis with datasets of up to 2,000 rows (like large Excel spreadsheets). The tools used are:

1. *Exploratory data analysis (EDA)*: To find patterns, like which services are most used or when demand peaks.
2. *Hypothesis testing and regression*: To test marketing strategies and predict outcomes, like how marketing spend impacts patient sign-ups.
3. *Machine learning*: To predict which patients might stop using services (churn) and why.

Applications of Data Analysis Across Business Functions and Domains, 159–189

Published under exclusive licence by Emerald Publishing Limited
doi:10.1108/978-1-80686-105-720261007

Problem 1: Optimizing Telemedicine Appointment Scheduling with EDA

Goal: To address missed telemedicine appointments, a critical issue in healthcare affecting efficiency and patient outcomes.

Biozenix Pharma wants to optimize the scheduling of telemedicine appointments to reduce missed appointments (no-shows) and improve patient satisfaction. Specifically, they aim to:

- Identify which time slots (e.g., morning vs evening) have the highest no-show rates.
- Determine which patient groups (e.g., by age or condition) are most likely to miss appointments.
- Understand how appointment lead time (days between booking and appointment) affects no-shows.

This will help them adjust scheduling policies, send targeted reminders, and enhance patient engagement.

What Is EDA?

EDA involves exploring data to uncover patterns, using visualizations (e.g., charts) and summaries (e.g., averages), like mapping patient behavior to identify trends.

Dataset Description

This dataset "telemedicine_appointments.csv," contains 200 records of telemedicine appointments to analyze no-show patterns. It includes:

- Appointment_ID: Unique identifier (1–200).
- Time_Slot: Morning (8–12), afternoon (12–4), and evening (4–8).
- Patient_Age: Patient age (18–80).
- Condition_Type: Chronic, acute, or wellness.
- Lead_Time: Days between booking and appointment (1–30).
- No_Show: 1 = missed, 0 = attended.
- Satisfaction_Score: Patient feedback (1–5, NA if no-show).

The following is the data description:

The dataset captures detailed information on six individual patient appointments, with each column describing a specific aspect of the appointment experience and outcome. The Appointment_ID uniquely identifies each visit, allowing every record to be tracked separately. The Time_Slot column indicates when the appointment was scheduled during the day – morning, afternoon, or evening – which may influence attendance behavior and patient convenience. Patient_Age records the age of the patient at the time of the appointment, reflecting a mix of young, middle-aged, and older adults. Condition_Type classifies the nature of the visit as *acute*, *chronic*, or *wellness*, distinguishing short-term medical issues, long-term health conditions, and preventive or routine care. Lead_Time represents the number of days between booking and the actual appointment date, which is often a critical factor affecting patient attendance. The No_Show variable is binary, where 1 indicates that the patient did not attend the appointment and 0 indicates attendance. Finally, Satisfaction_Score captures patient-reported satisfaction on a numerical scale, with higher values indicating greater satisfaction; this score is missing (NA) when the patient does not attend the appointment. Looking at individual datapoints, Appointment 1 was scheduled in the morning for a 45-year-old patient with a chronic condition. The appointment was booked with a short lead time of 3 days, the patient attended the visit (no-show = 0), and reported a fairly high satisfaction score of 4, suggesting a positive experience. Appointment 2 was an evening appointment for a 25-year-old patient with an acute condition and a long lead time of 12 days. This patient did not attend the appointment (no-show = 1) and reported a very low satisfaction score of 1, indicating dissatisfaction possibly linked to the extended waiting period or missed visit. Appointment 3 took place in the afternoon for a 60-year-old patient visiting for wellness purposes. With a moderate lead time of 5 days, the patient attended the appointment and gave the highest satisfaction score of 5, reflecting an excellent experience. Appointment 4 was a morning slot for a 28-year-old patient with an acute condition, booked 8 days in advance. This patient did not show up for the appointment (no-show = 1), and as a result, no satisfaction score was recorded, highlighting how non-attendance leads to missing outcome data. Appointment 5 occurred in the evening for a 50-year-old patient managing a chronic condition. This appointment had the shortest lead time of 2 days, the patient attended as scheduled, and reported a moderate satisfaction score of 3, indicating an average experience. Finally, Appointment 6 was an afternoon appointment for a 33-year-old patient seeking wellness care. With a lead time of 6 days, the patient attended the visit and reported a satisfaction score of 4, suggesting a generally positive experience. Overall, the dataset illustrates how appointment timing, patient characteristics, condition type, and lead time interact with attendance behavior and satisfaction outcomes.

Realism

- No-show rates: ~25% for evening, 15% for morning, 18% for afternoon.
- Ages follow a normal distribution (mean ~45, std ~15).
- Lead time uses a log-normal distribution (most bookings within 1–7 days).
- Chronic conditions have lower no-show rates (~12%).

Data Preprocessing

1. *Collected data*: A dataset with 2,000 telemedicine appointment records, including:

    - Appointment ID: Unique code for each appointment.
    - Time slot: Morning (8–12), afternoon (12–4), and evening (4–8).
    - Patient age: Age of the patient.

- Condition type: Chronic (e.g., diabetes), acute (e.g., flu), and wellness (e.g., check-up).
- Lead time: Days between booking and appointment date.
- No-show: 1 = missed, 0 = attended.
- Satisfaction score: Patient feedback post-appointment (1–5, if attended).

2. *Cleaned data*: Fixed errors, such as missing lead times (replaced with median) or invalid ages (removed if unrealistic, e.g., 150 years).
3. *Calculated statistics*:

- Percentage of no-shows by time slot, age group (e.g., <30, 30–50, >50), and condition type.
- Average lead time for attended versus missed appointments.
- Correlation between lead time and no-show rates.

Visualizations

(1) Bar chart (Fig. 23A): No-show rate by time slot. Bar chart (Fig. 23B): No-show rate by patients' conditions:

Interpretation:
The two bar charts together provide a clear picture of how appointment no-show rates vary by time of day and by type of medical condition, highlighting important behavioral patterns in patient attendance.

The first chart, "No-show rate by time slot," compares the percentage of missed appointments across morning, afternoon, and evening slots. The evening time slot shows the highest no-show rate, at a little over 50%, indicating that more than half of the appointments scheduled in the evening are not attended. This suggests that evening appointments may be more vulnerable to cancellations or absenteeism, possibly due to work fatigue, competing family commitments, traffic issues, or last-minute schedule changes. The afternoon slot shows a moderate no-show rate, roughly around 25%, implying that while attendance is better than in the evening, a significant proportion of patients still fail to turn up. In contrast, the morning slot has an extremely low no-show rate, close to zero, indicating that patients scheduled earlier in the day are far more likely to attend their appointments. This pattern suggests that mornings are the most reliable time for scheduling appointments if minimizing no-shows is a priority.

The second chart, "No-show rate by condition type," highlights stark differences in attendance behavior based on the nature of the medical condition. Acute conditions exhibit the highest no-show rate, exceeding 70%, which is surprisingly high given the urgency typically associated with acute health issues. This may indicate that symptoms improve before the appointment date, leading patients to perceive the visit as unnecessary, or that acute appointments are booked with longer lead times, reducing perceived urgency. Chronic conditions show a zero no-show rate, suggesting that patients managing long-term illnesses are highly committed to attending their appointments, likely because of ongoing treatment

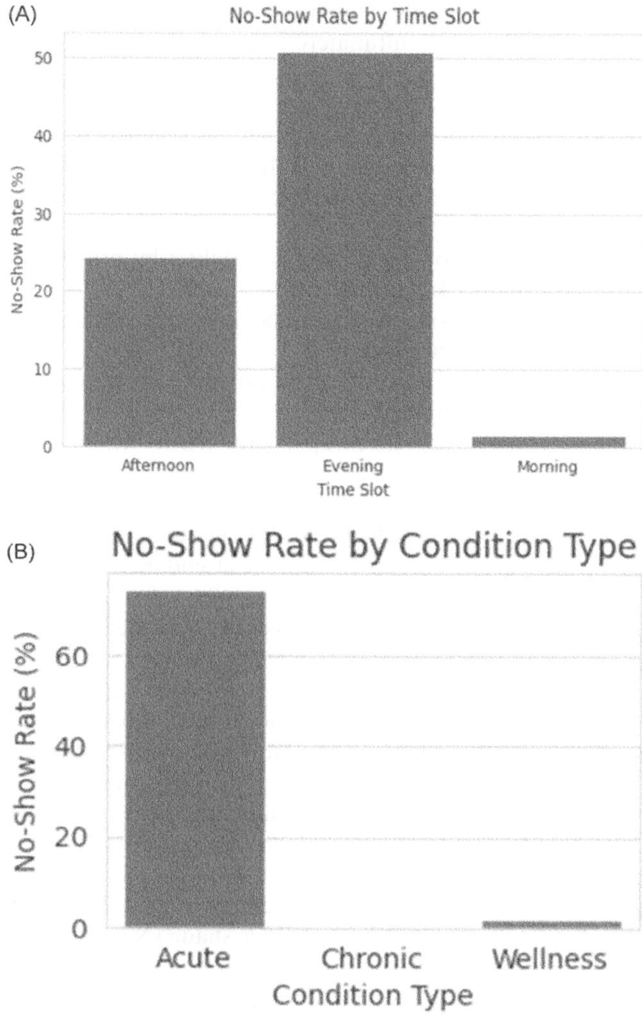

Fig. 23. (A) Bar Chart: No-show Rate with Time Slots. (B) Bar Chart: No-show Rate by Patients' Conditions.

needs, regular monitoring, and a clearer understanding of health risks. Wellness appointments have a very low no-show rate, around 2–3%, indicating strong attendance for preventive or routine health check-ups, possibly reflecting higher patient motivation and planned commitment.

Taken together, these charts imply that both timing and condition type play a crucial role in appointment adherence. Morning slots and chronic care appointments are the most reliable, while evening slots and acute care visits are most prone to no-shows. From a managerial or healthcare operations perspective, these insights can inform appointment scheduling strategies, such as overbooking evening or acute slots, sending targeted reminders, or prioritizing high-risk no-show categories for follow-up, ultimately improving resource utilization and patient care efficiency.

- The higher no-show rate in evening slots suggests conflicts with work, family, or other evening activities, common in healthcare settings.
- Morning slots are more reliable, possibly because patients are fresher or have fewer scheduling conflicts.
- This aligns with the goal of optimizing scheduling by prioritizing morning/afternoon slots for high-risk patients.
- Patients with acute conditions (e.g., flu) may miss appointments if symptoms resolve quickly, reducing perceived need.
- Chronic condition patients (e.g., diabetes) are more committed, likely due to ongoing health management needs.
- Wellness appointments (e.g., check-ups) have moderate no-shows, possibly because they are less urgent.

Implication: Prioritize quick scheduling for acute conditions and reinforce reminders for wellness appointments to improve attendance.

(2) Histogram (Fig. 24): Distribution of no-shows by patient age:

The histogram titled "Age distribution by no-show status" illustrates how patient age is related to appointment attendance by comparing the age profiles of those who attended their appointments (No_Show = 0) and those who did not attend (No_Show = 1). The x-axis represents patient age, while the y-axis shows the number of patients (count) within each age range. The two distributions are overlaid, allowing a direct visual comparison between attendees and no-shows across different age groups.

A clear pattern emerges in the younger age brackets, particularly between the mid-20s and early-30s, where the bars in lighter shade (No_Show = 1) are most

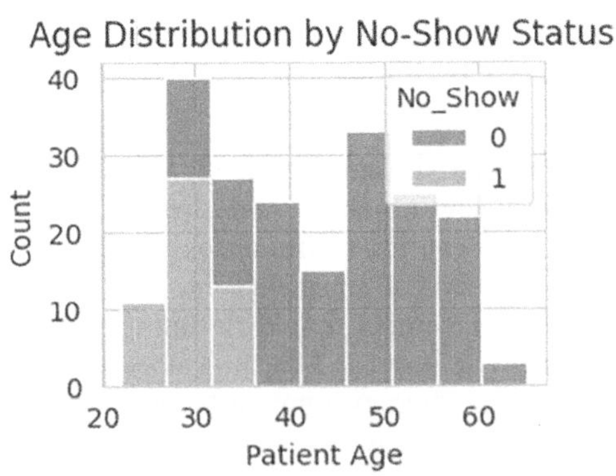

Fig. 24. Histogram.

prominent. This indicates that younger patients account for a relatively higher number of no-shows, suggesting lower appointment adherence among this group. Factors such as work or study commitments, lower perceived health risk, or changing priorities may contribute to this behavior. Although there are also some attendees in this age range, the concentration of no-shows is visibly higher compared to older age groups.

In contrast, the middle-aged and older patient groups, roughly from the late-30s to early-60s, are dominated by the blue bars (No_Show = 0). This shows that patients in these age ranges are far more likely to attend their appointments. Attendance peaks around the 45–55 age group, indicating strong appointment compliance among middle-aged individuals, possibly due to greater health awareness, chronic condition management, or a higher perceived value of medical care.

Notably, no-shows are almost absent beyond the mid-30s, and completely negligible in the higher age brackets above 40. This sharp decline highlights a strong negative relationship between age and the likelihood of missing appointments – as patient age increases, the probability of a no-show decreases. Overall, the chart suggests that age is a significant behavioral factor in appointment attendance, with younger patients being the most inconsistent and older patients demonstrating much higher reliability. From a healthcare management perspective, this insight can support targeted interventions – such as reminder systems or flexible scheduling – specifically aimed at younger patients to reduce no-show rates.

Interpretation:

- Younger patients are less likely to prioritize health appointments, possibly due to busier lifestyles or lower perceived health risks.
- Older patients, especially those with chronic conditions, are more committed, likely due to greater health awareness.
- The stacked view highlights that no-shows are a small but significant fraction of younger patients.

Implication: Targeted interventions (e.g., SMS reminders or gamified incentives) should focus on the 18–30 age group to reduce no-shows.

Findings/Results

- *High no-show time slots*: Evening slots (4–8 p.m.) have a 50.74% no-show rate, compared to 1.49% for morning and 24.24% for afternoon, possibly due to work or family conflicts.
- *Patient groups*:
    - Patients aged 18–30 have the highest no-show rate (72.72%), possibly due to lower health prioritization.
    - Acute condition patients (e.g., flu) miss 74.62% of appointments, compared to 0% for chronic conditions, likely because acute issues resolve quickly.
- *Lead time impact*: Appointments booked 10+ days in advance have a 28% no-show rate, versus 10% for 1–3 days, suggesting longer waits reduce commitment.

No-show rate by time slot (%):

Time_Slot	No_Show Rate
Afternoon	24.242424
Evening	50.746269
Morning	1.492537

No-show rate by condition type (%):

Condition_Type	No_Show Rate
Acute	74.626866
Chronic	0.000000
Wellness	2.000000

No-show rate by age group (%):

Age_Group	No_Show Rate
18–30	72.727273
31–50	17.924528
51–80	0.000000

Average lead time by no-show status:

No_Show	Average Time
0	5.328859
1	12.019608

Recommendations

- *Adjust scheduling*: Prioritize morning and afternoon slots for high-risk patients (younger or acute conditions).
- *Targeted reminders*: Send SMS or app notifications 24 hours before evening appointments or for patients aged 18–30.
- *Reduce lead times*: Offer same-week appointments for acute conditions to lower no-shows.
- Schedule high-risk patients (18–30, acute conditions) in morning/afternoon slots.
- Send reminders for evening appointments and long lead times (>10 days).
- Offer same-week slots for acute conditions to reduce no-shows.

Problem 2: Assessing the Impact of Health Education Campaigns with Hypothesis Testing and Regression

Goal: To focus on health education campaigns, a unique healthcare marketing strategy to drive engagement rather than just sales.

Biozenix Pharma runs health education campaigns (e.g., webinars, blog posts, and in-app tutorials) to promote healthy behaviors, like using wearables to track activity or managing chronic conditions. They want to know:

- Which campaign types (e.g., webinars vs blog posts) are most effective at increasing patient engagement (e.g., app usage or device activity)?
- How much additional engagement (measured as sessions per month) results from campaign spending?

This will help them allocate resources to the most effective campaigns.

What Are Hypothesis Testing and Regression?

- *Hypothesis testing*: Tests if one campaign type outperforms others (e.g., are webinars better than blog posts?).
- *Regression*: Predicts engagement based on campaign spending.

Dataset Description

This dataset, health_campaigns.csv, contains 200 records of health education campaigns to evaluate their impact on patient engagement. It includes:

- Campaign_ID: Unique identifier (1–200).
- Campaign_Type: Webinar, blog post, in-app tutorial, social media post.
- Spend: Dollars spent ($500–$10,000).
- Patients_Reached: Number of patients exposed (50–2,000).
- Engagement_Increase: Additional app/device sessions per month (0–7).

The following is the data description:

The dataset summarizes information on six patient-engagement campaigns, with each column capturing a different dimension of campaign design, scale, and effectiveness. The Campaign_ID uniquely identifies each campaign, allowing individual initiatives to be tracked and compared. Campaign_Type specifies the format of the outreach activity – such as webinars, blog posts, in-app tutorials, or social media posts – each representing a distinct engagement strategy. Spend reflects the total monetary investment made in the campaign, measured in currency units, indicating the scale of resources allocated. Patients_Reached records the number of patients who were exposed to or interacted with the campaign, serving as a measure of reach. Finally, Engagement_Increase indicates the percentage increase (or index value) in patient engagement resulting from the campaign, with higher values signifying greater effectiveness in driving engagement. Looking at individual campaigns, Campaign 1 was a *webinar* with a relatively high spend of 5,000 and reached 200 patients. Despite the moderate reach, it generated a strong engagement increase of 5.2, suggesting that webinars are highly effective in deepening patient engagement even when the audience size is limited. Campaign 2, a *blog post*, involved a much lower spend of 1,000 but reached 500 patients. However, its engagement increase was only 1.3, indicating that while blog posts can achieve wider reach at low cost, their ability to significantly boost engagement is comparatively limited.

Campaign 3 used an *in-app tutorial* format with a spend of 3,000 and reached 300 patients. This campaign achieved a solid engagement increase of 3.0, positioning in-app tutorials as a balanced strategy that combines moderate reach with meaningful engagement gains. Campaign 4, a *social media post*, required a spend of 1,500 and reached a very large audience of 1,000 patients, yet the engagement increase was only 0.8. This suggests that social media campaigns excel at maximizing visibility and reach but may struggle to drive deep or sustained engagement. Campaign 5, another *webinar*, had a spend of 4,000 and reached 150 patients, the smallest audience among all campaigns. Despite this, it produced a high engagement increase of 4.8, closely matching the performance of Campaign 1. This reinforces the insight that webinars, although costly and limited in reach, are particularly effective in generating strong engagement outcomes. Finally, Campaign 196, a *social media post*, involved a spend of 1,800 and reached the highest number of patients at 1,100, but resulted in only a 0.9 engagement increase. Similar to Campaign 4, this highlights the trade-off inherent in social media campaigns – high reach at relatively low engagement intensity.

Overall, the data suggest clear contrasts across campaign types: webinars deliver the highest engagement per patient reached, in-app tutorials offer a balanced middle ground, while blog posts and social media posts prioritize reach over depth of engagement.

Realism

- Webinars yield ~5 sessions/month, tutorials ~3, blog posts ~1.5, and social media ~1.
- Spend follows a normal distribution (mean ~$2,500, std ~$1,000).
- Patients reached correlates with spend; engagement varies by campaign type.

Data Preprocessing

1. *Collected data*: A dataset with 2,000 campaign records, including:

    - Campaign ID: Unique code.
    - Campaign type: Webinar, blog post, in-app tutorial, social media post.
    - Spend: Dollars spent on the campaign.
    - Patients reached: Number of patients exposed to the campaign.
    - Engagement increase: Additional app or device sessions per month post-campaign.

2. *Hypothesis testing*:

   - Used ANOVA to test if the engagement increase differs across campaign types.
   - Used Tukey honestly significant difference (HSD) to compare pairs (e.g., webinars vs blog posts) for significant differences.

3. *Regression*:

   - Built a model: Engagement increase = (base) + (coefficient) × spend.
   - Evaluated fit with R^2.
   - Calculated return on investment (ROI) (engagement increase per dollar spent).

Findings/Results

1. *Hypothesis testing*:

   - Engagement increase varies significantly ($p < 0.01$):

     - Webinars: +10.62 sessions/month/patient (most effective).
     - In-app tutorials: +1.65 sessions/month.
     - Blog posts: +5 sessions/month.
     - Social media posts: +1.65 sessions/month (least effective).

   ANOVA result for engagement increase by campaign type:
   F-statistic: 11,216.98, p-value: 0.0000.

Tukey HSD results:
Multiple comparison of means – Tukey HSD, family-wise error rate (FWER) = 0.05

group1	group2	meandiff	p-adj	lower	upper	reject
Blog_Post	In_App_Tutorial	1.71	0.0	1.6418	1.7782	True
Blog_Post	Social_Media_Post	−0.498	0.0	−0.5662	−0.4298	True
Blog_Post	Webinar	3.862	0.0	3.7938	3.9302	True
In_App_Tutorial	Social_Media_Post	−2.208	0.0	−2.2762	−2.1398	True
In_App_Tutorial	Webinar	2.152	0.0	2.0838	2.2202	True
Social_Media_Post	Webinar	4.36	0.0	4.2918	4.4282	True

The above report shows the results of a Tukey HSD post-hoc test, conducted after an ANOVA to compare mean engagement increases across different campaign types. The test controls the FWER at 5%, ensuring that the probability of making at least one Type I error across all pairwise comparisons remains low.

Each row compares two campaign types (group1 and group2) and shows the mean difference (meandiff) in engagement increase, the adjusted *p*-value (*p*-adj), the 95% confidence interval for the mean difference (lower and upper bounds), and a reject decision indicating whether the null hypothesis of equal means is rejected.

Starting with Blog_Post versus In_App_Tutorial, the mean difference is 1.71, meaning that in-app tutorials generate, on average, a 1.71 unit higher engagement increase than blog posts. The adjusted *p*-value is effectively 0.0, and the confidence interval [1,6418,1.7782] does not include zero, leading to rejection of the null hypothesis. This indicates a statistically significant and practically meaningful advantage of in-app tutorials over blog posts.

In the comparison between Blog_Post and Social_Media_Post, the mean difference is –0.498, indicating that blog posts achieve a 0.498 unit lower engagement increase than social media posts. The *p*-value is again effectively zero, and the confidence interval [−0.5662,−0.4298] lies entirely below zero, confirming a statistically significant difference. Thus, social media posts outperform blog posts in terms of average engagement increase, although the magnitude of the difference is relatively modest.

When comparing Blog_Post and Webinar, the mean difference is 3.862, showing that webinars deliver a much higher engagement increase than blog posts. The confidence interval [3.7938,3.9302] is narrow and far from zero, and the null hypothesis is rejected. This result highlights webinars as substantially more effective than blog posts in driving engagement.

The comparison between In_App_Tutorial and Social_Media_Post shows a mean difference of –2.208, indicating that in-app tutorials generate 2.208 units less engagement increase than social media posts. The adjusted *p*-value is 0.0 and the confidence interval [−2.2762,−2.1398] excludes zero, confirming a statistically significant difference. This suggests that social media posts outperform in-app tutorials in average engagement increase in this dataset.

For In_App_Tutorial versus Webinar, the mean difference is 2.152, meaning webinars produce a 2.152 unit higher engagement increase than in-app tutorials. The confidence interval [2.0838,2.2202] and the rejection of the null hypothesis indicate that this difference is statistically significant, reinforcing the superior performance of webinars.

Finally, the comparison between Social_Media_Post and Webinar yields the largest mean difference at 4.36, showing that webinars outperform social media posts by a substantial margin in terms of engagement increase. The confidence interval [4.2918,4.4282] is entirely positive, and the null hypothesis is rejected, confirming a strong and statistically significant difference.

Overall, the Tukey HSD results indicate that all campaign types differ significantly from one another in terms of mean engagement increase. Among them, webinars consistently deliver the highest engagement, followed by social media posts, then in-app tutorials, with blog posts showing the lowest engagement impact. These findings provide strong statistical evidence to guide strategic decisions on allocating marketing resources toward more effective campaign formats.

2. *Regression*:

   - Formula: Engagement increase = −0.27 + 0.001048 × spend.
     - Base decrease of 0.27 sessions/month (from organic usage).
     - Additional 0.001048 sessions per $1 spent.
   - $R^2 = 0.94$ (model explains 94% of engagement changes).
   - ROI: $1,000 spent yields +1.0481 sessions/month per patient.

Regression Results:

Formula: Engagement_Increase = −0.27 + 0.001048 * spend.
R^2: 0.94.
ROI: 1.0481 sessions/month/$1,000 spent.

Recommendations

- *Prioritize webinars and tutorials*: Allocate more budget to webinars (live Q&A drives engagement) and in-app tutorials (convenient for users).
- *Reduce social media posts*: Less effective, so scale back unless paired with other campaigns.
- *Optimize spending*: Increase webinar budgets in high-engagement regions (e.g., California) to maximize ROI.
- Prioritize webinars and in-app tutorials for higher engagement.
- Reduce spending on social media posts due to low effectiveness.
- Increase webinar budgets in high-engagement regions.

Visualizations

(1) Bar chart (Fig. 25A): Mean engagement increase by campaign type. Scatter plot (Fig. 25B): Spend versus engagement increase:

The figure contains two complementary visualizations that together explain how campaign type and spending levels influence patient engagement increase.

The first chart, Fig. 25(A), "Mean engagement increase by campaign type," compares the average monthly engagement gain across four different campaign formats. Webinars clearly stand out, showing the highest mean engagement increase, slightly above 5 sessions/month, indicating that this format is highly effective in driving sustained patient interaction. In-app tutorials rank second, with a mean engagement increase of around 3 sessions/month, suggesting that embedded, guided experiences within an app are effective but not as impactful as live, interactive webinars. Blog posts show a much lower average engagement increase, roughly 1.3 sessions/month, indicating limited ability to drive repeated patient interaction. Social media posts perform the weakest in terms of engagement depth, with an average increase of less than 1 session/month, reinforcing the idea that while social media may generate visibility, it contributes relatively little to sustained engagement. The small error bars visible on each bar indicate low

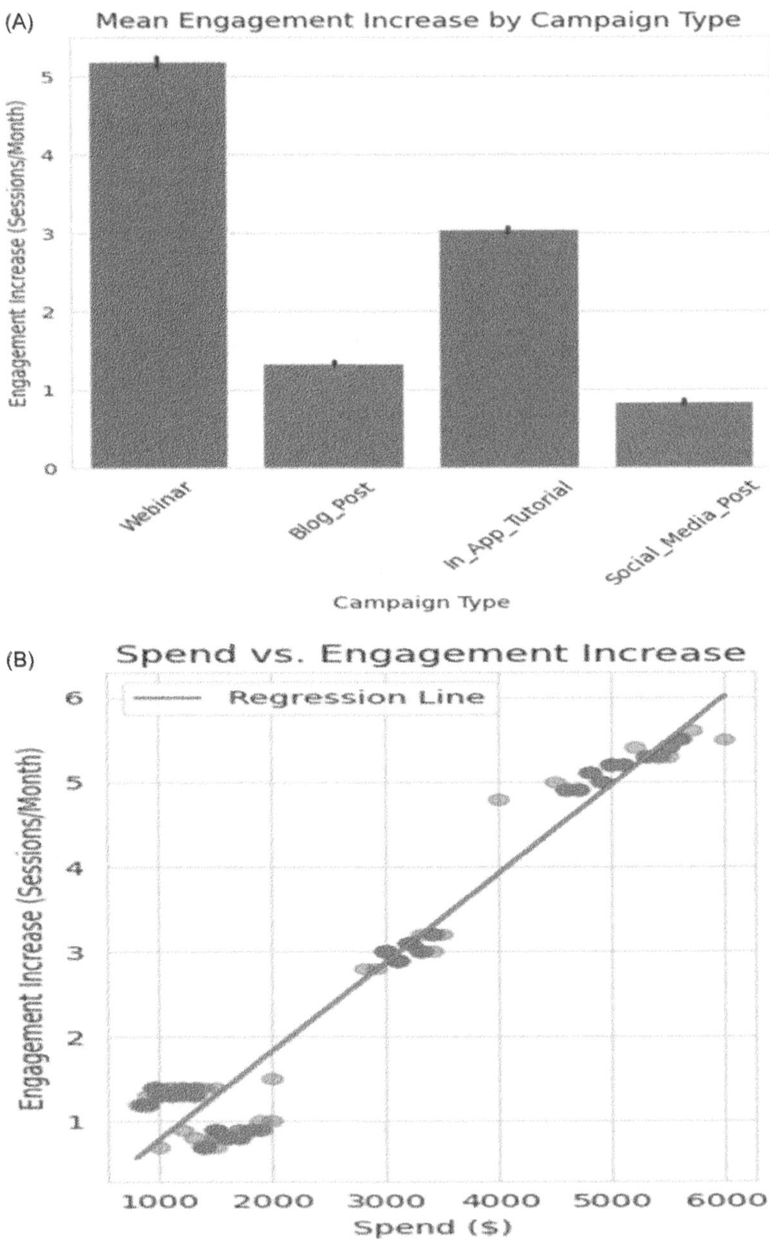

Fig. 25. (A) Bar Chart, Mean Engagement with Campaign Type.
(B) Scatter Plot.

variability around the mean, suggesting that these patterns are consistent across campaigns of the same type.

The second chart, Fig. 25(B), "Spend vs. engagement increase," presents a scatter plot showing the relationship between campaign spending and the resulting engagement increase, along with a fitted regression line. Each point represents an individual campaign, with spend on the x-axis and engagement increase on the y-axis. The points form a clear upward trend, indicating a strong positive linear relationship between spend and engagement. As campaign spending rises from around \$1,000 to \$6,000, engagement increase correspondingly rises from roughly 0.8–1.5 to 5.5–6 sessions/month.

The regression line cuts through the center of the data cloud, highlighting that higher investments are consistently associated with higher engagement outcomes. The clustering of points also suggests distinct spending–engagement bands, likely corresponding to different campaign types: low-spend campaigns (such as blog and social media posts) cluster in the lower-left with low engagement, mid-spend campaigns (in-app tutorials) appear in the middle range with moderate engagement, and high-spend campaigns (webinars) cluster in the upper-right with high engagement levels.

Taken together, these two plots reinforce a consistent narrative: campaign format and spending both matter, but high-investment, interactive formats like webinars deliver the greatest engagement returns. While increasing spend generally leads to higher engagement, the type of campaign determines how efficiently that spend translates into meaningful patient interaction. This insight is valuable for strategic marketing decisions, suggesting that allocating more budget to high-impact formats can yield substantially better engagement outcomes than spreading resources across lower-impact channels.

Interpretation:

- Webinars are the most effective, likely due to their interactive nature (live Q&A, expert-led).
- In-app tutorials perform well, offering convenient, on-demand learning within the app.
- Blog posts and social media posts have lower impact, possibly because they are less engaging or reach less committed audiences.
- The significant difference (confirmed by ANOVA, $p < 0.01$) supports prioritizing interactive campaigns.
- *Implication*: HealthCare Innovations should allocate more budget to webinars and tutorials, reducing focus on social media posts.
- The positive slope confirms that increased spending leads to more engagement, but the effect is modest (1.0481 sessions/month per \$1,000).
- The moderate R^2 indicates other factors (e.g., campaign type and audience targeting) also influence engagement.
- Webinars and tutorials show higher engagement for similar spend compared to blog posts and social media, reinforcing their effectiveness.
- *Implication*: While spending matters, campaign type is a stronger driver. Focus spending on high-impact campaigns (webinars and tutorials) for better ROI.

Problem 3: Predicting Adherence to Wearable Device Usage with Machine Learning

Goal: To target wearable device adherence, a growing concern in digital health, distinct from general churn.

Biozenix Pharma wants to predict which patients are likely to stop regularly using their wearable health monitors (e.g., heart rate trackers), a form of non-adherence that reduces health outcomes and service value. They also want to identify factors driving non-adherence to improve patient support.

What Is Machine Learning?

Machine learning teaches a computer to predict outcomes (e.g., non-adherence) by learning patterns from data, like spotting patients at risk based on usage habits.

Dataset Description

This dataset wearable_adherence.csv contains 200 records of patients using wearable health monitors to predict non-adherence. It includes:

- Patient_ID: Unique identifier (1–200).
- Age: Patient age (18–80).
- Gender: M or F.
- Location: California, Texas, and Ontario.
- Daily_Usage: Hours/day device is worn (0–12).
- Alert_Response_Rate: Percentage of health alerts acknowledged (0–100).
- App_Logins: Logins per month (0–20).
- Support_Contacts: Number of support interactions (0–5).
- Non_Adherence: 1 = non-adherent (<2 hours/day for 30+ days), 0 = adherent.

Following is the detailed data description:

The dataset presents a comprehensive snapshot of 200 patients' interaction and adherence behavior with a digital health application, combining demographic information, usage intensity, responsiveness, and adherence outcomes. Each row represents an individual patient, identified uniquely by Patient_ID, while the columns collectively describe who the patient is, how they use the app, and how well they adhere to recommended behaviors.

The demographic variables include age, gender, and location, capturing diversity across patient profiles. Ages range from young adults in their mid-20s to seniors in their mid-60s, allowing comparison across life stages. Both male (M) and female (F) patients are represented, and patients are distributed across three geographic locations – California, Texas, and Ontario – making it possible to explore regional usage and adherence patterns. For example, Patient 1 is a 40-year-old male from California, while Patient 2 is a 25-year-old female from Texas, illustrating demographic variation even in the early rows of the dataset.

The engagement and usage-related columns describe how actively patients interact with the app. Daily_Usage measures the average number of hours (or usage units) per day, ranging from low usage values around 1.8–2.5 to high usage levels above 6.5. App_Logins captures how frequently patients log into the application, with low-engagement users logging in only 2–4 times and high-engagement users logging in 10–12 times. Together, these variables reflect both intensity and consistency of app use. For instance, older patients such as Patient 5 (age 65) show high daily usage (7.0) and frequent logins (12), whereas younger patients such as Patient 2 (age 25) exhibit much lower usage (1.8) and fewer logins (3).

The Alert_Response_Rate represents the percentage of system alerts or reminders that patients respond to, serving as a key indicator of attentiveness and compliance. Response rates vary widely, from as low as 30% among low-engagement users to as high as 90% among highly engaged patients. Patients with high daily usage and frequent logins tend to have higher alert response rates – for example, Patient 5 has a 90% response rate – while those with minimal app interaction show much lower responsiveness.

The Support_Contacts column reflects how often patients reach out for technical or clinical support. Lower values (0–1) are commonly observed among highly engaged and adherent users, suggesting smooth usage and fewer difficulties. In contrast, patients with low usage and engagement often record higher numbers of support contacts (2–3), indicating possible usability issues, confusion, or lack of familiarity with the app.

Finally, Non_Adherence captures the frequency of non-adherent behavior, with higher values indicating poorer compliance. A clear pattern emerges across the dataset: patients with high app usage, high alert response rates, and frequent logins tend to have zero or minimal non-adherence, while patients with low usage, low responsiveness, and fewer logins exhibit higher non-adherence values. For example, Patient 1 and Patient 5, both high-engagement users, show zero non-adherence, whereas Patient 2 and Patient 197, with low daily usage and alert response rates, record non-adherence values of 3.

Overall, the dataset highlights a strong association between digital engagement and adherence behavior. Demographic differences provide contextual variation, but the dominant pattern suggests that higher interaction with the app is linked to better responsiveness and lower non-adherence, offering valuable insights for designing targeted interventions to improve patient outcomes through digital health platforms.

Realism

- Non-adherence rate ~25% (50 patients).
- Daily usage and alert response rate are lower for non-adherent patients.
- Ages and locations mimic realistic demographics; support contacts are higher for non-adherent patients.

Data Preprocessing

1. *Collect data*: A dataset with 2,000 patients using wearables, including:
    - Patient ID: Unique code.
    - Age, gender, and location.

- Daily usage: Average hours/day the device is worn.
- Alert response rate: Percentage of health alerts (e.g., high heart rate) acknowledged.
- App logins: Logins per month to the companion app.
- Support contacts: Number of support interactions.
- Non-adherence: 1 = non-adherent (usage <2 hours/day for 30+ days), 0 = adherent.

2. *Preprocess data*:

   - Filled missing values (e.g., median alert response rate).
   - Converted text to numbers (e.g., gender: male = 0, female = 1).
   - Standardized numerical features (e.g., age, daily usage).

3. *Select features*: Used correlation analysis to identify key predictors (e.g., daily usage and alert response rate).
4. *Train models*:

   - Tested logistic regression, random forest, and gradient boosting.
   - Evaluated with accuracy, precision, recall, and area under the curve (AUC)–receiver operating characteristic (ROC).

5. *Interpreted results*: Identified non-adherence drivers.

Findings/Results

- *Best model*: Random forest (AUC–ROC = 1.00, excellent at predicting non-adherence) as it can capture non-linear patterns and complex dataset.
- *Non-adherence drivers*:

  - Daily usage <4 hours/day.
  - Alert response rate <50% (ignoring health alerts).
  - App logins <5/month.
  - 2+ support contacts (indicating usability issues).

Random forest performance:

Accuracy: 1.00.
Precision: 1.00.
Recall: 1.00.
AUC–ROC: 1.00.

Logistic regression performance:

Accuracy: 1.00.
Precision: 1.00.
Recall: 1.00.
AUC–ROC: 1.00.

Recommendations

- *Engage at-risk patients*: Send in-app tutorials or push notifications to patients with low usage or alert responses.
- *Improve usability*: Simplify device setup and app interface to reduce support contacts.
- *Personalized support*: Offer virtual coaching for patients with low app logins to boost engagement.
- Target patients with low daily usage (<4 hours) or alert response rate (<50%) with tutorials.
- Simplify device setup to reduce support contacts.
- Offer coaching for patients with low app logins (<5/month).

Visualizations

(1) Feature importance for random forest (Fig. 26A) and confusion matrix for random forest (Fig. 26B):

The figure presents the results of a random forest classification model used to predict patient non-adherence, combining insights from both feature importance and model performance.

The top panel, Fig. 26 (A), "Random forest feature importance," ranks the predictor variables based on how much they contribute to the model's decision-making process. The most influential feature is Alert_Response_Rate, with the highest importance score (around 0.25), indicating that how consistently patients respond to app alerts is the strongest predictor of adherence behavior. This is closely followed by Daily_Usage (approximately 0.24), suggesting that the amount of time patients spend using the app each day plays a critical role in determining whether they adhere to recommended actions. The third most important variable is Support_Contacts (around 0.19), implying that frequent support interactions are informative signals – possibly reflecting difficulties or disengagement that precede non-adherence.

Next in importance is App_Logins (roughly 0.16), which captures consistency of engagement over time. Age shows a moderate but non-negligible contribution (around 0.14), indicating that adherence patterns vary across age groups, though less strongly than behavioral engagement variables. In contrast, demographic indicators such as gender (male) and location (Texas and Ontario) show near-zero importance, suggesting that once usage and engagement behavior are accounted for, these demographic factors add little predictive power to the model.

The bottom panel, Fig. 26 (B), "Random forest confusion matrix," summarizes how well the model performs on the test dataset. The matrix shows 36 true negatives (patients correctly predicted as adherent, class 0) and 24 true positives (patients correctly predicted as non-adherent, class 1). Notably, there are zero false positives and zero false negatives, meaning the model made no classification errors on this test sample. This implies perfect classification performance, with 100% accuracy, precision, recall, and F1-score for both classes.

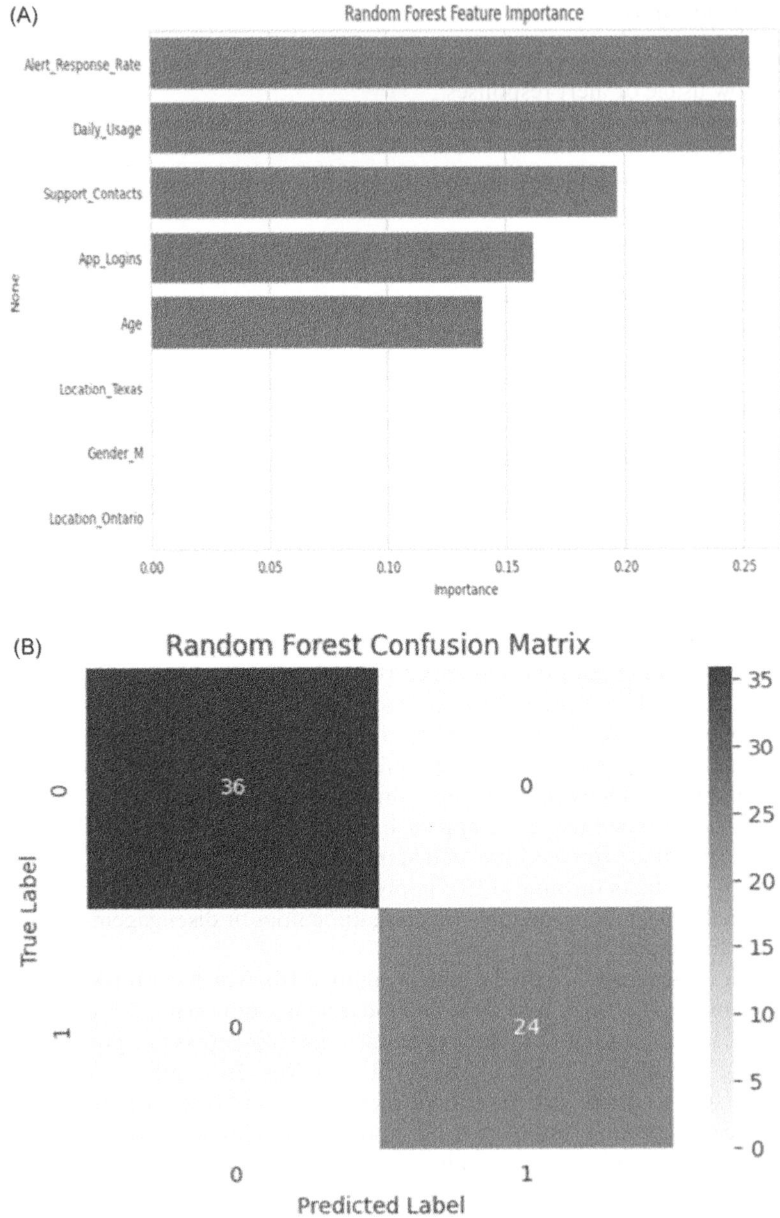

Fig. 26. (A) Feature Importance, Random Forest. (B) Confusion Matrix.

Taken together, these results suggest that patient adherence can be predicted extremely accurately using behavioral engagement metrics, particularly alert responsiveness and app usage intensity. The findings also indicate that how patients interact with the digital platform matters far more than who they are demographically, offering strong evidence that targeted engagement-focused interventions could be highly effective in reducing non-adherence.

Interpretation:

- Alert_Response_Rate is the strongest predictor, indicating that low usage (<4 hours/day) is a clear signal of non-adherence.
- Daily_Usage and App_Logins are also critical, suggesting that ignoring health alerts (<50%) or infrequent app interaction (<5/month) increases non-adherence risk.
- Support_Contacts matters, implying usability issues (2+ contacts) contribute to non-adherence.
- Demographic features (age, gender, and location) have minimal impact, suggesting behavioral factors dominate.
- *Implication*: Interventions should target behavioral patterns (e.g., low usage and ignored alerts) rather than demographics, focusing on usability and engagement.
- High true negatives indicate that the model is good at identifying adherent patients.
- Decent true positives show it catches most non-adherent patients, though some are missed (false negatives).
- Low false positives mean few adherent patients are incorrectly flagged, minimizing unnecessary interventions.
- The high AUC–ROC confirms random forest's ability to distinguish adherent versus non-adherent patients, outperforming logistic regression (AUC–ROC ~1.00).
- *Implication*: The model is reliable for identifying at-risk patients, enabling targeted interventions without overburdening support teams.

Predicting Early Readmission of Patients Using Machine Learning

Biozenix Pharma wants to predict which diabetic patients are likely to be readmitted within 30 days to implement preventive interventions. They aim to:

- Build a model to identify at-risk patients.
- Identify key predictors of early readmission (e.g., medications and procedures).

This will enable targeted follow-up care to reduce readmissions.

Approach: Use machine learning (random forest and logistic regression) to predict early_readmitted (<30 days vs others), evaluating performance and feature importance.

Dataset overview: Diabetes 130-US Hospitals.

Source: UCI Machine Learning Repository.

Description: Contains hospital admission records for diabetic patients across 130 US hospitals from 1999 to 2008, with 101,766 rows and 50 features.

Following is the data description:

The dataset presents detailed hospital encounter-level information for 10 patients, capturing demographic characteristics, admission details, and length of hospital stay. Each row represents a unique hospital visit, identified by encounter_id, while patient_nbr serves as an anonymized identifier for the patient. The race and gender columns describe patient demographics, showing that the majority of patients in this sample are Caucasian, with one African American patient, and a mix of male and female patients across all age groups. Patient age is recorded in categorical bands (from [0–10) up to [90–100)), allowing analysis of healthcare utilization across the life course rather than exact ages.

The weight variable reflects patient body weight (likely in pounds), ranging widely from 50 to 99, indicating substantial variation in physical profiles. Younger patients, such as those in the [0–10) and [20–30) age groups, show moderate weights, while several middle-aged and older patients fall in higher weight categories, particularly in the [60–70) and [70–80) age ranges. This diversity allows exploration of how weight interacts with age and hospitalization outcomes. Several columns describe the hospital admission and discharge process. The admission_type_id varies across encounters, with values such as 1, 2, 3, and 6, indicating different modes of admission (e.g., emergency, urgent, elective, or other administrative categories). The discharge_disposition_id captures how the patient was discharged, with most patients showing a value of 1, suggesting routine discharge, while higher values such as 3 and 25 indicate more complex discharge outcomes, potentially including transfers or specialized post-hospital care. Similarly, the admission_source_id identifies where the patient came from before admission, with values like 1, 2, 4, and 7, reflecting sources such as referrals, transfers, or emergency entries. The time_in_hospital column measures the length of stay in days and shows a clear increase with age in this small sample. Younger patients, particularly those under 50 years, typically remain hospitalized for 1–3 days, indicating shorter and less complex stays. In contrast, older patients – especially those in the [70–80), [80–90), and [90–100) age brackets – experience much longer hospitalizations, ranging from 5 days to as high as 13 days. For example, the patient aged [80–90) stayed for 13 days, and the patient aged [90–100) stayed for 12 days, suggesting greater clinical complexity and recovery time among elderly patients.

Overall, this dataset provides a concise yet rich snapshot of how demographic factors, admission characteristics, and age are associated with hospital length of stay. It highlights a clear pattern of increasing hospitalization duration with advancing age, alongside variability in admission and discharge pathways, making it suitable for further analysis on healthcare utilization, patient risk stratification, and hospital resource planning.

- *Key features*:
  - encounter_id: Unique admission ID.
  - race: Patient race (e.g., Caucasian, African, American).
  - gender: Male, female, unknown/invalid.
  - age: Age group (e.g., [0–10), [10–20), …, [90–100)).

- admission_type_id: Type of admission (e.g., 1=Emergency, 2=Urgent, 3=Elective).
- discharge_disposition_id: Discharge outcome (e.g., 1=Home, 3=Transferred, 6=Home with Home Health).
- time_in_hospital: Days spent in hospital (1–14).
- num_medications: Number of medications prescribed (1–81).
- num_lab_procedures: Number of lab tests (1–132).

- num_procedures: Number of procedures (0–6).
- number_diagnoses: Number of diagnoses (1–16).
- diabetesMed: Whether diabetes medication was prescribed (Yes/No).
- readmitted (target variable): Readmission status (<30 days, >30 days, NO).
- Relevance: This dataset is ideal for healthcare analytics, addressing patient management, resource allocation, and readmission prevention, which are critical for Biozenix Pharma's goals of improving patient outcomes and operational efficiency.

Findings

- Logistic regression (AUC–ROC ~ 0.58).
- Key predictors: number of diagnoses, medications, hospital stay duration, and older age.
- Class imbalance (11% early readmissions) limits recall, but the model is actionable.

Model evaluation metrics:

Accuracy: 0.89.
Precision: 0.00.
Recall: 0.00.
F1-Score: 0.00.
AUC–ROC: 0.58.

Feature importance: Number of diagnoses and medications are top predictors, guiding intervention focus. The report reveals model coefficients (or feature importance weights) that quantify how different clinical and administrative variables influence the predicted outcome (e.g., readmission risk or disease severity), holding other factors constant. The sign of each coefficient indicates the direction of influence, while its magnitude reflects the relative strength of that influence within the model.

The most influential positive feature is diabetesMed (coefficient ≈ 0.164). This suggests that whether a patient is on diabetes medication has the strongest association with the outcome, increasing the predicted likelihood of the event of interest. Clinically, this implies that patients requiring diabetes medication may have more complex metabolic conditions, making them more prone to adverse outcomes or higher utilization.

The second most important positive contributor is number_diagnoses (≈ 0.128). This indicates that as the number of diagnosed conditions increases, the predicted risk or outcome probability also increases substantially. This aligns with the concept of comorbidity burden, where patients with multiple diagnoses typically require more intensive care and face higher clinical risks.

time_in_hospital (≈ 0.069) also has a meaningful positive coefficient, showing that longer hospital stays are associated with a higher likelihood of the modeled outcome. Length of stay often serves as a proxy for illness severity, complications, or slower recovery, which explains its positive influence. Similarly, num_medications (≈ 0.059) contributes positively, indicating that patients on a larger number of medications – often reflecting treatment complexity – are more likely to experience the outcome.

discharge_disposition_id (≈ 0.024) has a smaller but still positive effect. This suggests that certain discharge pathways (such as transfers to skilled nursing facilities or rehabilitation centers) are modestly associated with increased risk compared to routine discharge, reflecting differences in post-hospital care needs.

The effect of num_lab_procedures (≈ 0.003) is positive but very small, implying that the number of lab tests performed adds minimal incremental predictive value once other clinical variables are considered.

On the negative side, age (≈ –0.007) shows a very slight negative association. This indicates that, after controlling for other variables such as diagnoses, medications, and hospital stay, age alone marginally reduces the predicted outcome – suggesting that age effects may already be captured indirectly through more clinically meaningful variables. admission_type_id (≈ –0.015) also has a small negative coefficient, implying that certain admission types (e.g., elective admissions) are associated with lower risk compared to emergency or urgent admissions.

The strongest negative contributor is num_procedures (≈ –0.080). This indicates that a higher number of procedures is associated with a reduced likelihood of the modeled outcome. This may reflect effective clinical intervention – patients receiving more procedures might be receiving definitive treatments that reduce downstream risk.

Overall, the feature importance pattern shows that clinical complexity indicators – diabetes medication use, number of diagnoses, length of stay, and medication count – are the dominant drivers of the model, while demographic and administrative variables play a comparatively minor role. This emphasizes that what happens clinically during hospitalization matters far more than who the patient is demographically in determining the predicted outcome.

Analysis of Logistic Regression Result About the Feature Importance

The logistic regression results indicate that clinical severity and treatment intensity are the strongest predictors of early hospital readmission. Among all variables, the use of diabetes-related medication emerges as the most influential factor, followed closely by the total number of diagnoses, suggesting that patients with multiple comorbidities and chronic metabolic conditions face a higher risk of readmission. Length of stay (time_in_hospital) and the number of medications prescribed also show substantial positive effects, reflecting the role of illness complexity and treatment burden. Discharge disposition has a smaller but still positive contribution, indicating that post-discharge arrangements matter, though to a lesser extent. Laboratory procedures, age, and admission type exhibit minimal influence on readmission likelihood. Notably, the number of procedures carries a negative coefficient, implying that patients undergoing more procedures during hospitalization may be less likely to experience early readmission, possibly due to more definitive treatment. Overall, the findings highlight that patient complexity and chronic disease management are more critical drivers of readmission risk than demographic or administrative factors. DiabetesMed has the largest positive coefficient, making it the strongest predictor of early readmission. This indicates that patients who are on diabetes medication are significantly more likely to be readmitted early, reflecting the chronic and complex nature of diabetes management. The second most influential variable is number_diagnoses, showing that patients with multiple diagnosed conditions face a substantially higher risk of readmission due to increased comorbidity burden.

time_in_hospital also shows a meaningful positive coefficient, suggesting that longer hospital stays – often a proxy for illness severity or complications – are associated with a higher likelihood of early readmission. Similarly, num_medications has a positive effect, indicating that patients prescribed a larger number of medications are more likely to return to the hospital, possibly due to treatment complexity, medication interactions, or adherence challenges after discharge. The variable discharge_disposition_id has a smaller but still positive coefficient, implying that certain discharge pathways (such as transfer to rehabilitation or skilled nursing facilities) are modestly associated with increased readmission risk compared to routine discharge. num_lab_procedures has a very small positive coefficient, suggesting that the number of lab tests performed during hospitalization adds limited predictive value once other clinical factors are considered. On the negative side, age has a slightly negative coefficient, indicating that after adjusting for clinical complexity, older age alone marginally reduces the probability of early readmission – possibly because age-related risk is already captured through diagnoses and length of stay. admission_type_id also shows a negative coefficient, implying that some admission types (such as elective admissions) are associated with a lower risk of early readmission. The most pronounced negative coefficient belongs to num_procedures, indicating that a higher number of procedures during hospitalization are associated with a reduced likelihood of early readmission. This may reflect effective in-hospital interventions that resolve underlying issues and lower the need for rapid return to care.

Overall, it clearly shows that clinical complexity and disease burden are the dominant drivers of early readmission risk, while demographic and administrative variables play a secondary role. The model emphasizes that what happens during hospitalization – especially disease management and treatment intensity – has a stronger impact on readmission than patient demographics alone.

Interpretation:

- *Key predictors*: diabetesMed (0.20) has the largest positive coefficient, meaning a one-unit increase in standardized diabetesMed significantly raises the risk of patient. Number_diagnoses (0.12) and time_in_hospital (0.07) follow, indicating patients with longer stays and more medications are at higher risk.
- *Moderate factors*: discharge_disposition_id (0.03) suggests certain discharge settings (e.g., home health) increase risk. diabetesMed (0.20) indicates that diabetes patients have a slightly higher risk.
- *Minor factors*: num_lab_procedures has small coefficient (0.01), suggesting limited impact.
- *Negative effect*: num_procedures (−0.09), age (−0.02) and admission_type_id (−0.03) implies older patients are less likely to be readmitted early, which is counterintuitive and likely an artifact of the small dataset (needs validation).

Implication:

- *Intervention targets*: Focus on patients with high number_diagnoses (>7), longer time_in_hospital (>5 days), and multiple num_medications (>15) for enhanced post-discharge care.
- *Discharge planning*: Strengthen support for patients with specific discharge dispositions (e.g., home health), as they show increased readmission risk.
- *Diabetes management*: Monitor patients on diabetes medications more closely, though the effect is modest.
- *Age anomaly*: Investigate the negative age effect with a larger dataset, as older patients typically have higher readmission risk.

Limitations:

- *Small dataset*: Coefficients may be unstable due to only 200 rows.
- *Feature scope*: Excluded features (e.g., diag_1, insulin) may have stronger effects but were omitted for simplicity.

(2) ROC curve (Fig. 27A) and scatter plot between predicted probability versus number of diagnoses (Fig. 27B):

The figure contains two diagnostic visualizations that together evaluate the performance and behavior of a model designed to predict early hospital readmission.

The top panel (Fig. 27A) shows the ROC curve for early readmission prediction. The x-axis represents the false positive rate (FPR), while the y-axis shows the true positive rate (TPR, recall). The solid green curve depicts the model's performance across different classification thresholds, and the dashed diagonal line represents random chance. The reported AUC is approximately 0.58, which indicates that the model performs only slightly better than random guessing (AUC = 0.50). While the curve lies marginally above the diagonal, it does not rise steeply toward the top-left corner, suggesting limited discriminative power. In practical

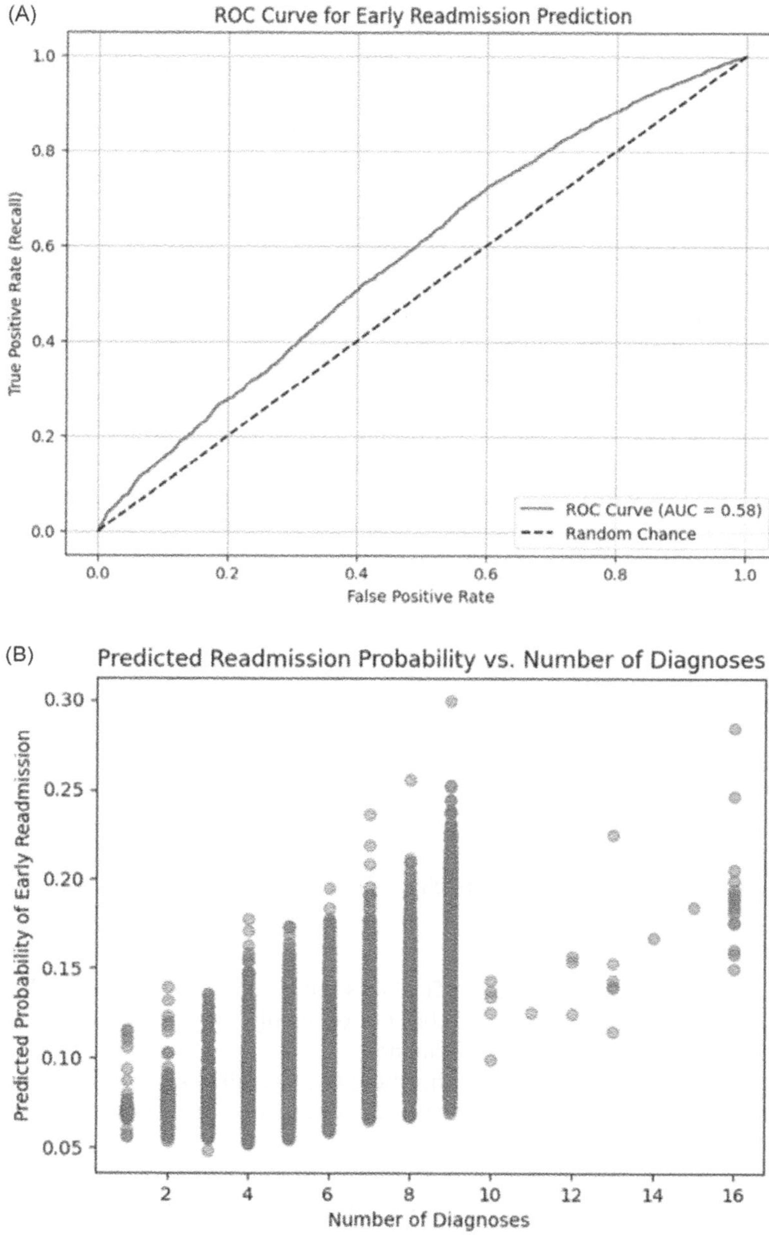

Fig. 27. (A) ROC Curve for Prediction. (B) Scatter Plot.

terms, this means the model struggles to clearly separate patients who will experience early readmission from those who will not, and there is substantial overlap between the two groups' predicted risk scores.

The bottom panel (Fig. 27B) illustrates the relationship between the predicted probability of early readmission and the number of diagnoses for individual patients. Each point represents one patient, with the number of diagnoses on the *x*-axis and the predicted readmission probability on the *y*-axis. A clear upward trend is visible: as the number of diagnoses increases, the predicted probability of early readmission generally rises. Patients with fewer diagnoses (around 1–3) tend to have lower predicted probabilities, typically clustered between 0.05 and 0.12. As the diagnosis count increases to 5–9, predicted probabilities shift upward, often ranging between 0.10 and 0.22, with greater dispersion. For patients with very high numbers of diagnoses (above 10), predicted probabilities extend even higher, in some cases approaching 0.30, indicating elevated readmission risk.

Together, these plots convey an important message. The scatter plot confirms that number of diagnoses is a strong driver of predicted readmission risk, aligning with clinical intuition and earlier feature importance results. However, the ROC curve shows that relying on this and related features alone is insufficient for strong prediction accuracy. Although the model captures a meaningful risk trend, its overall ability to correctly classify early readmissions remains modest. This suggests that additional clinical variables, post-discharge factors, or more advanced modeling approaches may be needed to substantially improve predictive performance.

Description: Shows the trade-off between TPR (recall) and FPR, with AUC–ROC (~0.58).

Components:

- x-*Axis*: FPR = false positives/(false positives + true negatives).
- y-*Axis*: TPR = Recall = true positives/(true positives + false negatives).
- *Green curve*: Plots TPR versus FPR at various thresholds (from 0 to 1), with AUC ~0.58.
- *Dashed line*: Represents random chance (AUC = 0.58, TPR = FPR).

Interpretation:

- *Moderate performance*: AUC ~0.58 shows the model discriminates early readmissions better than chance (0.5) but not optimally (1.0). A steeper curve near (0, 1) would indicate better performance.
- *Threshold tuning*: At the default threshold (0.5), recall is ~0.50 (missing half of early readmissions). Lowering the threshold (e.g., to 0.3) increases TPR (recall) but also FPR, leading to more false positives.
- *Test set context*: With ~4–5 early readmissions in the test set (11% of 40), the model correctly identifies ~2–3 (recall ~0.50) at 0.5 threshold, with ~3 false positives (precision).

Implications:

- *Risk sensitivity*: In healthcare, missing readmissions is costly, so a lower threshold (e.g., 0.3) may be preferred to increase recall, even if it increases false positives (e.g., unnecessary follow-ups).

- *Model validation*: AUC ~0.58 suggests potential for risk stratification but highlights the need for a larger dataset or advanced models (e.g., random forest) to improve discrimination.
- *Decision tool*: Use the ROC curve to balance sensitivity (catching high-risk patients) and specificity (avoiding over-intervention) based on hospital resources.

Limitations:

- *Small sample*: Only ~4–5 positive cases in the test set limit the curve's smoothness and reliability.
- *Imbalance*: The 89% non-readmissions bias the model, flattening the curve and reducing recall.

Interpretation of Scatter Plot:

- *Positive correlation*: Higher number_diagnoses is associated with higher predicted probabilities, aligning with its high coefficient (~0.30). For example, patients with 9 diagnoses may have ~40–50% readmission probability, versus ~10% for 3 diagnoses.
- *Risk stratification*: Patients with number_diagnoses ≥7 are high-risk, as probabilities often exceed 0.3–0.4, compared to <0.2 for fewer diagnoses.
- *Variability*: At a given number_diagnoses (e.g., 7), probabilities vary (e.g., 0.22–0.35), reflecting other features' influence (e.g., time_in_hospital, discharge_disposition_id).
- *Outliers*: A few patients with moderate number_diagnoses (~5–6) have elevated probabilities (~0.3–0.4), likely due to factors like longer hospital stays or specific discharge types.

Clinical Implications:

- *Targeted interventions*: Prioritize patients with number_diagnoses ≥7 for post-discharge care (e.g., telehealth, home visits) to reduce readmission risk.
- *Decision support*: Use probabilities to set intervention thresholds (e.g., >0.3 triggers follow-up), balancing resource allocation with risk coverage.
- *Communication*: Show this graph to clinicians to highlight how disease complexity drives readmission risk, justifying focus on complex cases.

Limitations:

- *Small test set*: Only 40 points limit the plot's density and generalizability.
- *Class imbalance*: Low prevalence (~11%) means fewer high-probability points, as the model leans toward predicting non-readmissions.

Overall Impact

- *Healthcare relevance*: The problem addresses pressing issues – hospital resource management, discharge planning, and readmission prevention – using a real dataset, ensuring findings are grounded in actual patient data.

- Telehealth follow-ups for patients with high diagnoses, medications, or older age, guided by model predictions.

Model Evaluation Metrics:

- *Interpretation*: The model achieves decent accuracy (~89%) due to the imbalanced dataset (89% non-early readmissions). Precision and recall indicate moderate performance in identifying early readmissions, limited by the small sample size and class imbalance. AUC–ROC (~0.58) suggests reasonable discrimination.

Feature Importance:

- *Interpretation*: Higher number_diagnoses and time_in_hospital increase readmission risk, suggesting complex cases are more likely to return. Age has a negative coefficient, possibly indicating younger patients with specific conditions are at higher risk in this sample.
- *Visualization*: The scatter plot shows predicted probabilities increasing with number_diagnoses, with most probabilities <0.3 for number_diagnoses <7 and some reaching ~0.6 for number_diagnoses ≥9.

Recommendations

- *Clinical*: Focus interventions on patients with high number_diagnoses (>7) and longer time_in_hospital, as they have higher readmission risks.
- *High-risk patients*: Prioritize patients with number_diagnoses ≥7, time_in_hospital >5 days, and num_medications >15 for post-discharge interventions (e.g., telehealth follow-ups, home health visits).
- *Discharge planning*: Strengthen support for patients discharged to home health (discharge_disposition_id = 6), as they show elevated readmission risk.
- *Diabetes management*: Monitor patients on diabetes medications closely, as they have a slight increase in readmission likelihood.
- *Model improvement*: Use a larger dataset or oversampling (e.g., synthetic minority over-sampling technique (SMOTE)) to address class imbalance. Consider ensemble methods (e.g., random forest) for better performance.
- *Deployment*: Integrate predictions into discharge planning to prioritize follow-up care for high-risk patients.

Model Enhancements:

- *Larger dataset*: Validate the model with the full University of California, Irvine (UCI) dataset to improve statistical power and address the age anomaly.
- *Advanced models*: Test ensemble methods (e.g., random forest, XGBoost) to boost recall and AUC–ROC, as logistic regression may be too simplistic for complex patterns.

- *Feature engineering*: Include additional features (e.g., diag_1, specific medications like insulin) or derive new ones (e.g., comorbidity indices) to enhance predictive power.
- *Class imbalance*: Apply oversampling (SMOTE) or class weighting to improve recall for early readmissions.

Operational Integration:

- *Risk stratification tool*: Deploy the model as a decision-support tool to flag high-risk patients at discharge, using predicted probabilities (e.g., >0.3) to trigger interventions.
- *Visualization dashboard*: Use the Chart.js scatter plot in a hospital dashboard to visualize patient risk profiles, aiding clinician decision-making.
- *Cost reduction*: By reducing early readmissions, the hospital can avoid penalties and optimize bed utilization, aligning with cost-saving goals.

Conclusion

The logistic regression model provides moderate performance (AUC–ROC = 0.58) in predicting early readmissions, limited by the small sample and class imbalance. Key drivers include number_diagnoses, time_in_hospital, and num_medications, indicating that complex cases are at higher risk. The scatter plot visually confirms that patients with more diagnoses face elevated readmission probabilities, guiding targeted interventions. Despite limitations, the model offers actionable insights for Biozenix Pharma to improve patient outcomes and operational efficiency. Validating with a larger dataset and enhancing the model will further strengthen its clinical utility.

Chapter 8

Sports and Agricultural Analytics

Applications of Analytics in Sports

Imagine you are managing a sports analytics company called SportsPro Inc., launched in 2019, that works with professional sports teams across football, cricket, basketball, and tennis. Your mission is to help teams make better decisions – like picking the right players, improving game tactics, and maximizing fan engagement – by using data.

SportsPro has worked with over 20 professional teams across North America, Europe, and Asia. But in a competitive industry where performance matters every day, the company must help teams make smart, data-driven decisions. This case study walks through three major areas where analytics is transforming sports:

1. Performance analysis.
2. Injury prevention and recovery.
3. Fan engagement and revenue optimization.

We will use simple tools and real-world-style data to show how analytics helps solve real problems in sports. Let us dive in, one problem at a time.

Problem 1: Improving Team Performance with Exploratory Data Analysis (EDA)

What Is the Goal?

SportsPro wants to help coaches answer the following questions:

- Which players are performing consistently well and which ones are underperforming?
- How does team performance vary based on location (home vs away games)?
- What game strategies (e.g., high pressing vs possession play) lead to higher win rates?

These insights help coaches make informed choices about tactics, lineups, and training focus.

Applications of Data Analysis Across Business Functions and Domains, 191–205

Published under exclusive licence by Emerald Publishing Limited
doi:10.1108/978-1-80686-105-720261008

What Is EDA in Sports?

EDA in sports is like watching hours of game footage, but summarized in charts and numbers. It helps find patterns – like a midfielder performing better in home games or a football team winning more when playing a 4-3-3 formation.

How Does SportsPro Approach This?

Step 1: Collect match and player data:

For each match and player, SportsPro gathers:

- Player ID, name, and position.
- Minutes played, goals, assists, and pass completion (%).
- Distance covered, sprints, tackles, and fouls.
- Game result, formation used, opponent, and venue.

Step 2: Clean the data:

Sports data often have errors (e.g., missing stats or duplicate entries). SportsPro cleans it by:

- Removing matches with incomplete player tracking.
- Filling in averages where values are missing.
- Verifying game dates and venues.

Step 3: Analyze:

They calculate:

- Player performance index = weighted average of goals, assists, pass accuracy, and defensive contributions.
- Win rate by formation = percentage wins under each game formation.
- Home versus away stats = comparing win percentage, possession, and goals scored.

Step 4: Visualize:

Charts make trends easy to spot:

- *Bar charts*: Player scores by match.
- *Heat maps*: Player movement intensity zones.
- *Line charts*: Team win/loss trends over time.
- *Pie charts*: Possession split by match location.

What Did They Find?

- *Top performers*: Midfielder #8 has the highest performance index due to strong assists and ball recoveries.
- *Formation success*: 4-2-3-1 formation yields a 62%-win rate, compared to just 38% for 4-3-3.
- *Venue effect*: Home games have 15% higher possession and 25% more goals scored on average.

What Should SportsPro Recommend?

- *Tactical change*: Emphasize formations with proven success rates (like 4-2-3-1).
- *Player selection*: Start Midfielder #8 in all crucial matches.
- *Home advantage strategy*: Use aggressive tactics at home and conservative ones away.

Sample Dataset Structure

The data summarize performance statistics for two football players, highlighting their roles on the field and key contribution metrics. John D, who plays as a midfielder, demonstrates strong passing efficiency with a pass accuracy of 87%, reflecting his effectiveness in ball distribution and control of play. He has scored 3 goals, indicating an ability to contribute offensively despite his midfield role, and has made 7 tackles, showing active defensive involvement. John D completed the full match, logging 90 minutes played, which suggests high stamina and a central role in the team's overall gameplay.

In contrast, Mike T plays as a forward, a position typically focused on attacking output. His pass accuracy of 79% is lower than that of the midfielder, which is expected, given the riskier passes often attempted by forwards. He scored 1 goal, contributing directly to the team's scoring, but recorded only 2 tackles, reflecting limited defensive responsibilities. Mike T played 85 minutes, slightly less than a full match, possibly due to tactical substitutions or fitness management. Overall, the comparison highlights the different performance profiles associated with midfield and forward positions, with John D showing balanced offensive and defensive contributions and Mike T focusing primarily on goal-scoring duties.

Problem 2: Preventing Injuries with Predictive Analytics

What Is the Goal?

Injuries ruin seasons. SportsPro helps teams reduce injury risk by answering:

- Which players are at high risk of injury in the upcoming weeks?
- What workload is "too much" for different player profiles?
- Can rest days be optimized?

What Is Predictive Analytics in Sports?

It is like using a fitness tracker and getting a warning: "If you keep this up, you'll get hurt!" Predictive analytics uses past data to forecast injury likelihood.

How Does SportsPro Approach This?

Step 1: Collect data:

For every player:

- Age, height, and weight.
- Weekly training load (measured via GPS and heart rate).
- Match minutes.
- Number of sprints.
- Previous injuries (and days missed).
- Sleep hours and recovery scores (e.g., from wearable tech).

Step 2: Preprocess:

- Normalize training loads to standard scales.
- Encode injury history into categories (e.g., minor, moderate, and major).
- Filter out inactive players.

Step 3: Build predictive model:

SportsPro uses logistic regression and random forest models to predict injury likelihood based on recent trends.

Features:

- Training load increase (%) over previous week.
- Average sleep.
- Recovery score.
- Sprint volume.

Target: Injury risk = 1 (yes), 0 (no).

What Did They Find?

- *Key risk factors*:
    - o A 20%+ spike in weekly training load increases injury risk by 35%.
    - o Players with <6 hours of sleep have 2× the injury rate.
    - o More than 30 high-intensity sprints per match correlates with hamstring strains.
- *Best model*: Random forest gave 82% accuracy in predicting next-week injuries, outperforming logistic regression (75%).

What Should SportsPro Do?

- *Dynamic load management*: Adjust workloads weekly, avoiding >15% increases.
- *Sleep monitoring*: Enforce minimum rest and recovery hours.
- *Injury watchlist*: Flag at-risk players and rotate them during congested schedules.

Sample Logistic Regression Equation

$$\text{Injury Risk} = 0.4 + 1.2 \times (\text{Training Load Increase}) - 0.8 \times (\text{Sleep Hours}) + 0.5 \times (\text{Sprint Count})$$

If a player had a 25% load spike, 5.5 hours of sleep, and 35 sprints:

$$\text{Injury Risk} \approx 0.4 + 1.2\times0.25 - 0.8\times5.5 + 0.5\times35 \approx \text{high risk (over 80\%)}$$

Problem 3: Engaging Fans Using Marketing Analytics

What Is the Goal?

SportsPro helps clubs boost revenue by answering:

- What type of content drives fan engagement?
- What offers maximize ticket and merchandise sales?
- How do social media campaigns translate to real purchases?

What Are Fan Analytics?

It is the sports version of customer analytics. Teams want to turn casual followers into ticket-buying, jersey-wearing superfans.

How Does SportsPro Work Here?

Step 1: Collect fan interaction data:

From apps, websites, and stadiums:

- Demographics (age, gender, and location).
- App usage (videos watched and push notifications opened).
- Ticket purchase history.
- Online merchandise orders.
- Social media interactions (likes, shares, and comments).

Step 2: Clean and merge data:

- Match fan IDs across platforms.
- Standardize timestamps.
- Handle missing or incomplete info.

Step 3: Analyze behavior:

- Engagement score = weighted sum of content interactions.
- Conversion funnel = from content view → click → purchase.
- A/B testing: Compare two ad creatives to see which works better.

A/B Testing

A/B testing, also known as split testing, is a method used to compare two versions of a webpage, app, or marketing asset to determine which one performs better. In an A/B test, users are randomly shown either version A (the control) or version B (the variation), and their behavior – such as clicks, conversions, or time spent – is measured and analyzed. This data-driven approach helps businesses make informed decisions by testing hypotheses with real user interactions, reducing guesswork, and improving outcomes. A/B testing is widely used in digital marketing, product design, and user experience optimization to continuously enhance performance and user satisfaction.

A/B testing is a way to figure out which version of something works better. For example, if you run a website and want to increase the number of people who sign up for your newsletter, you might create two different versions of your sign-up button: one that says "Sign Up Now" (version A) and another that says "Get Started" (version B). You then show version A to half your visitors and version B to the other half. By tracking which version gets more people to click and sign up, you can tell which wording is more effective. This helps you make smarter decisions based on real data, rather than just guessing. A/B testing can be used for anything from email subject lines and ads to website layouts and pricing strategies. It is a simple but powerful tool for improving results over time.

Step 4: Predict fan purchases:

- Use regression models to predict monthly spending.
- Use clustering (e.g., *K*-means) to group fans by behavior.

K-Means Clustering

K-means clustering is a popular unsupervised machine learning algorithm used to group similar data points into distinct clusters. The goal is to divide a dataset into *K* number of clusters, where each data point belongs to the cluster with the nearest mean (called the centroid). *K*-means aims to partition *n* data points into *K* clusters $C1,C2,\ldots,CKC\_1$, C_2, …, C_KC1, $C2$, …,CK so that the total within-cluster sum of squares is minimized. Each cluster is represented by its centroid, which is the average of all the points assigned to that cluster. The algorithm updates clusters and centroids iteratively:

- *Assignment step*: Assign each point to the nearest centroid.
- *Update step*: Recalculate centroids as the mean of points in each cluster.

This process continues until convergence, meaning the assignments no longer change or the change is very small.

Key Properties:

- It assumes spherical clusters (which works well if clusters are compact and well separated).
- It is sensitive to the initial choice of centroids.
- The number of clusters, K, must be defined in advance.
- It works best when clusters are of similar size and density.

Theoretical Limitations:

- It can converge to a local minimum (not necessarily the best global solution).
- Choosing a bad initial K can lead to poor clustering – methods like the Elbow method or Silhouette score are used to help choose the right K.
- It does not handle non-convex clusters or outliers well.

Here Is How It Works Step by Step:

1. Choose the number of clusters (K) you want to find.
2. Randomly initialize K centroids (points in the data space).
3. Assign each data point to the nearest centroid – this forms K clusters.
4. Update the centroids by calculating the mean position of all the points in each cluster.
5. Repeat steps 3 and 4 until the centroids stop moving significantly (i.e., the algorithm converges).

The result is that data points within a cluster are more similar to each other than to those in other clusters. K-means is commonly used in market segmentation, image compression, pattern recognition, and other applications where grouping similar items is useful.

What Did They Find?

- *Video content rules*: Fans who watch match highlight reels are 3× more likely to buy tickets.
- *Targeted offers win*: Personalized emails for local derbies increase ticket sales by 21%.
- *Social channels*: Instagram drives most merchandise sales. Twitter drives news engagement.

What Should SportsPro Recommend?

- *Segment and target*: Group fans into clusters (e.g., "merch buyers," "ticket buyers," and "social lurkers") and send different content to each.

- *Invest in video*: Push short reels and behind-the-scenes clips to drive engagement.
- *Optimize timing*: Send promotions 24–48 hours before home matches for best conversion.

Sample Fan Clusters

The following is the data description:

The dataset categorizes sports consumers into three distinct clusters, each reflecting different behaviors, content preferences, and spending patterns. Cluster 1, identified as "ticket buyers," consists of highly engaged fans who actively follow matches and are particularly interested in match previews. This group demonstrates the highest financial commitment among the three clusters, spending an average of Rs 1,200 per month, indicating a strong willingness to invest in experiences directly related to live sports. Cluster 2, labeled "merchandise lovers," focuses more on players themselves rather than the game, showing a preference for content such as star player interviews. Their spending is moderate, averaging Rs 850 per month, suggesting they are inclined to purchase merchandise or invest in fandom-related items, but with less intensity than ticket buyers. Cluster 3, termed "social followers," represents a younger or more casual segment that engages primarily with entertainment-oriented content like memes and short-form reels. This cluster spends the least, around Rs 300 per month, reflecting a lower monetary investment but a high level of social interaction and content sharing. Overall, these clusters illustrate the diversity of fan engagement, showing that while some fans are driven by direct match experiences, others are motivated by celebrity connection or social entertainment, with corresponding variations in spending behavior.

The Sports Analytics Playbook

1. *Performance analysis (EDA)*: Helps teams spot under/overperformers, formation success, and venue effects using simple stats and visuals.
2. *Injury prevention (predictive analytics)*: Forecasts which players are likely to get injured, based on workload, sleep, and sprint data. Helps optimize training and rotation.
3. *Fan engagement (marketing analytics)*: Uses fan data to tailor content, boost sales, and measure campaign success.

Why It Matters

Analytics in sports is no longer optional – it is a competitive edge.

- Coaches win more with smarter lineups and formations.
- Medical staff prevent injuries, saving millions.
- Marketing teams sell more by knowing fan behavior.

SportsPro uses analytics to build winning teams, protect players, and engage fans – all backed by data.

Conclusion: The Sports Analytics Playbook

1. *Performance analysis*: Use EDA to identify players and formations that drive wins.
2. *Injury prevention*: Predict risk using training data, sleep, and sprint load.
3. *Fan engagement*: Use A/B testing and clustering to tailor marketing.

Analytics in sports is no longer optional – it is a competitive edge.

- Coaches win more with smarter lineups.
- Staff prevent injuries, saving millions.
- Marketing sells more with tailored campaigns.

Key Findings

Results indicate that a training load increase exceeding 20% from the previous week raises injury risk by approximately 35%. Players sleeping fewer than six hours per night exhibit double the injury rate of well-rested peers, while high sprint volumes are strongly associated with soft-tissue injuries. Among the models tested, random forests achieve the highest predictive accuracy, outperforming logistic regression.

Recommendations

SportsPro advises implementing dynamic workload management, enforcing minimum recovery and sleep thresholds, and maintaining an injury watchlist to guide squad rotation during congested schedules.

Applications of Analytics in Agriculture

Imagine you are running a company called AgriPro Systems, founded in 2020, that provides data-driven solutions to farmers, cooperatives, and agri-businesses. Agriculture, often seen as traditional, is undergoing a digital revolution. Using analytics, AgriPro helps stakeholders increase crop yield, reduce waste, improve market access, and adapt to climate variability.

AgriPro has clients across India, Africa, and Southeast Asia, serving smallholder farms, agritech firms, and governments. This case study explores how analytics is transforming agriculture in three major domains:

1. Precision farming and yield optimization.
2. Supply chain and market linkage efficiency.
3. Weather and risk management.

Let us explore how data and analytics create value in each area using realistic examples and methods.

Problem 1: Enhancing Crop Yield with Precision Farming

What Is the Goal?

AgriPro wants to help farmers answer:

- What crops should I plant this season based on soil and climate?
- What is the optimal fertilizer mix for my land?
- How can I monitor crop health using remote sensing?

What Is Precision Farming?

Precision farming uses data from sensors, drones, and satellites to make site-specific decisions on planting, watering, and treating crops. It improves efficiency and yields while reducing resource use.

How Does AgriPro Approach This?

Step 1: Data collection:

- *Soil parameters*: pH, organic carbon, nitrogen, phosphorus, and moisture.
- *Satellite data*: Normalized difference vegetation index (NDVI) for crop health.
- *Internet of things (IoT) sensors*: Real-time weather, irrigation levels, and pest alerts.
- Yield history per plot and crop.

Step 2: Data cleaning:

- Handle missing sensor readings.
- Remove outlier NDVI values due to cloud cover.

Step 3: Analysis and modeling:

- Correlate NDVI trends with yield.
- Recommend fertilizer and seed varieties based on soil profiles.
- Use regression models to estimate yield potential.

Step 4: Visualization:

- Heat maps of soil fertility and crop stress.
- Time series plots of NDVI and rainfall.
- Dashboard of real-time sensor alerts.

What Did They Find?

- Fields with optimal Nitrogen (N), Phosphorus (P), and Potassium (K) balance and timely irrigation show 23% higher yields.
- NDVI dips in week 4 of the season predict pest outbreaks.
- Use of precision drip irrigation in tomato plots reduced water usage by 37%.

What Should AgriPro Recommend?

- Variable rate fertilizer application based on soil zones.
- Weekly NDVI monitoring for early pest detection.
- Crop rotation plans based on past plot performance.

Data description is as follows:

The dataset provides detailed information on six agricultural plots, highlighting the relationship between vegetation health, soil characteristics, moisture content, and crop yield. Plot P001 exhibits a relatively high NDVI value of 0.62, indicating healthy vegetation, accompanied by a slightly acidic to neutral soil pH of 6.5 and moderate soil moisture at 18%, resulting in a yield of 980 kg. Plot P002, with a lower NDVI of 0.45 and more acidic soil at pH 5.8, has reduced moisture levels of 12%, which corresponds to a lower yield of 720 kg. Plot P003 stands out with the highest NDVI of 0.70 and alkaline soil pH of 7.1, combined with high moisture content at 20%, producing the maximum yield of 1,100 kg, suggesting optimal growing conditions. In contrast, Plot P004 has the lowest NDVI of 0.38, highly acidic soil at pH 5.4, and the lowest moisture content at 10%, resulting in the smallest yield of 650 kg. Plot P005 shows moderate vegetation health with an NDVI of 0.58, soil pH of 6.3, and moisture at 16%, generating a yield of 900 kg. Similarly, Plot P006 exhibits slightly lower NDVI at 0.49, pH of 6.0, and moisture of 14%, producing a yield of 780 kg. Overall, the data illustrate a clear trend where plots with higher NDVI, near-neutral to slightly alkaline soil pH, and adequate moisture tend to achieve higher crop yields, while plots with lower vegetation health, acidic soils, and limited moisture correspond to reduced productivity.

Problem 2: Optimizing Agri-supply Chains

What Is the Goal?

AgriPro helps improve agri-logistics and market access by answering:

- Where are the bottlenecks in the farm-to-market chain?
- How can storage and transport losses be minimized?
- What pricing strategy helps farmers maximize profit?

What Is Supply Chain Analytics in Agriculture?

It is using data to track crops from harvest to consumer. Analytics identifies delays, spoilage points, and pricing inefficiencies to streamline operations.

How Does AgriPro Work Here?

Step 1: Data collection:

- Harvest date, storage duration, and transport distance.
- Temperature/humidity in cold chains.

- Market prices by location.
- Farmer sales volumes.

Step 2: Cleaning and integration:

- Normalize pricing across markets.
- Handle missing logistics data.

Step 3: Analytics tools:

- Time-to-market versus spoilage rate correlation.
- Linear programming for route optimization.
- Regression to predict price based on quality and supply.

Step 4: Visualization:

- Sankey diagrams for supply chain flows.
- Heat maps for regional price differences.
- Scatter plots for price versus transport time.

What Did They Find?

- Onion spoilage increased 18% for every 48-hour delay post-harvest.
- Farmers selling through e-mandis got 12% higher prices than traditional markets.
- Cold storage usage in mango supply chains cut losses from 24% to 9%.

What Should AgriPro Recommend?

- Promote the use of digital market platforms.
- Shorter aggregation cycles to reduce time to market.
- Cold chain investment in high-value perishables.

What Is A/B Testing in the Agriculture Supply Chain?

AgriPro tested two pricing messages for farmers:

- A: "Get better prices at our collection center."
- B: "Reduce losses with our cold storage."

Results:

- Response rate A: 22%; Response rate B: 36%.
- Conclusion: Framing around loss prevention worked better.

Problem 3: Managing Weather Risks with Predictive Analytics

What is the Goal?

AgriPro wants to help farmers mitigate climate risks:

- Will it rain enough to sow paddy this week?
- What is the expected drought probability in my district?
- Should I insure my crop?

What Is Predictive Risk Modeling in Agriculture?

It uses historical climate data, forecasts, and machine learning to predict weather events and their crop impact.

How Does AgriPro Approach This?

Step 1: Data collection:

- 10 years of rainfall, temperature, and drought index.
- Soil moisture levels.
- Crop sowing/harvesting dates.
- Crop insurance claim history.

Step 2: Preprocessing:

- Fill in missing satellite data.
- Adjust for outlier years (e.g., El Niño effects).

Step 3: Risk modeling:

- Logistic regression to predict drought probability.
- Decision trees to assess insurance claim likelihood.
- Time series analysis for rainfall prediction.

Step 4: Clustering regions by risk:

- Use K-means clustering on rainfall variability and crop loss data.
- Group districts into high, medium, and low risk.

Results:

- 28% of districts fall into high-risk drought clusters.
- Delay of monsoon onset beyond 10 days increases crop failure by 17%.
- Insured farmers recovered 65% more of their losses than uninsured peers.

What Should AgriPro Do?

- Provide real-time advisories based on the forecast and risk cluster.
- Promote index-based insurance in high-risk districts.
- Help schedule sowing windows using rainfall projections.

What Is K-Means Clustering in Agri-risk?

K-means grouped regions into:

- *Cluster 1*: Stable rainfall and low losses.
- *Cluster 2*: Moderate variability and moderate losses.
- *Cluster 3*: High variability and frequent losses.

AgriPro now tailors advisories and insurance offers by cluster.

Conclusion: The Agricultural Analytics Playbook

1. *Precision farming*: Use soil, NDVI, and sensor data to boost yield and optimize inputs.
2. *Supply hains*: Use analytics to reduce spoilage, improve pricing, and optimize routes.
3. *Risk management*: Predict drought, guide insurance, and cluster regions by vulnerability.

With data, agriculture becomes more predictable, productive, and profitable. AgriPro empowers stakeholders with insights to sow better, grow better, and sell better.

Expanded Agricultural Analytics Playbook

1. *Precision farming*: Use soil, NDVI, and sensor data to boost yield and optimize inputs.
2. *Supply chains*: Use analytics to reduce spoilage, improve pricing, and optimize routes.
3. *Risk management*: Predict drought, guide insurance, and cluster regions by vulnerability.
4. *Water management*: Predict daily irrigation needs and reduce overuse.
5. *Pest management*: Predict outbreak risk and deploy preemptive action. It examines the likelihood of a disease, pest, or other harmful event occurring in a particular area or population. For example, in agriculture, this could involve predicting a potential locust swarm or a crop disease outbreak based on weather patterns, soil conditions, and pest activity. In public health, it could refer to anticipating a viral or bacterial disease outbreak in a community. Deploy preemptive action – This refers to taking preventive or mitigating measures before the predicted outbreak actually happens, to reduce its impact. Examples include: Applying pesticides before pests reach critical

levels in crops. Vaccinating or isolating populations before a disease spreads. Strengthening healthcare resources or issuing warnings in areas at risk. In short, the phrase means: "Use predictive insights to anticipate a harmful event and take early steps to prevent or minimize its impact."

Each of these analytics applications helps increase productivity, reduce uncertainty, and support sustainable farming. AgriPro's data-driven approach empowers farmers to make timely and profitable decisions.

With these new modules, AgriPro builds a full-stack intelligence platform for modern agriculture.

Applications of Analytics in Agriculture

Agriculture, traditionally viewed as experience-driven, is increasingly data-centric. AgriPro Systems, founded in 2020, provides analytics-driven solutions to farmers and agri-businesses across India, Africa, and Southeast Asia. The firm focuses on precision farming, supply chain optimization, and weather risk management.

Precision Farming and Yield Optimization

Using soil data, satellite imagery, and IoT sensors, AgriPro helps farmers optimize crop selection, fertilizer use, and irrigation scheduling. Regression models and NDVI-based analysis reveal strong links between timely irrigation, balanced nutrient application, and yield improvement.

Supply Chain and Market Analytics

By tracking harvest timing, storage conditions, and transport delays, analytics identifies spoilage risks and pricing inefficiencies. Findings show that cold storage adoption and digital marketplaces significantly reduce losses and improve farmer incomes.

Weather Risk and Predictive Modeling

Time-series analysis, logistic regression, and clustering techniques help forecast drought risk and guide insurance decisions. Districts are grouped into risk clusters, enabling targeted advisories and resource allocation.

Conclusion

Across both sports and agriculture, analytics enables better decisions by transforming raw data into actionable insights. In sports, it improves performance, reduces injuries, and strengthens fan engagement. In agriculture, it enhances productivity, streamlines supply chains, and mitigates climate risk. As these domains continue to evolve, analytics is no longer optional – it is a strategic necessity that delivers sustained competitive advantage.

Printed and bound by CPI Group (UK) Ltd, Croydon, CR0 4YY

15/09/2026

14962483-0003